Fighting for A Home & Country

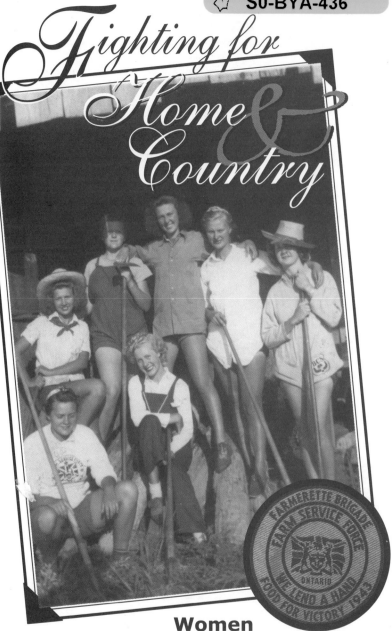

**Women
Remember World War II**

 Edited by Janine Roelens-Grant

i

With Appreciation

The Federated Women's Institutes of Ontario
extend a heartfelt thank you to all members who took the time
to record and submit a story.

© 2004 Federated Women's Institutes of Ontario (FWIO)
7382 Wellington Road 30, RR 5, Guelph, Ontario N1H 6J2   519-836-3078

Library and Archives Canada Cataloguing in Publication

Main entry under title:
Fighting for home & country : women remember World War II
/ edited by Janine Roelens-Grant.

Includes index.
ISBN 0-9698693-8-X

1. World War, 1939-1945--Women--Canada. 2. World War, 1939-1945--Personal narratives, Canadian. 3. World War, 1939-1945--Women. 4. World War, 1939-1945--Personal narratives. I. Roelens-Grant, Janine II. Federated Women's Institutes of Ontario

D811.5.F44 2004   940.53'161'0820971   C2004-906099-6

Front Cover Photograph: *War bride Patricia Woodruff (p. 215) and her husband Milford are stepping into an army vehicle in Selsdon, Surrey, England.*

Back Cover Photograph: *Ruth Metcalf (p. 145) and fellow nurses with their equipment for gas warfare practice.*

Title Page Photograph: *Margaret Archer (p. 3) and girls from Farm Service Camp in Thedford, Ontario.*

Cover and book design by Debbie Thompson Wilson, Willustration

Printed in Canada by Moffitt Print Craft Limited
240 Woodlawn Road West, Guelph, Ontario N1H 1B6

While great care has been taken to ensure the accuracy of the accounts within, this book is comprised of personal stories and thus reflects the individual's memories, opinions and perspectives.

For copies of this book, write or call the FWIO at the above address.

Introduction

Fighting for Home & Country: Women Remember World War II, published by the Federated Women's Institutes of Ontario (FWIO), documents some of its members' wartime experiences. The aim of *Fighting for Home & Country* is to reconstruct a sense of time and place experienced by Women's Institute (WI) members as young girls and women during the years of World War II from 1939 to 1945.

WI members from across Ontario have shared their wartime stories. Many lived in another province or country at the time of the war, including Alberta, Saskatchewan, Manitoba, Quebec, England, Scotland, Holland, Belgium, Germany, Poland, Croatia, Estonia, Latvia and the Ukraine. Some stories are told from the perspective of a child; others encompass growing-up years from a "just turned teen" to a married woman. Others experienced these years as war brides, factory workers, Land Army girls or farmerettes, mechanics, refugees and prisoners of war. Many served in various capacities – as nurses, cooks, truck drivers, wireless operators, mechanics, etc. - in the army, navy or air force.

Depending on where they lived, the degree that these young girls and women were touched by war varied. Almost all of them wrote about blackouts, the rationing of food, clothing and gasoline, air raid shelters and gas masks. These things became matter of fact; many even became blasé about these war measures. Others recorded living in constant fear of the devastation caused by V-1s or buzz bombs, V-2 rockets and other weapons of war. Many chronicled the real horrors of war - death and destruction, suffering and starvation and the grim cruelties and realities that engulfed their days.

Resilience, perseverance and undying hope are also documented in these stories. In Europe, young girls relay their mothers' daily struggle to keep families fed and clothed with a roof over their heads amidst the chaos. Driven from their homes, these young girls wandered with their families for the duration of the war seeking refuge wherever they could find it. For many, the uncertainty of their lives was the only constant.

Women on the home front were resilient and determined as they stepped up to do a "man's" job and as they fervently undertook voluntary war work. During this period, some women tackled jobs they never dreamed of doing. For the most part, these wives, mothers and young girls felt appreciated as they did their "bit" for the war effort. At the same time, many spoke about developing a sense of independence and confidence in their abilities to be self-sufficient.

Within are accounts of altruism. They pendulum from the 5-year-old who so freely parted with her favourite doll which was sent to a needy little girl overseas to the young nurse who tended to soldiers, broken physically and spiritually, trying to make their last moments peaceful. There are numerous recollections about the impressive volunteer work of patriotic school children and women who faithfully collected tinfoil and milkweed pods, bought War Savings Stamps and knit miles of yarn into socks, scarves and other essential items. Many of these recollections are simply about giving.

Other stories are about the taking of peoples' homes, dignity and lives. There are accounts of losing a beloved cousin, childhood friend, Father, brother or husband who went missing in action. Some told about families being picked up by the Germans and herded into cattle-cars never to be seen again, simply because they were Jewish. There are stories of brothers and fathers who were hunted down by the razzias, or Secret Police, and forced into the military or shipped off to work in German factories. Others speak of women and children surviving in Eastern Europe as Allied Forces retook a conquered land.

Undoubtedly, these stories will test your emotions criss-crossing the spectrum from grim lows to glorious highs.

For all of the women who so generously took the time to record and submit a story and share their photographs and memorabilia, FWIO thanks you. Some members were spurred to document their story for the first time simply because they were asked. Space did not allow all of the stories to be included, nor did it allow for those selected to be printed in their entirety. The stories were edited. These stories together with the photographs give war a human face.

The front cover photograph suitably portrays the title of the book – *Fighting for Home & Country: Women Remember World War II* – and much more. The irony of a young war bride Patricia Woodruff and her husband Milford stepping into an army vehicle as their "bridal car" is clearly evident – a newly married couple building their life together in contrast to the inevitable loss of life from vehicles of war. The photograph testifies to a belief in survival and the war's end.

Neysa E. Clark upon concluding her submission noted, "Writing this makes me realize, more than ever, that ordinary people doing extraordinary things won the war." Indeed, this is what *Fighting for Home & Country* is all about – ordinary women and their daughters doing extraordinary things as they fought for home and country.

❧ E. Ruth Algire

When World War II was declared, I was 15-years-old, ready to start Grade 13 at Nepean High School in Ottawa. I was terrified at the thought of another war. I had four uncles in World War I and had heard about guns, barbed wire, trenches, poisonous gas and death. It worried me to think that my brothers, cousins and school friends might soon be involved in war. There was no glamour or romance for anyone in the announcement in early September 1939, "Canada is at War!"

Daily life goes on, war or no war. In 1940, National Registration became compulsory in Canada. A wallet-sized registration card was issued to each adult to be carried at all times for identification. My sister and I volunteered to help with registration. Next came ration books for everyone. As one book became out-dated, it was turned in and another one was issued. A ration book contained B coupons for butter, M coupons for meat, S coupons for sugar, and so on. Gas, beer and liquor coupons were in other books. Nylon stockings were scarce, as was flannelette for diapers. When I needed the flannelette in 1946 for my baby, I could only get three yards at a time. When requesting flannelette, some girls even had to open their coats to show that they were really pregnant.

In February of 1941, my older sister began nurse's training at the Ottawa Civic Hospital. In May, my brother graduated from Queens University and soon joined the Royal Canadian Engineers. I started Normal School in the fall and boarded in Ottawa and came home on weekends. My first school was on the Ferry Road in Fitzroy Township. Teachers were expected to sell War Savings Stamps, keep track of the money and purchase certificates for the children. I was impressed with one little boy who brought American buffalo nickels week after week; I discovered later that he was draining his uncle's collection. We had Junior Red Cross meetings and I taught the children how to knit squares for an afghan, which we donated.

Since many of the farmers' sons were in the services, German prisoners of war were made available to work on the farms. My father and brother, with a little help from us girls, didn't need any extra help. But we often saw POWs who worked a few miles away, dressed in blue jeans with a red stripe down each leg and a large red circle on the back of their jacket. At first people were afraid of them, but gradually realized that they were young men similar to our relatives and friends. We were warned not to socialize with them. Some of the farmers allowed them to wear civilian clothes and drive the farm truck on errands, but this was against the rules. The men were polite and well-behaved and some were well-educated. They worked hard, although some were shocked to find they were expected to clean cow stables and pigpens.

When he had to go overseas in the summer of '43, my older brother sold his 1929 Model A Ford to my second brother and me for $75. My friend Marion coaxed me to take a school near Williamsburg, about 60 miles from home, so I found it handy to drive back and forth on some weekends. Soon my brother realized he was getting the short end of the deal and sold me his share. At the end of the school year, the tires were so bare I was lucky to find someone who gave me $50 for the car. The next fall, Marion helped me find a boarding house near the school. Soon I was involved in various projects for the war effort. We gathered milkweed pods and dried them in bags hung along the fence; they were used to stuff life jackets. Again I found myself selling War Savings Stamps and keeping track of nickels and dimes. We made a quilt for the Red Cross, with some help from a lady in the community.

One night I went to a wedding reception in the local hall and I was introduced to a young airman who became important in my life. Clair was the youngest of a farm family in my school section and he was stationed at Bagotville, Quebec, near Chicoutimi. He made the long journey home by train as often as possible and we wrote many letters between visits. We were married on July 15, 1944, in the Dunrobin United Church and I went to live in Bagotville for the summer. For my wedding I wore a white silk-jersey street-length dress, which was useful for several years afterward as my "good dress." I was lucky to have a pair of nylons for which my cousin had stood in line for an hour at an Ottawa store. The reception was country style on the lawn at the farm with about 70 guests. Several of the ladies insisted on bringing food and one neighbour made my wedding cake.

I returned to Ontario in time to start teaching in the school I had attended as a child and I boarded with my parents in our old farmhouse. I taught in this school for two terms with visits from my husband once a month. I kept busy with school and community work, and I even made a quilt.

Meanwhile the war raged in Europe. Every day the radio and newspapers reported great victories for the Allies, but also listed the names of many servicemen killed or missing in action. My beloved cousin, a friend since childhood, went missing over the Irish Sea and was never found. Another cousin married a lovely English girl and eventually brought her home to Saskatchewan.

My older brother Russ was in the midst of the fighting in Northwest Europe. He was the Reconnaissance Officer for the 23rd Field Company of Engineers and was awarded the Military Cross for service at Arnhem in Holland. The news of Russ's decoration came by telephone and Mother calmly said, "Well, I'm not surprised." We were lucky to be in Canada where we ate well and were safe from shells and bombs. We kept in touch with our military friends by writing letters on flimsy blue airmail forms and watched anxiously for replies.

Clair was stationed at Torbay, Newfoundland, in 1945, so I made plans to join him for the summer. VE Day came on May 8, but the war with Japan continued. Clair was still in Torbay, so off I went by train to Moncton and then flew the Trans Canada Airlines to Torbay. Newfoundland was considered overseas as it still had not joined Canada. I was getting quite able to travel by myself and had no trouble until I arrived at my destination and found no husband waiting! I had a phone number so I got out a nickel and approached a phone booth only to find that the coin would not fit in the slot. Newfoundland had its own coins, including small 5 and 20 cent pieces. Eventually, I got my message through and a Jeep arrived to collect me. We went directly to our summer home near the airport. It was a crude little cottage, but good enough for a short stay.

Our summer was disrupted when we heard that Clair's squadron was to be moved to the Pacific Theatre of war. We immediately began to make arrangements for me to get home to Ontario. On August 6, we heard that the atomic bomb had been dropped on Hiroshima and within days the war was over. Clair would soon be discharged so I once again got on a plane and was heading home. In Moncton I boarded a train loaded with soldiers going home. I was fortunate to meet an older lady and we travelled together to Montreal where I changed trains for Ottawa.

When "the boys came home," many women lost their jobs. I was fortunate to be able to keep teaching and eventually became principal of an eight-room school. Many other females, despite the competition, were able to achieve success due to their wartime experience and this led the way for younger women to try careers other than nursing and teaching. My wartime experiences certainly made me more independent and gave me a chance to travel.

🍁 Margaret Archer

I worked for the Ontario Farm Service Force the last three years of the war. It was organized to help the farmers in the summertime because the young men had gone to war. There were camps in the Niagara district and in the area of Forest and Thedford. We picked cherries and peaches. In the bogs at Thedford, onions, celery, carrots and mint were grown; we weeded and harvested these crops. It was great fun and we were helping the war effort.

The camaraderie among the girls was wonderful. We could leave high school early if we promised to stay at the Farm Service Camp for 13 weeks. High school girls came from as far away as Timmins and Napanee. We were paid 25 cents an hour. Room and board was $3.25 a week and was paid to the Farm Service Camp. During 1943 and 1944, we were housed in the high school in Forest. We slept on bunks in the gymnasium and ate in the Home Economics room. My sister Shirley also came to camp in 1945. One time our Recreation Committee decided to have a dance, so they invited an equal number of soldiers from Camp Ipperwash. But double the number came.

Margaret (far left) with cadet friends, VE Day, 1945.

The first time I rode in a half-ton truck was when I started to go to the market in Sarnia to help sell fruit and vegetables. Often on weekends, we would hitchhike to Ipperwash beach for a swim. Hitchhiking was a most unusual thing for girls to do. We also went into the local poolroom to play pool. And sometimes, we played baseball with the girls in Thedford.

In high school I joined cadets for girls. We wore navy blue skirts, a white blouse and a navy wedge cap. We studied the different kinds of airplanes, so we could recognize if they were our planes or belonged to the enemy. We marched on VE Day. I remember soldiers from Holland were stationed in Stratford and Princess Juliana came to see them. I went to the railway station to see "a real, live princess." She was wearing red sandals and my Aunt Elizabeth said, "Imagine, a princess wearing red sandals." They looked okay to me!

As cadets we helped prepare parcels to send overseas. I remember sending a parcel to one particular soldier, Bill Moses, who later became my husband. The parcel contained cookies, Christmas cake, chocolate bars, razor blades and septic sticks to fill in the tiny spaces in the box. A septic stick is used when a man cuts himself shaving. One stick would last a long time. He told me I had sent enough to supply almost the whole Third Field Regiment.

When Bill got back to Canada from Europe in the summer of 1945, he volunteered to go fight the Japanese. Bill was a dispatch rider in the army. We were married in September 1945.

🍁 Sarah Edna Armstrong

Two of my brothers enlisted to serve their country; both were in the air force. Jim arrived in England in 1941 and Austin in 1943. Austin had been given leave to marry a girl from Scotland, but he was called into action. His plane was shot down over the Bay of Biscay in 1944. No trace of the plane or crew was ever found. I will never forget the day the telegram arrived. Prior to this, all telegrams had been mailed from Shelburne, a town close to where we lived. But this one was delivered to the door by the telegraph operator. My mother and father were never the same, always expecting to see Austin come through the door. "Killed in action" is much easier to deal with than "missing in action" and presumed dead. Jim arrived home safely, with many memories.

❦ Leata Ashby

My first war related experience occurred in 1941. Our family had our land expropriated by the Department of National Defence for an Army Training Centre. Altogether, 94 Lots on Concessions 6 through 12 in St. Vincent Township were designated, in total 17,000 acres. There were 11 Lots in Sydenham Township expropriated, plus another 2,000 acres. More than 100 families had their lives changed forever.

My family lived on the north half of the 9th Concession. The 175-acre farm had been in our family for three generations. This expropriation closed four schools, five churches and two cemeteries. The Defence Department promised to fence and care for all the cemetery stones found on the different farms. They also allowed family members to visit the cemeteries of their descendants whenever possible. After a lot of speculation, my father was given notice that we would be the first to move as they were going to use our large stone house as a temporary headquarters. Three more families had to move in six weeks and everyone had vacated their properties by September 30, 1942. Imagine, over 100 families looking for a new home or farm at the same time. The valuator assured everybody that they would receive a fair price. My parents' farm was valued at $100 less than what they paid my grandfather in 1924.

We looked as far away as Stayner for a new home, but found our new farm on the 7th Line South, with 100 acres on the Big Head River. Mr. Picot was the real estate agent who showed us the farm. My mother had one look at the house and sent me flying to tell my dad the house was in a state of disrepair. However, my father was so impressed with this land that had a river running through it, he promised if Mother would take a chance, they would rebuild the house. He kept his word. We now had electricity, something we never had before, a wood furnace that would go all night and running water with indoor plumbing.

The home issue was settled and we all went on with the war effort. Rationing was not a real hardship on the farm. Although extra gas was coloured and was to be used only in our tractor, it sometimes found its way into our car. As children we received War Savings Stamps for Christmas. My mother worked in both the Women's Institute and the Red Cross. It was due to a letter received by the Institute about the government experimenting with the use of a fluffy material from inside milkweed pods that children were given the task of picking as much milkweed as they could find.

George Bishop, my father's youngest brother, was an officer in the air force. He was sent overseas and was shot down over Germany. My grandparents received word that he was missing in action. This came in a black-etched telegram. It was several weeks later that word was received that he had been captured and interned in a German prisoner of war camp. When the war was finally over he returned home safely. He would not talk about his internship at the prison camp, but spoke about how wonderful the Salvation Army was to him.

Finally, after much sorrow for many, the war was over. I was in high school when our town bell rang joyously. One of my favourite teachers started crying. I looked at her and said, "Why are you crying now?" Her answer was, "These are tears of thankfulness and happiness - my man will be coming home." But sadly, so many did not.

🍁 Gwen Banks

I will always remember Sunday, September 3, 1939, the day when Britain declared war on Germany, the start of World War II. I was in church at the time, when the service was interrupted to relay the news that war had been declared. Life was never to be the same again.

The first months of the war were known as the "Phoney War," as nothing seemed to be happening. This changed in May 1940 when the French defences were breached and the British and Allied troops were forced to retreat to Dunkirk. On May 26, 1940, hundreds of boats, including a fleet of fishing boats and anything else that was seaworthy, put out across the English Channel to rescue the hundreds of thousands of troops from the beach at Dunkirk. The sea remained calm, as though by a miracle. Once in England, the troops were billeted in private homes and hotels. Anyone with a spare room was expected to take in one or more of the rescued troops.

On the home front, young men were recruited into the Forces and women were expected to take up war work. I had always wanted to train as a registered nurse. I joined the British Red Cross when I was 16 and had a certification in first aid, home nursing and procedures in case of a gas attack. The Civil Nurse Reserve was formed under the auspices of the Red Cross. I lost no time in volunteering for this service and was accepted.

I was posted to the Nottingham City Hospital, a first-class teaching hospital where I received an excellent training as a practical nurse. Two or three 36-bed wards were available in preparation for casualties. After the fall of France, the beds were filled. The fighting and the air raids began in earnest. I recall walking to work and watching a dogfight between a Spitfire and a German plane. Shrapnel fell nearby, but I didn't fully realize how easily I could have been badly injured if a piece of it had hit me.

In January 1941, I joined the Women's Auxiliary Air Force (WAAF). I did my initial training in Morecomb, a town by the sea. Training, known as "Square Bashing," entailed daily marching up and down the sea front, learning drills and sitting in on lectures in various places. Eventually I was assigned to go to a Royal Air Force (RAF) Hospital at a large reception camp near the Welsh border, where I received more training.

We slept in bunks in Nissen huts. I vividly remember one portly WAAF Warrant Officer who used to arrive at 6:00 a.m. bellowing, "Wakey! Wakey!" If one were slow getting up, she would strip off the sheet and shake you awake. After ablutions and dressing, we made our bunk beds. We then stood to attention at the side of the bunk while the Duty Officer inspected.

My next posting was to a Bomber Command Station, where I was to work in sick quarters. One evening at about midnight a call was received for myself and two other orderlies to go immediately to the main sick quarters as there had been a crash. Two planes, one a Lancaster ready for take off and a Manchester coming down the runway, met head on and exploded. The results were grievous. Several of the aircrew were severely burned. Surgeons arrived from the burn unit of the nearest RAF Hospital. I will never forget the odour of burnt flesh. One of the WAAF nursing orderlies had the sad task of writing a letter dictated by one of the seriously injured aircrew. The letter was to be given to his wife; he died shortly after.

The following year I was transferred to RAF Coningsby, still a bomber command. While there, I met a member of an aircrew whom I eventually married on June 6, 1944, D-Day. Our leave was not cancelled because the Allied Command did not wish to draw enemy attention to invasion plans, as cancelling all leave would have done. Our marriage took place after a considerable wait for the vicar to arrive. He apologized for his late arrival as he had been listening to the news of the D-Day invasion landings. Ten weeks later, on the night of August 26, I became a widow. My husband was a member of a Pathfinder Squadron. They were always first over the target and the last out. A German fighter plane shot them down over Denmark as they return from a raid over East Germany.

An RAF Psychiatric Hospital, a lovely old building and former spa in Derbyshire, was my next posting. Making night rounds, along a corridor lit only by a bulb at each end, was eerie. Often one would suddenly see a figure approaching, someone would be sleepwalking and would give you quite a start. The station adjutant added to the eerie feeling by practising his flute during the night. Our patients were chiefly aircrew. Some had flown too many tours of duty; many had seen too many friends die. Others suffered mentally from the stress of overseas duty in places such as Malta, which was under constant bombardment by enemy planes.

My last posting was to a blood transfusion unit stationed at Nottingham University. From there, I was sent to a discharge unit. The war had finished. After more than six years, I was a civilian again.

❧ Nora Barber

Even though I was only 7-years-old when war was declared in 1939, I have some vivid memories of World War II and related events in my Alberta hometown of Elk Point. My first memory was the day after Prime Minister Chamberlain of Great Britain had returned to London from the meeting where Hitler was given the go-ahead to take over the Sudetenland. A particular man in our village was upset and came storming to our house to talk with my father. He said that Chamberlain was a fool and how could he even think that he was bringing "peace in our time."

After war was declared, many young men from the village and surrounding area enlisted – mostly in the air force and the navy and a few in the army. It must have been when one or some of them had been home on leave that the young boys in the community learned rifle drill. A lot of the young kids, including the girls, used to march and drill with our broomsticks. That was part of our play for a while.

My mother had come to Canada from the Netherlands and we had relatives there. I'll never forget the morning in May 1940 when she came into our bedroom in tears and told us that the German Air Force was bombing Rotterdam. And then it wasn't long before the whole country had capitulated and the Dutch Royal Family had fled to England. I think my mother was grateful that Canada had offered refuge to Princess Juliana and her children.

In the summer of 1941 we made a brief holiday trip to Edmonton. While there, we heard an appeal on the radio that the Canadian Air Force needed anyone to enlist to train in radio. My father had trained in radio and electricity and he thought that he should go. My mother was upset and said that they wouldn't take him because he was too old. He was 57.

Even so, he went to Edmonton that fall and offered himself. He was at the stage of the physical examination when the doctor asked him, matter-of-factly, his age. Everything up to that stage had been positive and it looked as if he would be accepted. But when the doctor heard his age he was amazed because my father didn't look 57. The doctor then said that the air force wasn't that desperate so they didn't take him. You can imagine my mother's relief when he came home.

On December 7, 1941, as we were about to eat supper we heard the news that Pearl Harbour had been bombed by the Japanese Forces. From then on the news broadcasts became the basis of many a geography lesson. Many of those names I still remember today - Corregidor, Tobruk, Midway, etc. At that time, I found it hard to understand why Southeast Asia was called the Far East. My father liked to hear the BBC broadcast from London. I can still hear the sound of Big Ben at the beginning of the news broadcasts.

I think it was the following winter of 1942-'43 that we had practice blackouts, even in Alberta which was hundreds of miles from the West Coast. Also, the Alaska Highway was being pushed through as fast as possible. Some of the men from our town went to work on it.

At school we had a Junior Red Cross. Children were encouraged to buy War Savings Stamps; they were 25 cents each and 20 made up a War Savings Certificate. At the end of the war they were to be worth $5. Wage earners were encouraged to buy Victory Bonds. In 1943, because our car was a real luxury, my parents decided to sell our 1940 Model Ford, a two-door sedan, and put the money into Victory Bonds. They got $900 for it. But, much to my mother's dismay and indignation, my parents found out about a month later that the man who had bought it sold it again for $1,200. There were no more trips to the lake for a summer swim or visits to my two uncles' farms, visits that I thoroughly enjoyed.

When he finished high school, my cousin John, who was a first class student and had been accepted into the Faculty of Medicine at the University of Alberta, joined the Royal Canadian Air Force (RCAF). Because he was good in mathematics, he was put in the Navigator class. When John came home on leave, he always stayed with us the night he arrived, and the next morning my uncle would come to get him with a team and either a buggy or cutter, depending on the season. John went overseas in the late winter, early spring of 1944. Unfortunately, that was the last time we ever saw him. His plane was shot down over Germany that fall; he was listed as "missing in action." All the other crew members turned up in prisoner of war camps, but John's body was found floating in a canal, so the report said. He had made the supreme sacrifice just weeks before his 21st birthday.

Late in August 1944, we moved to Victoria because my father had been advised for medical reasons to move to a lower altitude. As the Netherlands had been liberated, my mother was anxious to contact our relatives. The Red Cross certainly helped in that regard. All had survived the occupation, except one cousin who had been conscripted into the German Army and had been killed on the Russian front. The family that lived in Amsterdam had a particularly tough time. When the armistice in Europe was declared, there was great rejoicing in our household.

The day after VE Day, there was a great parade in Victoria and all the Boy Scouts and Girl Guides were invited to take part. I marched with our Girl Guide Company; it was one of the happiest experiences of my life. I was at Girl Guide camp when VJ Day was announced. This day too was a happy one, but not as happy as before because I knew my special cousin John would not be coming home.

❦ Gwendolyn Boles

I was 14-years-old when I started Grade 11 at the Continuation School in Belmont, Ontario, in September 1939. Our teacher sat on one of the front desks and told us Canada was at war with Germany. This meant little to me at that time as that country was a long way away and I was a girl with no close relatives in the age group for service. The next two years passed, with Grandma complaining about sugar rationing and Dad about the shortage of gasoline for the car.

After graduation, I went to Beal Technical School in London for a special commercial course, riding the bus back and forth or carpooling. I took a job in the Bank of Nova Scotia in Belmont for a year and then I went to work at the London Life Insurance Company in April 1943.

There, events were organized to entertain the servicemen. I was too late to join their troop show, but went to the dances at the surrounding army, navy and air force bases. We were bused both ways. Later, I got to make dates with the boys. In addition to working at the Insurance Company, I helped in the canteen at Westminster Hospital. I also tried packing vehicle parts at General Motors for overseas, but I found two jobs too tiring!

In October 1944, at a dance held at Queens Park in London with the Alf Tibbs orchestra playing, I met a shy soldier – Bill Boles - from Estevan, Saskatchewan. He was stationed at the barracks on the fairgrounds and was taking a motorcycle repair course. Bill had been stationed at St. John's, Newfoundland, in the artillery for two years and then transferred to the Armoured Corps. He was on embarkation leave en route to Hamilton for another course, after which he was scheduled to go to Camp Borden for a driver mechanic course before going overseas.

Every leave, Bill returned to London and finally got permission for us to marry in the parsonage of the United Church in Belmont on February 3, 1945. Bill and his best man, a friend from Saskatchewan, had bought my wedding ring and a silver heart-shaped locket in Toronto after pawning Bill's watch. They arrived at my father's farm after the snowplow had cleared the road. Bill and I drove to the parsonage with my father, the best man, Fred Simpson, and the bridesmaid, Freda Abbott. Rev. Oliver married us and refused payment from all servicemen.

We had a small reception at home and, after chores, Dad drove us to my apartment in London. Bill went back to Camp Borden Sunday afternoon and I went to work Monday morning.

I gave up my apartment and moved in with two single girls who worked at London Life. On weekend leaves, Bill and I spent Friday nights with friends and Saturday nights on the farm. One April day I received a call from Bill saying he had been given his order for overseas. It was a sad day. However, a few days later the war in Europe ended. I received many letters from England, with words and sentences cut out, while Bill waited for his return to Canada.

To occupy my evenings, I took the Red Cross Home Nursing and a First Aid Course and volunteered at Victoria Hospital. My most undesirable job was scrubbing the iron beds and mattresses for new patients. I learned how to empty bedpans and give back rubs, enemas and bed baths. I had applied at the hospital for a nursing career before going to Beal Tech, but the class was full. VJ Day came in August; it was a glorious happy day with everyone celebrating in the streets.

Then, in January, I received a postcard saying my husband was coming home on the *Queen Elizabeth* docking at New York Harbour. I had to call the armouries to see when the train was to arrive in London. On February 4, 1946, I took the bus to the CPR station and lined up behind the letter "B" - relatives on one side and soldiers on the other. Bill was very thin and trembled from head to foot as he hugged me. He was probably just as frightened as I was of the years ahead, since we had spent only a few weekends together after marrying.

Somehow I had managed to find a place to live - 753 Princess Ave, with a woodstove, a pantry, a pullout sofa in the main room and a shared bathroom with only cold running water. I went to work every day, while Bill stayed home on leave listening to the radio and drawing with pastel crayons. I still have the pictures. The war and separation were over and the future lay ahead.

🍁 Joan Bosomworth

When the Kingsway Store opened in Elora, Ontario, on March 29, 1940, the war had been going on for six months. Young men and women were joining the services. The effects of the Depression were still evident in the low prices and in the minds and purses of the customers. People were getting war work and it seemed as though times were improving. Goods gradually became scarce and rationing was imposed. Most customers accepted this with resignation. Compared to the sacrifices of the enlisted men and women and their families and the severe rationing and food shortages in Britain and Europe, we were fairly well off.

Sometimes, after unpacking a large carton of dry goods in the store, women would gather around hoping for some kitchen towels or some other needed article. But scarcity brought out greed in a few people. Like the woman who bought a gross of shoelaces, although they were not hard to get, or the woman who shouted at us because hairnets were not coming in from China, or the customer who blamed us every week because we could not supply the English dishes she needed for her large family.

During those years, most homes had oilcloth on their kitchen tables. One farmwoman had repeatedly asked for oilcloth week after week. When it finally came in, we were unwrapping it at the back of the store, but had not yet put any on the rack. When the woman came in the front door, she stopped and said, "You got the oilcloth. I can smell it." We were glad to have it for her and others.

The large display windows of the Kingsway Store had small holes for ventilation. Sometimes we could hear snatches of conversation on the street. Some humorous, such as, "Let's go into the new store; a couple of crazy kids run this one." My parents owned the business, but my sister Dora and I were often alone in the store. Other remarks were insulting to Elora, like the conversation between two women from the city: "Let's try to buy it in here. They probably don't even know there is a war on."

People like this and customers who could not stay loyal to one store, led retailers to believe there was a larger demand than there actually was. So when goods became available after the war, some storekeepers overstocked. A regular customer was Hannah McLean who purchased socks, handkerchiefs, etc., on behalf of the Ladies Auxiliary of the Legion who regularly sent parcels overseas. The Auxiliary raised part of its money by having bingos in homes and giving prizes like tea biscuits or homemade jams.

During World War I there had been some profiteering so the Canadian Government set up the Wartime Prices and Trade Board to control prices. We received reams of paper with long lists of prices for almost everything – whether we sold it or not. One year, a day or so before a wartime Christmas, one of the officials of the Board came to the Burt Brothers' Department Store and took up hours of valuable selling time checking prices. When the man asked if there was another dry goods store in Elora, the frustrated Charlie Burt said, "No." He told me later that, because we sold a minimum of yard goods, it wasn't really a lie. We were grateful to a kind competitor.

Stores were put on a quota by wholesalers and manufacturers. Being new, when our one supplier had fewer goods for us and we had no quota elsewhere, we were in trouble. Fortunately, the Gorden Mackay Wholesale Company kindly gave us some quota and increased it over the years so we were able to supply the community with many needed items. Toys, however, were scarce because many were manufactured in Germany, Japan and Britain.

We became friends with our customers and had time to listen to lonely wives and worried mothers. We grieved with the rest of the community when sad news came. Mother and I were at home doing the washing when news came of the end of the war. We rushed down to help Dora decorate the store with bunting and flags.

Isabel (left) and sister, VJ Day, 1945.

🍁 Isabel Bospoort

I was born early in 1939. My dad was approaching 60 and my mom was close to 40. Mom stayed home, as most moms did at that time. Dad was employed at the Parker Pen Company as a production engineer. Soon after the war began, Parkers re-tooled and began to produce shell casings for the Canadian Army, instead of their sleek and beautiful pens and pencils.

At an early age I sat on the sofa with Dad at our home in Parkdale and listened to Mathew Halton, the CBC's war correspondent, grimly reporting the latest news from the battlefront in Europe through the static and war noises emanating from our handsome wooden radio. Our quiet, tree-shaded neighbourhood soon began to change. The uncles, brothers and young fathers of my friends started appearing in the khaki (army), grey-blue (air force) or navy blue (navy) uniforms. The navy also had a white uniform, which impressed little girls, and big ones too!

The next thing I knew, they were boarding troop trains at Sunnyside or Parkdale stations, both close to our neighbourhood. I wept along with my friends and their parents as they said goodbye. At first I was a wee bit ashamed that my dad wasn't going anywhere but to his day job. I learned when I was grown up that he too felt that he should be going but he was already 60-years-old and contributed to the war effort in many other ways.

Then the neighbourhood mothers, aunts and older sisters began to leave their safe, secure homes and low-paying jobs. They went to work in the factories and the munitions plants to replace their menfolk who had gone to war. I watched them in the morning, dozens of them, with white turban-like kerchiefs to protect their long 1940s hairdos from dangerous machines. They strode purposefully along to catch the streetcars, swinging big metal man-size lunch boxes.

Older mothers, like mine, stayed at home and provided daycare for their neighbours' small kids and a safe after-school haven for the bigger ones. I had mixed feelings about sharing my mom, but she was a trained nurse and trusted babysitter, so I got used to having a house full of playmates,

Some neighbours began to get the dreaded telegrams delivered to their doors by uniformed officers and we knew that another daddy or big brother had been killed in action. We wept with them, and we comforted them, and we helped them carry on. Then it didn't seem so bad having my dad stay home in Canada. I had him home every evening to sing to me and tuck me in at bedtime.

Some time during those years, War Savings Stamps and food and gas coupons became an accepted part of our daily lives. "Don't leave home without it," referred to your ration book, not your credit card. Those round blue tokens with the holes were fun to play with, but they also got us scarce food items at the grocery store. Black market butcher shops flourished. My little girlfriends and I, being cute and appealing, went to the meat store with our mom or dad to ask in our "sweet little way" for a chicken or the Sunday roast that the adults found hard to obtain.

At that time my father still owned an old house in a village about an hour north of Toronto, where he had lived with his first wife. We often went there on weekends if we could stretch the gas ration that week. Once you got to the country you could always get a little gas from a farmer. We bought eggs, chickens and turkeys from those same farmers for our neighbours. We enjoyed rich cream and fresh ripe berries not available in the city. It was my proud duty to deliver the eggs in six-quart baskets to the neighbours when we got home Sunday night.

It seemed to me that every home had pictures on their walls of those wartime political leaders, Roosevelt (US) and Churchill (Britain). I don't know if the Canadian leader wasn't considered as important, but I don't remember him on the wall, only in the daily papers.

There was always a quilt-in-progress in our big front room where Mom and her friends held frequent quilting bees, using up all their good scraps to keep their families or "the boys" warm. Oh, how I loved those lunches they served. That's when you tasted some of the little treats they might have hoarded. They all did a lot of sock and scarf knitting and bandage rolling for the Red Cross. My elderly aunt, who lived with us from time to time, was always busy making warm coats for children from my dad's old suits and overcoats. New wool fabric was not available. It all went to the war effort.

I dreaded the evenings when we were required by law to close our blackout curtains, which were probably a quilt or tar paper, or shut off all the lights after the air raid siren sounded. The alarms were usually just practice runs, but when we peeked out at the night sky, it was totally criss-crossed with searchlight beams. Failure to comply with the lights-out rule brought an immediate visit from the Air Raid Warden. Dad and he had frequent noisy arguments. The Warden always won.

The first "Very Important Person" in my family, except for my parents, was a student who lived upstairs with his parents on the second floor of our triplex, our huge old Parkdale house, which had been turned into flats. He helped Dad and other neighbours with heavy projects, played baseball with the boys, pushed my swing and pulled my wagon. He had just always been there, this tall, brown-haired, friendly boy who was like a big brother. Then one day, he came home in uniform and it was my turn to say goodbye.

Soon, it was school time for me. One vivid memory remains of our kindergarten classroom one day per week becoming a temporary chapel, where a white wooden cross and a little war memorial were set up in the centre. All of the staff and student body stood around it, while the last post was played, hymns were sung and prayers were said in memory of the teachers, former students, brothers and fathers who had perished overseas that week.

We always went to Saturday matinees at the local movie theatre. The war news documentary films came on first, before the cartoon and the main feature. The news was pure propaganda, but because it was our propaganda it was okay. It gave us a chance to hurl insults at Hitler and Mussolini. If you'll pardon this terrible racist slur – our favourite was "Whistle while you work – Hitler is a jerk – Mussolini is a sheeny – Whistle while you work!" Even our skipping songs were full of insults to "the enemy."

The war brides were a great novelty to us. Their accents, their different clothes and shoes and their beautiful babies in high-wheeled British prams fascinated us. Several English girls came to our neighbourhood and we grew to love them for their sense of fun and their fresh new approach to life in Canada.

We were fairly close to Malton and Downsview, and every day fighter planes and bombers passed over our house bound for who knows where. There were also huge dark dirigibles which floated low overhead and made no sound, except for the ones fitted with loudspeakers, which broadcast propaganda messages with rousing "march" music.

The day the war ended we got the message on the school PA. Teachers immediately let us all loose. I don't think they could have stopped us anyway. Everyone was deliriously happy. When I got home, my mom gave my sister and me each a wee flag to wave and took our photo for posterity. The streets were jammed with autos which couldn't move for happy mobs of people, so drivers just left their cars and joined the throngs. Streetcars were overflowing with people hanging out the windows and clinging to the sides. Even the trolley roofs were crowded with people throwing confetti and tickertape, blowing horns and singing. Everyone left their jobs, dropped what they were doing and went into the streets.

The boys came home in bunches. We would go down to the station and watch them greeted by happy wives and parents, and children they hadn't seen since they were babies. The boy upstairs came home quietly and surprised us all. I ran to meet him and he threw me up in the air like when I was little, but now I was a great big 7-year-old. His cap fell off and I saw that his hair had turned completely white. His face was deeply lined and he looked like a thin, old man. His mom's cooking fattened him up again, but he never spoke of the terrible things he had seen and he didn't play and joke anymore.

We all moved to the country house. Dad finished up his working years as a commuter to Toronto. After four years of high school, I trained at Sunnybrook Veterans Hospital as a Department of Veterans Affairs RNA. I was finally "in uniform," but this uniform and my English-type veil had to be starched. I whistled "march" music as I worked in the wards and some of the veterans happily joined in.

By this time, wounded veterans of the Korean Conflict had joined World War I and II veterans. Just before our graduation we were given forms to sign if we wished to join a branch of the armed services. This sounded right up my alley but a young Dutch veteran and recent immigrant I was dating said, "No way, that's no life for a woman. You're going to marry me," and I did!

🍁 Catharina Bouwhuis

I was 10-years-old when World War II started. I lived on a small farm in Friesland Province in Holland, along with my five brothers and two sisters. The German soldiers overtook our country in five days. In 1942, they started to send our young men, aged 19 to 25, to France and Germany to build airfields, dig manholes and work in factories that manufactured war materials. Three of my brothers were in France and later one of them was sent to Germany. After one year, the two came home from France on leave and never went back.

We had to learn to be extremely careful and close-mouthed. However, the underground or the resistance movement was active and plotted against the Germans throughout the war. They did brave things. They would hide escaped Allied prisoners and help them get back to England.

The German Army took almost everything, leaving us with few resources. We were on food rations and only given enough food coupons for our family of eight. My father worked off the farm, leaving my mother and the children to do the farmwork growing potatoes and vegetables, etc. It was difficult when the underground brought eight other young people from the cities in the south for us to take care of and to share what we had with them.

Although girls were taught home economics in school, there was no material available for us to sew, so we practiced our fine stitches on paper. Sometimes we were fortunate enough to get some sugar bags that we bleached; we made articles out of that heavy material. There were three spinning wheels in our house. When we made articles from yarn and sold them, half of the profit went to the sheep farmer where we got the wool. Everyone dealt in the black market. Salt was $20 a pound and we needed salt to cure our meat and to use as a preservative.

The winter of 1943 to 1944 was a hard winter. We were required to take three children from the city for six weeks, then another three for six weeks, and so on. These children were malnourished and thin and some had scurvy.

My parents fed and clothed them. One night in 1944, we were approached to hide some Jewish people, but we already had all we could feed. People from the city would walk for days with wheelbarrows to get some vegetables from the farms. They had to pass the guarded bridge. Some guards would let them pass on the way back, but others would take what they had for themselves. There were good and bad Germans.

One day, we met some young German soldiers retreating on our side road. They evidently were avoiding the main road in hopes for escape. They told us, "You will soon be liberated."

🍁 Corinne Boyce

I remember standing in the backyard of our home in Sudbury, Ontario. I was holding my baby brother in my arms and the tears were streaming down my face. I had just heard the terrible news on the radio and the words "We are at war" rocked my safe world.

I was 13-years-old and had no experience of war and knew of no one who had been to war. But for some reason, it created an awful feeling that we would be touched somehow. My older brother was 14 at the time and I had no idea that in a few short years I would be watching him leave our home for the battlefield.

The years passed quickly and my brother joined the army. He spent a few short weeks training at Camp Borden. My family had moved to Toronto by this time and we were able to see him a few times on leave. He still looked like a young boy. As we waved goodbye to him at the train station, we had no idea where he was destined. We spent a lot of anxious days waiting for his first letter to learn that he had been sent off to England.

I have many letters from my brother while he was overseas. I recall one in particular he wrote to my grandmother telling her of sitting in Flanders Fields among the poppies. How sad to think of a young soldier sitting among those who were gone due to war. Another letter came as the war ended and he said he had signed up to go to Burma. My mother was so upset about it that my brother asked me to calm her down.

We soon were notified that he would be among the homecoming soldiers at Union Station in Toronto. We were all on hand to welcome him home and surprised to find he had grown to be a man. He soon advised us that the only way to get home quickly was to sign up, as they knew it would all be over before long. He did not talk much about the war, but did tell us that he had met our elementary school principal one day in the trenches and it was like finding an old friend.

Gladys in Northern Ontario, 1942.

❧ Gladys F. Bracey

I was born and raised on a farm in Saskatchewan. Due to medical reasons, my two brothers were rejected by the services, so being a proud Canadian I felt I should represent our family. I enlisted in the air force in April 1942 in Regina, Saskatchewan, and went to Toronto for basic training. I was so homesick! After basic training, I went to Guelph to train as a chef. I lived at the Cutten Fields Golf Course and we had many of our classes at the College.

My first posting was to Yorkton, Saskatchewan, which was only 40 miles from my home. It was # 11 SFTS, a Pilot Training School. There were many Australian, New Zealand and British airmen in training. There were a lot of activities on our station – bowling, badminton, tennis, shows and dances. There was never a chance to get bored.

I was there two years before going to the Paulson Bombing & Gunnery School in Dauphin, Manitoba. I was there for VE Day. What celebrating? I had to work! From there, I went to Moncton, New Brunswick. VJ Day happened while I was in Moncton, and I had to work there too! I moved on to Dartmouth, Nova Scotia, and was discharged in October of 1945.

❧ Harriet Broeze

I was born in a town 17 kilometres from the Rhine River, about the centre of the Netherlands, called Ede. There was a military base located there. In the summer of 1939 there were a lot more soldiers on the road than usual, which naturally to an 8-year-old was interesting. I remember on May 10, 1940, our mother called us out of bed to tell us that war had broken out.

We lived between two military bases and were told that our farm community was not safe and we had to move into town. My parents and their seven children packed a few necessary items into a cart pulled by a bicycle and with two or three other bicycles we started the 5 kilometre trip into Ede. It wasn't an easy task to find homes for all the evacuated families. I believe it was less than a week when our country capitulated and another week before we were able to return to our homes unsure of what we might find. As we made our way back, we passed home after home that had been damaged, but our home was okay.

To me, we lived a relatively normal life for the next two years of German occupation. We saw many more soldiers; they were just in a different uniform. The Jewish people had to wear a sticker on their clothes for identification. Then things began to change. Many Jewish people began to disappear. They were sent to camps or went into hiding. However, life went on and another sibling was added to our family in 1941.

We began to hear of people suffering from severe hunger and disease due to poor nutrition. In the summer of 1942, five of my seven siblings and I got sick with diphtheria. We all recovered; many did not. We had a quarantine sign on our door while we were sick and I remember mother saying that at least no one would bother us for a while. She was referring to the enemies or traitors.

During the summer, churches brought children between the ages of 7 and 12 from the cities to stay with farm families. A 7-year-old boy stayed with us for three summers. My parents invited his parents three or four times a year to come to visit. One time his mother and his aunt came for a visit. They came by train and then had to walk half an hour to our farm. They arrived at 10:30 a.m. and my mother served them coffee and a sandwich. The ladies bowed their heads and asked God's blessing for this food. The next day, Mom told me that they had had no breakfast and probably little supper the night before, if anything at all. These were the people who really knew about hunger. My mother always had food for them to take home. We learned fast what war was about.

We were farmers and were fortunate to have enough to eat most of the time, but we still lacked much of the nutritional needs of a growing family. We had to give most of our milk, grain and meat to the so-called "food bank." I remember my father slaughtering a pig, a sheep or calf during the night and hiding it from the soldiers so that we didn't have to give it to them.

In September of 1944, our Allies were stalled on the south side of the Rhine. The south of Holland was free, but our side of the river was still under German occupation. The war intensified for us. Many homes near the river were bombed and families fled inland for safety. The food supply depleted terribly. Our family took in 10 refugees. We managed to find places for them to sleep in our cramped quarters and we shared what little food we had. Our porridge became thinner. There was no feed for our cows or hens and they produced much less. Any food rations we received were minimal. Our bread looked like dark brown beans to me. I remember how beautiful white bread looked when the war ended.

After every meal, people came knocking on our door looking for leftovers. I recall one particular knock left me heartbroken when we opened it to one of my classmates looking for anything at all to eat. We had nothing left to give her. That winter all the horses that were left were taken from the farmers. As for the few farmers that still had some food to sell, they would only trade, as money was worthless.

A busy railway station was located about three kilometres from our home. The railway line ran about a kilometre behind our house and was often a target for bombing and people were killed. The bombs were released from the airplanes above our home in hopes of hitting the tracks. They often missed. One bomb landed so close to our house that the explosion shattered our windowpanes. These bombings were frequent during the last year of the war. We did not lose any family members to the war. Our neighbour however, was not so fortunate. They lost three of their sons. They worked in the underground trying to help the Jewish people hide.

One day about 10 soldiers marched into our home and took over our living room and camped there with their radios and all kinds of paperwork. Of course, they had their rifles and all their gear with them. My mother was cooking something on the woodstove at the time and they pushed it aside and cooked something for themselves. We had another stove given to us and my parents set it up in our back kitchen for our use. The soldiers came and went during the day, but I don't recall where they slept. We woke up one morning about a week later to find that they had packed up their gear and were gone.

One Sunday morning we were surprised by another visitor, a German soldier who appeared in our living room. We did not see him coming and had no time to hide. The children were playing outside. He asked if we could give him something to eat. One of the women staying with us spoke German and angrily told him that there were 20 people living in this small farmhouse and there was no food for him. He got angry and said that if he was Dutch we would probably have food for him. He said that he was hungry too and didn't want this war anymore than we did. He hadn't seen his family in 18 months and if he ever attempted to flee he would be shot. He turned around and left. We shed a few tears for him and came to realize that he too was human, like us.

I clearly remember April 17, 1945. A woman who regularly came to get milk from us came that day. She told us that our town was free. We couldn't believe it, but she kept repeating it. "Yes, yes, we are free and the town is full of Canadian soldiers. I thought you would have heard by now." The next day we all walked to town. What a sight! Yes, we were free! But the war was still going on - just 10 kilometres north was still under occupation. Then on May 5, 1945, it was finally over. The Germans surrendered. I was 14-years-old.

🍁 Alice Brothers

Alice and Lyle, Quebec City, December, 1944.

We had just been married on December 27, 1939, and left our hometown of Brussels, Ontario. Lyle's basic training was carried out in Listowel, a town 18 miles away. After receiving basic training in a parking lot of an old furniture factory in Listowel, Lyle was attached to the 24th Field Ambulance and sent to Val Cartier Military Camp in Quebec City. While there, Major McKibbon from Wingham realized Lyle had an ear problem and so he was transferred to Ordinance Corp in the Citadel, Quebec City.

Lyle's civilian trade as a watchmaker was then discovered and he was placed with the Royal Canadian Electrical and Mechanical Engineers (RCEME). He was stationed at No. 5 Depot, St. Malo in Quebec City, where he serviced army instruments on guns. These boys were given subsistence allowances and had to find elsewhere to live. They were allowed to bring their wives with them. Thus, my life as a war bride began.

Our first home was in Hostess House operated by Major Lewis and his family of the Salvation Army. This was a home for servicemen and their wives for a six-week period prior to a departure overseas, after which time we had to find other lodgings. During our stay there, we had made a friend of Mildred Richardson who worked at Hostess House. She suggested that her mum might have a room to spare. This proved to be one of the best things that happened to us. They had a large family of ten and only four of them lived at home, so they opened their home to servicemen and their wives. Many evenings were spent at their home with games and singalongs.

During our stay in Quebec, our Darlene was born. My days (Oh, how wonderful they were!) were spent in community work and playing the organ for evening services at church. I also played for gym and craft classes at the YWCA.

I remember, most vividly, my nine-month stay in Arvida, north of Quebec

City. No. 5 Depot serviced the aluminum plant there. It also served the area along the St. Lawrence River through to the Gaspé. At this time, we lived with the Coffey family, who all worked for the aluminum company. There was a unit stationed there to guard the plant and keep everything in good repair. While guarding the St. Lawrence, there were several U-boats caught. They had been responsible for sinking numerous merchant ships. We never learned of this until after the war, as it was kept secret.

How well I remember our trips home to Brussels when Lyle had weekend passes. Gas was rationed, so we carried gas in cans in order to get home to visit our parents. We spent more hours on the road than in Brussels. Lyle was transferred to Ottawa in 1945. War was coming to a close and he was stationed at the National Defence Headquarters, where they serviced instruments for storage. I did not find Ottawa as friendly a place, nor were there as many interesting things to do. However, I had Darlene who was a year old and she kept me busy.

We really had only one sad time during the war and that was in May 1942 when Lyle's brother Monty was killed. There were seven lads in the Royal Canadian Air Force (RCAF) being sent to England when the plane they were on exploded over Goose Bay. At that time, this was considered sabotage.

🍁 Vera Brown

With the war not going well in 1942, I felt I should be doing something worthwhile to help. Many of my friends were engaged in the war effort. My two roommates were working for the Wartime Prices and Trade Board, while I was just a file clerk at an insurance agency. I heard that girls were being recruited to work in an ammunition plant in Ajax, Ontario, so I applied and was accepted. Off I went, not knowing a soul. On the train, I discovered I wasn't the only one. My travelling companion was also alone and by the time we reached Toronto we were good friends and shared a room for the next few months.

Our residence was adequate. There were about five or six residences in our area for girls from the West and a lot for those from the Maritimes. I worked on the "Cap and Det" line, where I made the small detonator at the tip of the shell. There were three shifts, each trying to outdo the other. And, since it was assembly work, there was a lot of pressure and sometimes it caused accidents and fingers were lost.

If we missed the bus, we would hitchhike rather than wait an hour or so for the next one. We hitchhiked mostly in twos, but one day I was alone. A well-dressed man about 60, driving a lovely big car, picked me up. He was probably a VIP from General Motors. He gave me quite a dressing-down about hiking alone. Sounded just like my dad! But he must have made an impression because I never did it again.

My mother wrote her cousin in Fergus and told her I was living in Ajax and I received an invitation to spend Christmas with them. They still had four girls at home and I had such a good time. When I was invited back at New Years and Easter, I jumped at the chance. At Easter, they told me of an opening at the Beatty Brothers Factory in the drafting department. My six months were up in Ajax, so I went back and handed in my resignation and went to Fergus. I was lucky to get the job; I could have been out of work. Later, I learned that they had given up training young men who only left to join the Forces. So really I was releasing a young man for the war effort.

I had an amusing experience on my first trip to Fergus. I boarded the train in Toronto and travelled quite a distance without seeing a conductor. I was beginning to wonder how much further I had to go when a conductor came through the door shouting, "Acton, Acton!" I was about to put up my hand when he said, "Next stop, Acton!" You see, my maiden name was Acton and I had never heard of the town Acton.

❧ Eileen Brydges

My father-in-law, a widower, had five sons in the Armed Forces in World War II. I recall when the oldest was in a military hospital in England, the second was a prisoner of war in Germany, the third was an instructor at Camp Borden, the fourth served in Italy and later in the army of occupation in Holland, and the youngest served in Europe and then signed up for the war in Japan. Father kept the home fires burning through many lonesome and worrisome days, weeks and months.

The middle son and I were married in March 1945 in Ottawa on his embarkation leave. A required gunnery course delayed his departure. Then came VE Day, and later VJ Day. The war was over. One by one the boys came home, were discharged and went job hunting.

Then came an invitation which read: "You and your family and friends are cordially invited to a "Welcome Home" for the men and women of the Armed Forces from the townships of Bagot and Blythfield to be held in the Separate School Hall, Calabogie, March 1, 1946, at 8:00 p.m." It was signed, Reeve, Councillors and Ladies of the Red Cross. The five sons, three with wives and two with girlfriends who later became their wives, all attended, as did their proud and happy Father.

I will never forget the look in his eyes and the expression on his face as he looked down the long table at his 10 loved ones and said, "I never dreamed I would ever see all my sons and their wives together again at one table."

💐 Judy Buma

In May 1940, the Germans invaded the Netherlands and the lives of people living in that small country were forever changed. The city in which I lived was the home of the Royal Dutch Navy, a port along the North Sea. When the Germans walked into our city, the entire navy fleet, along with all the marines and naval officers, left for the open sea and crossed over to Great Britain where they fought alongside the British Navy. The Germans took over the shipyards and used the dry docks for maintenance of their war machinery, such as destroyers and U-boats. The Germans used the U-boats to torpedo British Navy ships. The British, in turn, bombed the wharves almost daily in order to halt the work done in the dry docks. And also, almost daily, some of the bombs missed the wharves and fell on the city. Many civilians lost their lives during these bombings. Den Helder was a dangerous place to live.

At this time I was six, the oldest of four children. My sister was 4 and I had two little brothers, one who was 3 and one who was just a baby. So much changed because of the war. Gone were the carefree days of my childhood, replaced by constant fear. When airplanes were sighted off in the distance, the sirens would scream all across the city to tell people to look for cover. Dad had decided that the safest place in our home was under the staircase, far away from windows. All of us would crowd into this narrow space. The baby carriage was always ready with a few emergency items for the baby, as well as for the rest of us. A small storage place under the mattress held important papers and some money.

Janny, my sister, started to scream the minute she heard the sirens. If this happened during the night the two of us would dash out of our bed and run to Mom and Dad's room. I crouched down and put my fingers in my ears to reduce the noise of the sirens. The house shook when bombs fell nearby and Mom or Dad would guess which street was hit. Janny trembled and screamed and before long nightmares were part of our lives.

Oma, my grandma, lived in another part of Holland where things were relatively quiet. One day Janny and I went for a long train ride with Dad. We were going to Oma's place; it was much safer there and no sirens kept us awake at night. Dad's youngest sister was still living at home and both Oma and my aunt took care of us. That fall, Oma enrolled me in Grade 1 and my sister in Kindergarten. We were in a strange city, without our parents, in a new school where we knew no one. We did not know that we would stay at Oma's for a full year.

After a long, long time Dad visited and told Oma he was going to take us home again. Mom could not do without us any longer. There was no telephone in either home and we were too young to write letters. Mom was so happy to have us back again. A surprise was waiting for us when we

24

arrived. Mom showed us a new little brother. He was about 10-months-old. For us children, life was normal for a while. Bombings did not occur as often as before, there was food on the table and we had the clothes we needed. Dad, however, disappeared now and then. We did not know that the Germans were looking for him. They needed men to work in their ammunition factories in Germany. They drove their big trucks onto our streets, cordoned off the neighbourhood, knocked on every door, or broke down the door, and looked all over for young men. When they found some, they dragged or pushed them out of the house and shoved them into the trucks. Some never returned home.

One day a big green army truck drove onto our street and stopped a few doors away. Some Germans knocked on the door and pushed their way in. A few minutes later, they came outside and pushed an older lady into the street; someone inside the truck pulled her in. She had not done anything illegal; she was picked up because she was Jewish. She never returned. Her life likely ended in one of the gas chambers. I remember this day clearly.

Mom and Dad had made a hiding place for Dad. A little pot-belly stove stood in the corner of the kitchen; Mom could not use it because there was no coal. Dad would remove the stove, lift up the linoleum, take up some floorboards and disappear under the floor. Mom would replace the floor covering and the stove. We did not even know the hiding place was there because my parents made sure we were not in the room when they opened it up. When the Germans asked us where our Dad was we could not give it away. It was not until I was 9 that I found out about Dad's hiding place.

Many things started to change. Almost every month some new order was issued by the Germans to make life difficult. Keeping us in clothes and shoes was one of Mom's major problems. She had made a coat for me out of one of her own. I wore a cape made out of flour bags and Janny had a dress made from the same material. Dad made sandals for us from a piece of wood made into the shape of a foot, with straps made from part of a piece of belt and the whole thing kept together with shoelaces. Almost every evening Dad would fix some of them because the wood was soft and did not keep the small nails in place.

Oma knitted socks and underwear for us made from a crocheted bedspread. I still remember the feel of hard cotton underwear and socks. Sometime before the war started, Mom had bought a tent for use at the beach. The tent, made of coarse fabric in orange and white with black stripes in between, was large. One day Mom brought the tent from the attic and since we had outgrown, or simply worn out, our pyjamas, she decided to use it to make nightclothes for us. A friend of the family helped Mom make pyjamas and at the end of the day the five of us modelled our new clothes in the living room. Dad happened to walk in at that time, took one look at us all lined up in orange, white and black stripes, and with a funny look on his face said, "Oops, wrong place!" He walked out, returned and said, "For a minute, I thought I was in jail!"

D-Day came in June 1944. Some people who had managed to hide a radio listened to evening news from the BBC in London. News that the Allies had landed in Normandy filtered through. Every day the troops moved further north. Paris was liberated and a few days later the north of France was free. Canadian and British troops were in Belgium and Holland would be next. Everyone expected freedom within a few days. But Holland's big rivers stopped the advance. In September, troops got as far as Arnhem and Nynegen. The Germans controlled the bridges, the fighting was fierce and many Canadian boys lost their lives. The Americans were attacking the German homeland at the same time, which made the Germans desperate. They withdrew to the north with the advancement of the Allies. There were Germans everywhere!

By far the worst year of the war was 1944. There was so much suffering during that last winter, known as the "Hunger Winter." There was chaos everywhere. Holes were blown in dikes and lowlands were flooded to stop the advancement of the Allies. Gas was made available between 12:00 noon and 1:00 p.m. to cook dinner, but who had any food? We only had 400 grams of bread a day to eat, and even potatoes and cabbages were no longer available. A central kitchen provided one ladle of soup per day for each person. The soup contained mainly cabbage leaves floating in warm water. People owning homes with flowerbeds dug up their tulip bulbs to cook and eat. There were hardly any dogs or cats left - eating them kept some people alive.

Farms were visited by hundreds of hungry people hoping to find food, any food. They walked for miles and miles, some came on old tireless bikes, and others pushed a handcart or baby carriage. Sometimes they were given food to take home and other times they were fed before they left. Some had walked for days to receive some food, only to have it taken by hungry Germans. Some simply could not go on, they sat at the side of the road and died.

Canadians pushed north again in the spring of 1945. They managed to cross the rivers and day-after-day new towns were liberated. The soldiers were cheered by thousands of people. The Canadians handed chocolate bars to children and cigarettes to men.

The killing of innocent Dutch citizens, however, continued at a dizzying pace. When the Dutch underground killed a German officer, the whole male population of a small town was rounded up and sent to Germany. Only a handful returned later, and the town was left with widows, women and children.

The word capitulation was on everyone's tongue. Planes flew low over the city a few days before the war ended. Pamphlets came down from the sky like confetti and containers with bread - real, white delicious bread - fell from the sky like manna from heaven. Every family received some bread, just plain loaves of bread. But that bread was better than any cake I have ever tasted. We also received a container with milk powder, egg powder, which no one had ever seen before, and hard biscuits. In addition, our container had some canned food in it. We could not read the labels because they were printed in English, but on opening one can we found red beets.

On the seventh of May 1945, Germany capitulated. We were free! The Germans and their sympathizers were rounded up. Young men who had been working underground, or were in hiding, came home. Many parents waited for children to come home; wives waited for husbands. Jews, hidden by Dutch citizens, hoped for the return of their loved ones. Most times, they hoped in vain.

Churches held special services thanking God for keeping us safe during those terrible years, thanking God for new-found freedom, but also asking God to help all those who had lost family members.

All through the war, we were not allowed to sing the Dutch National Anthem. Our church organist gave a beautiful rendition of our Anthem, a song we had not heard for five years. Some people could hardly sing without crying. We were finally free!

Lucienne, 1946.

🍁 Lucienne Bunda

I was born and raised in Ghent, East Flanders, Belgium. I obtained my teacher's degree in July 1944. We were handed our diplomas and told, "Go home!" We could hear the big guns in the distance.

During my school years, the Germans occupied part of our building and for some classes we went across the street to a private boarding school for girls. The rooms they supplied were not heated, so we sat with our coats, scarves and gloves on during the cold days. While in school I would circulate underground newspapers, such as *La Libre Belgique* and *Vrij*. I do not know how the principal, Miss Mestdagh, became aware of it, but she asked me, "Are you aware that you are putting yourself and the school in danger?" I stopped bringing the papers to school.

Regardless of the danger, we listened daily to the BBC news. And I would keep a daily journal of news and write down the words of the songs of that period. I wore a Belgian Flag pin. Once this was forbidden, I switched to an ivy leaf, with its special secret meaning - "I am attached to my country." I also kept chalk in my pockets and put "V" for Victory on walls.

Food rationing was severe in Belgium. We did not have a farm-oriented economy; it was more industrial. The quality and amounts of food continued to deteriorate as the German occupation dragged on. I used to make lists of what one ought to stockpile in case of another war. Before the war I was a finicky eater. But this changed as I often went to bed hungry. I was happy to eat plain boiled barley with a little, oh so little, sugar!

As the occupation continued, we learned where and how to obtain black market food products - potatoes, whole wheat, dried peas, dried beans and barley. It was always dangerous to either buy or sell, but you took your chances and were glad you could do it. With the information obtained by word of mouth, I would ride my bicycle to farms, quite a distance from home, to buy food. It was always a gamble to get back into the city and not be caught. Farmers or black market traders would also bring grains, peas, beans and barley to your house. The products were packed in special pockets sewn in their coats, which they would shake over a sheet laid out on the floor.

Towards the end of the war, the Germans forced my dad, a self-employed tradesman, to go work in the factory situated in the dockyard area of the city. One did not say "No," or they'd send you to forced labour camps in Germany. At least my dad could come home after work, even if it was a long bicycle ride home. Dad also tried to keep up with his other work. What kept him going was blood sausage. We could obtain it without food stamps because the butcher befriended us. I did not like eating those sausages.

I refused teaching jobs because they were in small towns and, while waiting for a better position, I took employment in a lawyer's office. Around the end of October 1944, or the beginning of November, the Third Canadian Division moved into Ghent for rest and regrouping after they cleared and opened the Scheldt Estuary, which gave the Allied Forces access to the inland Port of Antwerp. The battle-weary soldiers of the Third Canadian Division were welcomed and billeted in private homes in Ghent. The barracks in Ghent were already taken over by other troops.

My dad also owned a hardware store and we would hear about the worst of people from customers. The stories about the behaviour of some Canadian soldiers were not that great, so we did not put our name down to billet a soldier. Besides, we really had no spare bedroom and there were already two full apartments rented out. On Sunday, November 5, 1944, I was waiting by the door of our store for my mother to get ready for church when our next door neighbour called, "Lucienne, what does that soldier want?"

It was a Captain looking for billets for about 10 of his men. As we were talking, trying to figure out who might have accommodations still available, other neighbour ladies stopped by and helped with some names and addresses. Then, one of the ladies said, "But, Madame De Bruyker, you have no one." My mother replied, "We have no spare bed." "No problem," she said, "we will lend you a small mattress to put on the floor." This little mattress was for me and I would give up my bedroom to a soldier, who freed us from the Germans and deserved some comfortable rest for a few nights.

When my dad heard the news, he was not pleased. Some time after lunch, the Captain dropped off Sergeant Wesley F. Bunda at our home. I said as he walked in, "We like to keep the place clean!" He responded, "She did not say welcome, glad to see you. No, just we like to keep the place clean!"

This was our first meeting. But everyone liked Wes' version that he later told our children. His story: "Every day I had to go to Headquarters for new orders. Every time I came down the hill on my motorbike and turned on this street, I would see this young girl observing me - a good-looking Canadian soldier. The third day I drove by, this young girl snatched me off my motorbike with a big fish hook fastened to a big fishing pole. This young girl had asked her father to make the fishing pole for her so she could catch me."

That first evening Sergeant Bunda went out with his friends and I went with mine. When I came home, our soldier was not back yet. My dad's comments were not flattering. Anyway, I stayed up, but as night progressed I finally closed the store door and went to sleep on my cot. The next morning as my dad opened the store and took the shutters down, there came Sergeant Bunda to the door. He got lost coming from the park where their equipment was parked. The streets fanning out like the spokes of a wagon wheel confused him in the dark. Not having any luck obtaining directions, some lady took pity on him and let Wesley spend the night on a chair in her house. First thing the next morning, Sergeant Bunda went looking again and found our house.

I took some time off work, showed Wesley the city, especially all the historic sites, which he saw only as old stones. After that point, Wesley and I went out with my gang and their guest soldiers and visited with my parents. We certainly tried to make his stay enjoyable. Sergeant W.F. Bunda did not fit the stereotype of the "wild Canuck," he was always a gentleman. On Thursday, November 9, 1944, the Third Division left for Nynegen, Holland.

Wesley sent a letter thanking us for our hospitality. He added that I could write him if I wanted and he would like to hear from me. I was glad to oblige; I had an occasion to write in English and not forget what I had learned. So we stayed in friendly correspondence.

May 8, 1945, was VE Day, the end of all fighting in Europe. What a joy! We all joined the happy crowd laughing and dancing in the streets. Once the war was over and while he was still stationed in Holland, Sergeant Bunda hitchhiked to Ghent to visit. In June 1945, after I passed my examination, I was employed by the Belgian Office of Mutual Aid to work as a censor for the British Intelligence Service - military tag No.G-953-409. The work was done in Brugge, Belgium, and we were trucked back and forth every day.

Along the way, we must have fallen in love because at the end of August, when Wesley asked me to marry him I said yes. At the time, Wesley was stationed in Holland and was likely to be shipped back to Canada. In September 1945, our Unit No.1 District Censorship Station (DCS) moved from Bruge to Bonn, Germany, and was part of the British Army on the Rhine (BOAR). There, I was employed both as a censor and a translator.

While still in Holland, and later in England, Wesley started to take the necessary steps for us to be married. He left for Canada on November 9, 1945, on the *Queen Elizabeth I*. What we did not know or realize is that once Wesley returned to Canada, all the steps he had taken for us to be married were nullified and void. He had to start over again and make an application to obtain an immigration permit for me. A year later, in November 1946, I returned home to Ghent to prepare for my immigration to Canada.

I obtained second-class passage, Cabin 295, on a Swedish shipping line that was faster than any other. My three iron trunks came with me, but the crates had to be shipped separately and fumigated before being released from quarantine in Montreal. Before arriving in New York, the ship's doctor vaccinated everyone who had no valid smallpox vaccination papers. Once the ship docked, I started to look for Wesley. I looked over the crowd, thinking he would be close to shipside. There was a man standing by the gangway that I had to use to disembark and he seemed to be waiting for someone. I did not like his looks. I went back inside, came back on deck, back inside, back on deck, back inside, back on deck … and he was still standing there. Finally, I gazed over the crowd and further back I saw Wesley putting up his hand with the "V" sign. He had been wondering why I did not disembark.

We toured New York for the rest of the day. The following day we left for Canada by bus. We crossed into Canada on May 7, 1947, over the Rainbow Bridge at Niagara Falls, Ontario. It was snowing! Father Laverty, a priest at Our Lady of Help Christians' Church in Wallaceburg obtained special dispensation from the London Diocese to marry us on May 17. Coming to Wallaceburg, Ontario, was certainly a culture shock in more ways than one. It was a completely different way of living.

🍁 Liena Buys

On the morning of May 10, 1940, Hitler attacked Holland. My oldest sister Jo was sent to town to buy everything you would not be able to buy during wartime, such as coffee, tea, spices, etc. Soon after the invasion, the German soldiers rounded up the Jewish people. Every Sunday morning a cattle train stopped in our village and as they gathered the Jewish families, Mothers would cry out to people to take their children home. But nobody did. They were scared. Then the soldiers would grab the kids by their legs and arms and throw them in the train.

One afternoon, my dad's hired hand, Bart was his name, was digging out sugar beets by hand when he yelled, "They've come to take me away." There were two German officers, with another man between them. Bart knew him right away. He had given him plain clothes; he was a German deserter. So they took Bart behind our farm and dug up the German uniform. The next day, Bart went on a transport truck to Amesfoort where there was a prison camp; later he was put on a cattle train to the Dachau Concentration Camp. There his duty was to stand on guard every morning, where the crippled and the rich were separated and burned in the chambers. Then he had to go with the wheelbarrow and cleanup the bones and remains. He was there for two years. When he came back after the war was over, his body was covered with bruises and scars. He had typhus and was only 50 when he died.

Often during the war, when the air raid sirens sounded, my mom and dad with their family of six girls and two neighbours with sixteen children would run and hide in a safe basement-like structure in our orchard. It was covered with sugar beet stalks inside and there was a supply of sugar water too.

When the Canadian soldiers were stationed on our farm, we always waited for them to finish breakfast. We would be so happy to eat their leftovers - nice white bread and the Christmas cakes that were sent over from Canada. The Canadians cooked in our kitchen and slept in our barn.

After the war, I married my husband John. He was the oldest of a family of four boys. They lived in Huesden, a beautiful town on the Maar River. Before the war, there stood a beautiful town hall. Often, there were fights between Canadian soldiers on the south side of the river and the German soldiers on the north. The Germans relayed that everyone would be safe if they went to the basement of the town hall. One day, almost 500 people went there for shelter. Then the Germans blew up the town hall. Most of the people died instantly. My husband John was asked to come with his horse and wagon and load the remains and bring them to a mass grave. When the war was over, John received a beautiful certificate for his bravery.

🍁 Jean Cassan

At the outbreak of war in 1939, I was in my late teens and decided to go into training as a nurse. I graduated from Belleville General Hospital School of Nursing in 1942.

After graduation and spending some time in obstetrics, the war was still raging, so I decided to apply and was accepted at the hospital close to the major air station at Trenton. Later, I spent a few months at the Kingston, and then the Ottawa, Military Hospital.

In July 1944, I found myself aboard the SS *New Amsterdam*, a fully-loaded troopship including the complete staff for #24 Canadian Military Hospital. After 10 days, we arrived in Gaurach, Scotland, and some time

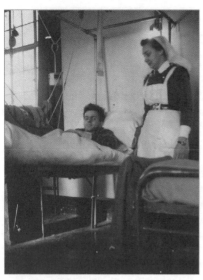

Jean with patient, November, 1944.

later went by train to London, England. My first sighting of London was from the back of an army truck. Eventually, we travelled to Horley, midway between London and Brighton.

Leaving home and travelling across the sea into a war zone was traumatic. I was an only daughter and my father had recently died. I am sure my mother was lonely. She always came through with the occasional box of goodies from the sparse rations. In England, we had what were called Canadian rations – dried eggs and grey bread.

Fortunately, no family members were casualties. Although my brother spent four years as a Spitfire pilot, he returned home safely. Following the signing of all the treaties and the return home of our patients, we were gradually released to go home as well. Along with another nurse and a doctor, I returned to Canada with a boatload of wives and children of Canadian soldiers. There were no serious illnesses on board, but we spent 10 days on the North Atlantic in November of 1945 on a small ship called the SS *Bayona*. Halifax looked really good when we arrived. Following a couple of months leave, I returned to Kingston where I was officially discharged.

🍁 Neysa E. Clark

I was 21 and living in Toronto when the war began in September 1939. The war filled our lives. My dad was 58 and his peacetime white-collar job disappeared. Because he could read blue prints, he found himself in a new world at the fast-expanding Victory Aircraft Ltd. in Malton, where they were building the gigantic Lancaster bombers. He became a lead-hand supervising a team of women aircraft workers – riveters, like those immortalized by the wartime song "Rosie the Riveter" and war production posters.

After I married, I was a homemaker until the pressures of war increased. I started to work in the office of a small B.F. Goodrich plant, which retreaded used tires with recycled rubber for civilian use. This was not a completely satisfactory process, but new tire production was exclusively for the Armed

Forces or essential services. The retreading factory where I worked was across the road from the stockyards and the meat-packing plants of Swifts and Canada Packers. When getting off the streetcar for work, the smell of the stockyards and the sickening steam rising from the drains on the street near the processing plants made me hold my breath until I entered the Goodrich plant. Once inside, the welcome smell of hot rubber overpowered the outside air and clung to my clothes and hair.

My sister-in-law was soon employed as one of the 5,000 women filling all kinds of ammunition shells at the immense General Engineering Company (GECO) plant, a self-contained mini-city in 172 camouflaged buildings with 16 kilometres of underground tunnels, covering over 117 hectares of former farmland southeast of the intersection of Eglinton and Warden Avenues in east Toronto. On arrival at the plant, everyone changed into the cotton underclothes, jumpsuits and turbans provided. They wore shoes without metal nails as a precaution against static electricity and sparks.

My husband Reg and both of his brothers, Bert and Alf, enlisted, as did my sister Verna, my brother Hedley, many cousins and almost all of our friends. Some experienced much danger and fighting; many had support roles. Some were sent far away; some did duty near home. Some were gone from home for years; others for a shorter period of time. Some were heroes; many were wounded; sadly, many died. Many returned home safely, profoundly changed by their experiences. Many men found their wives were no longer the familiar "girl they left behind," as she had also changed from her experiences during the years apart. Women's roles changed completely and forever, never to be the same again.

Reg enlisted in the air force in 1940, but was not called for duty until early in 1941. After his eye test he was disappointed to find out that he did not qualify for aircrew, so he entered as a clerk since he had office experience. As the war continued and the number of aircraft multiplied and casualties increased, there was a growing need for aircrew. From time to time, the requirements for the eye test became less stringent and Reg reapplied each time, still in hopes of the wild blue yonder. As the most needed replacements were for the vulnerable tail gunner's spot, I was always relieved - though Reg was disappointed - that he was not accepted.

After basic training, Reg was assigned to the Orderly Room or office at Manning Pool, where a staff of about 20 administered the daily business for the huge complex. Later on, he was posted to the #1 Training Command on York Street in Toronto. We were married by this time, and once again I worried for nothing about a distant move. This Training Command covered all the air force training for Ontario, as well as the thousands in the Air Cadet Program. Reg was attached to the Air Cadet section, where he remained for most of his time with the Royal Canadian Air Force (RCAF), spending his summers at Air Cadet camps at Trenton, Clinton and Aylmer air stations with about 10 other members. Here the large cadet groups, which changed every few weeks, continued their studies of the principles of flight and navigation and experienced the camaraderie of life on an air station – living in tents, drilling, playing games and recreation and flying in one of the hundreds of noisy training planes filling the sky overhead. These training planes were piloted by young men, not much older than the cadets, who were in the serious business of learning to fly for war.

When she was 20, my sister Verna took the great step of independence from the family and enlisted in the Women's Royal Naval Service (WRENS). After a few weeks of basic training at Galt, even including "swabbing the decks," she was posted to HMS *Cornwallis* and a huge naval training base in Nova Scotia. This base had literally been cut out of the bush and was a sea of mud in rainy weather. The sticky mud and frequent stones made marching and inspection parades especially difficult for women. Men wore big rubber boots, but women wore black stockings and shoes with rubbers, which often came off in the mud. This base was home to a transient population of about 10,000 seamen and about 600 women or Wrens. Dances in the drill hall, sometimes to the music of the big bands, were overwhelming at first!

Verna was posted to the Victualling Stores, where Naval Officer Helen McKercher, later Head of the Home Economics Branch of the Ontario Ministry of Agriculture, developed the menus for all the personnel on the station, as well as for the crews of the naval ships crossing the Atlantic on convoy duty from that port. Verna's job, using paper and pencil, was to arrive at the huge amounts of food to be ordered using a formula for the menus supplied – the number of men on board times the number of ounces of meat, potatoes, vegetables, bread, butter, sugar, tea, etc., per man, per day. For the base it was straightforward. But for the ships, the number of ships, number of crew and number of days at sea varied. Verna said she spent the war worrying that through some mistake of hers some ship's company on duty in the North Atlantic would go hungry!

Both Reg's brother Bert and my brother Hedley volunteered for the army. Both were married with children and both served in Canada. Bert became an army driver and Hedley was in charge of the battery shop at Camp Borden near Barrie, servicing hundreds of vehicles on the base. Both of their wives worked in war plants. Reg's brother Alf joined the army early in the war and was in England by Christmas of 1939. He eventually fought in North Africa in the long bitter fighting of the Italian campaign. He was credited with shooting down an attacking Stuka dive-bomber with a Bren gun. This may have seemed like a movie. But it was real and Alf was just an ordinary young man, far away from his wife and children. He had a little boy Bob, who was 2, and his daughter June was born after he left for England. She was 6-years-old before he saw her on his return home.

In later years, I went to Normandy with my sister Verna and I stood on that dreadful beach at Dieppe. I thought of those young men with their full packs and heavy equipment, struggling, shouting and swearing to reach dry land and all under heavy fire from fortified positions from the surrounding high ground. The raid was not a surprise to the Germans and nearly 1,000 Canadians were killed and hundreds wounded and captured. I stood there where they had fought and died and I thought bitter, bitter thoughts of the war.

There were so many heroes. And there were others who did their part. All had their lives greatly affected by the war. Writing this makes me realize, more than ever, that ordinary people doing extraordinary things won the war!

🍁 Shirley Crisp

The love of my life and I were 14-years-old in 1939 when World War II began. The thought that war would affect our lives was just a mere wisp in our minds. We were dreaming of our future together. Time marched on, as did the conflict; he worked in a foundry on machines of war, I in a shop making uniforms for the military. We were engaged. When my sweetheart turned 18, he joined the army. I was proud, but heartsick. Toronto was our home city. He was shipped to the East coast for training. Letters were written every day, which helped a little.

We planned a June wedding. He had permission from his commanding officer, but the situation in Europe escalated. So on his final leave in April 1943 we were married in a beautiful church ceremony with family and friends attending. In those days, the mail was fast. The invitations were sent Wednesday evening; all were received Thursday. The wedding was Saturday. My new husband left on Monday.

This is a love story about two teenagers caught in a conflict, not of their making. My husband did return to me in August of 1945. He was on his way from Europe to the Pacific Theatre of war after serving in the D-Day landings and the liberation of Holland. The war ended on his way home. His war experiences and the horror he saw, never left him. Following is a letter from myself, the 18-year-old bride to her 19-year-old husband of three days.

> *My Darling:*
> *As I sit and write, visions of you pass before me. Dreams of the past, memories of what has been. They hurt my tortured soul. But the tears that fall with their remembrance bathe the wounds that our parting has inflicted.*
>
> *You have gone, but the knowledge of your love is a great comfort to me. I must hold it and my memories ever near to me, for the future is not ours to foretell.*
>
> *Yes, you have gone and taken my heart with you. It has left a cavity in my breast that aches in its emptiness. But I*

*shall carry on, for you. My tears will water our love like a
plant and it will grow and bloom victorious over all else
forevermore.*

*Love Tequilla
(his pet name for me!)*

🍁 Marjorie Darling

The summer of 1939 seemed much like previous summers to a 16-year-old girl with eight weeks of carefree days to be enjoyed before returning to school in September for my final year. Warm sunny days were spent on the beach at Bournemouth with my three cousins, and then one morning a letter came from my father asking my aunt to put me on the train for London the next day. I returned to London and became aware of the mood of anxiety prevalent amongst the adults, although my father tried to reassure my mother by telling her no one in their right mind would bring about another war after the slaughter and carnage of the Great War, his war, World War I.

Late in the evening on August 31, my sister and I were hustled back to school in Surrey. The next morning we discovered some of our friends had arrived back before us. The morning of September 3 is still clear in my mind - the older girls were on the school grounds helping to fill sandbags to pile up in front of the basement windows. We were called to listen to the wireless and heard Neville Chamberlain declare that the country was at war with Germany. Almost immediately, there was the chilling sound of the air raid siren. I remember thinking I would never see my parents again. Fortunately, I was wrong on that score.

There were immediate changes. For instance, we never went anywhere without our gas mask and identity card - my number was DMFK/242/21. If you entered a room at dusk or later, you never turned on a light until you made sure the blackout curtains or screens were in place. Neither did you open an outside door before turning the hall light out. If you did, there was usually an Air Raid Warden around to warn you. A piece of black paper with a hole or slit covered the inside of the glass of our flashlights, so that just a ray of light shone through. And suddenly, there were no church bells, a real loss! The bells were to be rung only if there was an invasion by sea or air. Signposts at crossroads and intersections were removed and all place names at railway stations were taken down. This made travel difficult.

In the meantime, our house in London was given up and our belongings put in storage. It was not until June 1940 that we had a house again, this time in the north of England at Southport in Lancashire. For those of us who were in boarding school there was not the trauma of having to leave home for the first time, which many children suffered by being evacuated to private homes in the country. We were in familiar surroundings with our friends. This was the time of the "Phoney War," and apart from the odd air raid warning not much happened.

When the siren did go, and we always heard it because there was one on the roof of the school, we put on our dressing gown and took our pillow and eiderdown and went quickly and quietly to the cellar to our allotted bunk bed. The first time we went down, I looked for my sister who was only 6. I couldn't see her, so I asked the Sister. It turned out she had put on her dressing gown and slippers and had got back into bed and was fast asleep.

After the fall of France and the evacuation of troops from the beaches at Dunkirk, I remember our gym mistress describing the scene at the Dorking Railway Station as the trains slowed and stopped. People were giving the troops tea, sandwiches, cigarettes, and anything else they had to give these exhausted men who were so thrilled to be home again.

The fear of invasion was real. On June 29 my father came south to fetch my sister and I to take us north to join my mother in our new house. I had two or three weeks holiday and then one day my father came home and told me he had arranged for me to have a job interview. I knew I would have to earn my own living and I had just turned 17. It was time for me to get a job, but I had no idea what I wanted to do. I was too young to go into the services, so I became a Temporary Woman Clerk in the Ministry of Labour and National Service.

The house, which my parents had leased, was quite big and so it wasn't long before the Billeting Officer paid us a visit. We were required to take two billets - one was a colleague of mine at the office and the other a Corporal in the Royal Army Pay Corps whose outfit was stationed in Southport. This turned out to be a great benefit as my father had been transferred back to London, leaving my mother, my sister, our faithful maid and me without a man in the house.

During the time the Battle of Britain raged, we saw the newspaper vendor's placards with the number of fighter plane losses. We rejoiced at "theirs" and were saddened by "ours." We didn't even think that "theirs" were young men and were somebody's son or husband or father. We just thought of our young men.

Liverpool was only about 16 miles away, so when the port was being bombed we sometimes got the effects of being on the fringe of the main target. I remember the night when the Sunshine Home for blind babies on the next road took a direct hit and the little ones were all killed. Feelings ran high. Because of our close proximity to Liverpool, each office had firewatching duties. This, I think, was a voluntary commitment. We had to take a course in putting out fires, working a stirrup pump and making our way through a burning area on our stomachs, together with basic fire prevention exercises. We were fortunate in never being put to the test. The most onerous part of the training was wearing tin helmets; they were so heavy.

In 1940, in my particular section at the office there were seven clerks and one supervisor. All of us were in our teens and early twenties and over the next two years the young girls were called up and replaced by older, married women. As the time neared for my call up papers to arrive, I decided against the services and expressed a preference for nursing, much to my family's dismay. I applied to St. Mary's Hospital in Paddington and after various interviews and medicals was accepted to commence in October 1942.

Earlier that spring, in May 1942, my family had returned south and was now living in Surrey on the edge of London. My days with the Ministry of Labour and National Service continued in one of the London offices. I didn't start nursing in October, as late that summer I contracted cerebrospinal meningitis and spent many weeks in the hospital. Eventually, I was able to start at St. Mary's in February 1943. Because of the hospital's proximity to Paddington Station - railway terminals were prime targets for bombing - we were sent to the country for the first two months. After having passed the necessary probationary exams, I started in the hospital proper.

Many of the London hospitals had large facilities outside of London; some were regional mental hospitals taken over and used for civilian patients whose care was not an emergency. This arrangement was set up just prior to the outbreak of the war; it was called Emergency Hospital Service (EHS). Patients were sent to the country for both medical and surgical treatment and emergency patients who were admitted to the London hospital were operated on, and as soon as possible transferred to the country for continuation of their care. Many of the single-decker buses were turned into ambulances with three or four stretcher spaces each side of the bus. There were also large sections of these EHS hospitals reserved for servicemen and were used when there was an increase in casualties, such as after Dunkirk.

After six months at Paddington, my group was sent to the sector of the EHS which was staffed by St. Mary's. Most of our patients were servicemen and some women dressed in hospital blues. Many were recuperating from wounds and broken bones. Some stomped around in walking casts, cheerful, willing to please. The wards were large, consisting of 18 to 20 beds. The nurses swept the wards twice a day and nothing pleased these young men more than to sweep for a nurse who had taken their fancy. We were not allowed to go out with a patient, but it was amazing how many couples were seen in the local tea shops in the nearby town or at the local cinema.

This was a time when the UK had troops from all over the world, including thousands of Americans. The Allies were preparing for D-Day and we used to watch the planes and gliders practising in the clear April skies. We prepared, in our own way, with every spare minute used to make gauze squares, surgical swabs, splints, bandages, etc., for use when the casualties arrived.

Just a couple of weeks before D-Day my group was sent back to Paddington. We were so disappointed as we felt we would not be an important part of the invasion for which we had prepared. However, we need not have worried because soon after the invasion the V-1s and V-2s started arriving over London and the southeast coast. The V-1s were called buzz bombs or doodlebugs. There was something uncanny about them because there was no pilot. They were noisy, and the moment the engine cut out you ran for cover because it was going to drop somewhere near. The V-2, on the other hand, was a rocket with an explosive warhead and there was no advance warning. The first you knew about them was when they landed and exploded causing widespread damage.

With the doodlebugs and the rockets came many casualties, which kept our wards busy. The patients who were so brave and philosophical were starting to show signs of anxiety, especially during the night when they heard these wretched doodlebugs. They had already been dug out of bombed buildings and didn't want to go through it again.

I remember one woman patient - I even remember her name - discharging herself. Unheard of! She was not an air raid casualty, but she received a message that a V-1 bomb hit her house. She had to go home because she whispered to me that her life savings was hidden behind a loose brick by the fireplace. I often wondered if she found the money.

The war did not end as quickly as had been hoped, but eventually the end was in sight. With the troops' entry into Germany and the discovery of the concentration camps came the call for medical help. As soon as doctors had completed their year of internship, they were drafted into one of the services, so the medical students who were about to take their final exams filled the call for staff. I don't remember how many St. Mary's students, only male in those days, went over, but medical students were always a "devil-may-care" group. These young men went to Germany as a spirited, carefree group, ready to help. They came back some weeks later as a responsible, sober, changed group. Their weeks at the Bergen-Belsen Concentration Camp had left its mark on them forever. They brought back photographs of the horrors of what they found, which up to that point had not been published by the British Press.

Then came D-Day, May 8, 1945. Who can forget it? I came off duty at 6:00 p.m. and joined the crowds. I just went where the crowd took me, everyone singing and happy, hugging and kissing, doing the conga around Piccadilly Circus and being carried along to Buckingham Palace. I walked back through Hyde Park to Paddington and for once in our long years of training the doors of the nurses' home had been left unlocked that night. However terrible were those years of war, we worked hard and we played hard and we learned lessons we have never forgotten.

🍁 Joan Davison

The day was warm and sunny. The flowers and trees were in their full glory on that peaceful Sunday morning in Surrey, England. War with Germany had been announced earlier that day, still it was quite a shock to hear the sudden wailing of the air raid siren. It was September 3, 1939, and to a teenager, life looked good. I was part of the staff in a large house, under the cook's thumb in the morning and helping the housemaid in the afternoon. The alarm turned out to be false, but being so young, I found it all very exciting and fun.

Within a few months, England was engulfed in a sea of khaki, air force blue and navy blue. The Canadians made themselves at home and were glad to make friends and find a family they could visit. They received the most wonderful food parcels from Canada and would always share. It was like Christmas and gave us a change from the meagre rations. The Americans arrived later on and made their presence felt, not always in the best way. They earned the epithet, "Overpaid, oversexed and over here," from the resentful Tommies, or British soldiers. However, they all worked together in their one purpose of defeating the Germans.

The routine of my life remained fairly constant until a Canadian came to our home bringing his food parcels. He was able to play guitar and sing and yodel up a storm. We decided to get married. He had to get his Captain's permission and my parents said yes. They did suggest that we should not start a family until after the war. Upon reflection, it was rather a futile request to make to two very young, very much in love and very green sweethearts.

I was lucky to get a white wedding dress and two blue bridesmaid dresses and we were married three weeks after the bans were read. Thirteen months later we had a son. My husband came home as often as he could and we were happy. During this time I worked as a letter carrier for the Post Office, getting up at 5:00 a.m., sorting and then delivering letters on my bike, sometimes in the pouring rain. I was doing my bit for my country.

I eventually moved to Polegate in Sussex to be nearer to my husband. It was there, while I was bathing the baby in front of the fire, that we were

Wes and Joan, July 19, 1941.

bombed. A low-flying plane on its way back to Germany decided to drop its bombs. I immediately dove under the table with the baby as the noise and dirt rained around us. Thank God we were safe, but such a mess. The air was so thick with dust and dirt that you couldn't see anything.

In 1943, my husband was sent with the First Division to invade Italy. I was back in my hometown living in one room. I had rented the ground floor room, which was right next to a church. The room had been empty for a long time and was large and spacious. When I snuggled down for the night in the dark, the baby in his cot, the room came to life. I could hardly believe the army of mice running and scurrying over the floor, the bed, the curtains. They had taken over the room.

So I got myself dressed, made sure the baby was asleep and off I went to my parents' home two miles away. I borrowed their cat Mickey. It took about two weeks, but Mickey did his job well. No more mice. It is sad to say that he had eaten so many mice in such a short time that it was the death of him. But, as far as I was concerned, he did his bit for the war effort!

In the spring of 1944, an Army Chaplain came to talk to me about my husband's health. He was returning to England on a hospital ship. He was suffering from severe shell shock and could not be exposed to loud noises or war movies. He was to return to Canada, so arrangements were also made for our son and myself. I arrived in Halifax in November 1944, and came to Ottawa by train which had been dubbed "The Diaper Express" since it was full of war brides and their children.

I shared a tiny apartment with my mother-in-law and sister-in-law, who were kind to me. I was homesick but got over it. My husband was not able to come home from the hospital until May 1945, 10 days before our daughter was born. We eventually raised seven children. I am a grateful Canadian citizen and thankful for the sacrifice made for the good of mankind by so many unsung heroes.

🍁 Yfke de Gorter

In 1932, the Dutch built a barrier dike between the provinces of North Holland and Friesland in order to create a lake to the south of the dike. In this newly created lake, the Dutch Government built another dike and put up two pump stations. When the water was pumped out, they had reclaimed 18,000 hectares of good farmland, which they called a polder. I lived on a farm in the small village of Slootdorp with my parents, my four brothers and three sisters.

Early in the morning on May 10, 1940, the Germans invaded the Netherlands. They bombed the city of Rotterdam and fought at strategic points. The dike was one such point. My dad, younger sister Annie and I had seen the war preparations on the dike the day before while travelling to

Friesland to attend a wedding. There were soldiers at checkpoints, bunkers, barbwire constructions and piles of sand bags. The Dutch soldiers fought, but were no match for the Germans. After five days, the Netherlands surrendered.

My dad and sister had gone home right after the wedding, but I had stayed in Friesland at my grandparents' house. I had to stay with them for 10 days because the dike was closed. Downed airplanes and other debris had to be cleared away and the bridge had to be repaired. When the dike was passable again, Dad knew a truck driver who shipped goods over the dike regularly. He transported people too. I was told which town to go to, found the truck and climbed in the back, along with several others. We got over the dike and I arrived home safely. That summer I was 16-years-old.

We were now an occupied country. The Germans established an Administration Bureau to replace the local government. Nazi sympathizers were appointed to positions of mayor and council and they executed the orders of the Nazi Government. Our lives completely changed. The population was ordered to bring their brass and copper possessions to the mayor's office. These items were collected to send to Germany to be made into ammunition. Much of our food supply was also shipped to Germany and food became scarce, as did fuel.

On the farm at threshing time, an inspector from the Administration Bureau's Food Supply Office came and kept track of our harvest. We were allowed to keep enough grain for our family and the rest would be shipped to Germany. However, a kind inspector would often look the other way, so farmers could put some extra grain away for their own purposes. Later, we even had to turn over our radios to prevent us from listening to the BBC broadcasts. Not everyone complied with this order; many people hid radios in their homes or barns in order to listen to them in secret. The newspapers were full of German propaganda.

Then they started sending men to Germany to work for the war effort. Farmers and other people who were working in the food production industry were exempt, but men not deemed essential had to go to work in factories. No one wanted to go to Germany, which resulted in many men going into hiding; the so-called "onderduikers," literally meaning diving under. Many men obtained fake identification and hid on farms posing as farmhands. Onderduikers often worked for the underground resistance, sabotaging bridges, guarding ammunition, breaking into jails to free political prisoners and carrying out other dangerous missions.

The country became poorer and poorer. On the farm, we always had enough to eat because we had our own milk and wheat. It was not long before people in towns and cities began to think of their relatives in the country, though in the past they may not have ever admitted that they were related to lowly farmers. Now friends and acquaintances joined them on a trip out to the farms in the hopes of buying or trading their belongings for food. These "road people" came on bicycles or walked with handcarts or even baby carriages, anything that would hold food. The "road people" had to have a place to stay overnight. Dad had two places in the barn for such people. He took their identification cards and their matches. They got them back in the morning with a mug of milk and a slice of whole wheat bread.

One cold night, Dad invited a man into the kitchen. Dad said to him, "I don't think you are what your card says you are." The man admitted he was a watchmaker. It was not long before we rounded up all our broken watches and clocks. He took them and fixed them for us. When he brought them back, we suggested that he go up the road to our trustworthy neighbours who may also have need for his skill. After that, we learned that he continued to travel through the countryside trading his skill for food.

Wim and Alie were two "road people" who often slept over. We generally did not make conversation with the overnight "road people." The less you knew the better! But when Alie told us one day she was a seamstress, we put her to work. We had 10 people in our household with no new clothes and no material. We were constantly mending and making new from old. I got a spinning wheel and we traded grain for wool from my father's friend who kept sheep. I spun yarn and we had the kids in warm socks again.

We also took in two "hunger kids." The church and other groups in the cities gathered hundreds of these children and sent them to the country to be saved from starvation. We got two boys. Their father had worked in a butcher shop, but the Germans had taken him to Germany to work for the war effort. Jacob, the youngest, enjoyed himself at our house and soon grew quite chubby. But his brother Art was nervous, especially when he heard the English flying over. They flew very high; you could hear them, but not see them. Art would stand at the window crying, "They are going to kill my dad! They are going to kill my dad!" We tried to comfort him by telling him that Germany was so big, they would never find him.

The winter of 1944 to '45 was severe. In the country most farmers did what they could. Some never had the soup pot off the stove. One evening before Christmas, a girl came to the house with three children. The children seemed high-class. It was our guess the children were Jewish and the girl was probably working for the underground. We took them in and let them stay at the house. After a bath and supper, they went to bed. The next morning they headed out into the cold again. That day it started to snow and got nasty. We were concerned, but what could we do? We knew they had to go over the dike. Later, we heard a farmer had taken them in and let them stay until he found a trucker to take them safely over the dike.

The people working at the Administration Bureau were not all committed Nazis; some got inside information out. Dad was warned he was blacklisted for helping people. Before Christmas Dad decided that since there were not as many people on the roads anymore, he would remove the sleeping quarters in the barn for the time being. Besides, in the village there was a shelter fixed up to keep the "road people" overnight. That evening we heard the crunch of boots outside on the gravel. Fortunately, upon inspection, the Germans found no sign of hidden travellers in our barn.

In April of 1945, Canadian and Allied Forces had already freed the south part of the Netherlands. In the north, we were still waiting for the Germans to leave. We knew we were sitting on a time bomb; if the Germans blew up the dike, our entire polder would be flooded. On April 17, 1945, they did it. The Germans had planted dynamite in a specific spot in the dike around our polder and that morning we got warning that the dike was to be blown up. And so it happened, we heard a big bang and the water gushed back into the polder. The inundation of our polder was not a strategic move for the Germans, only an act of revenge.

Early that morning we were told to leave. Right away, we started to bake bread and prepare lots of food. Friends who lived about 12 kilometres away had said they would take us in if something ever happened. They lived outside the polder on the other side of the dike, where there was no danger of flooding. My friend Tinie and I were sent on our bicycles to the Nobel's farm to see if it was still okay for us to come.

It was all quite well-organized. Since Dad had three wagons and horses, he was responsible for our two neighbours, as they had none. The three wagons were loaded with food, bedding and children. The men drove the cattle. Late that afternoon, we all arrived at Mr. Nobel's farm. His cattle were put in the pasture, so that we could put our cattle in the stalls. The cows had to be milked and the children put to bed. Lying in bed that night, all I heard was the clop-clop of horses' feet up the road and wagons rattling by as other families fled the flooding polder.

Early the next morning, Tinie and her dad and I biked back to the farm. One wagon had already been driven back during the night. When we arrived at our farm, my brother was about to leave with a full load on the wagon. Dad was closing the doors to the house and my brother was anxious to get going. The water level was rising in the yard and he was afraid the horses might balk. But Tinie and I wanted to fetch a baby crib out of the house for our neighbour's infant. In our bare feet, we ran into the house, the water roaring into the basement. I took the crib apart, handed it down to Tinie through the open window and we took it to the wagon where my brother was waiting impatiently. He urged the horses down the lane and left with the full wagon.

Dad, my sister Annie and some others had stayed behind to carry furniture up to the second floor so that it would stay dry until we could pick it up by boat a few days later. Tinie and I followed the wagon on our bikes, but every so often we had to stop to pull debris out of our spokes. After awhile we came to higher ground and the going went better. It was the most beautiful spring morning with the canola fields yellow with bloom.

We lived in Mr. Nobel's new sheep barn until the fall, when we got a house in the nearby village of Winkel. The hole in the dike was fixed in December 1945 and the polder fell dry a second time. It was a dreary sight.

Villages were ruined and so were the farms. If the water had risen to the ceiling, the building went down. Our house was in ruins. The village was rebuilt with material from Scandinavia.

❧ Jean Deshane

On the night of September 3, 1939, the air raid sirens sounded for the first time. We grabbed our clothes and headed downstairs to go out to the air raid shelter in the back garden. But on the way down, we stopped to look out the window, and there caught in the glare of the searchlights was a shiny silver plane. We never did that again, but that sight has stayed in my mind all these years.

In 1939, I was 16. I worked in an office in the city of Glasgow, Scotland. I was scared and excited at the same time. I volunteered to do anything extra that I could. My friend and I volunteered at the Overseas Club. We got up before six o'clock in the morning, went to the Club and made breakfast for the servicemen. We still made it to work by 9:00 a.m.

Eventually, Britain turned to conscripting women because of the shortage of manpower. In the beginning, I was granted exemption because the firm I worked for claimed that I was in a responsible position that would be hard to replace. However, this excuse was finally rejected and I was called up for service. I chose to serve in the army with most of my friends. I had never left home before and being inducted into the army was a real scary experience.

I had always had my own bedroom and was now suddenly transported into a large Nissen hut with over 100 women of all shapes and sizes, manners and behaviours. The beds were wooden bunks set up in lines throughout the hut. Showers and wash basins were in a large adjoining room and there was no such thing as privacy. It was quite an adjustment, but we learned the rules and regulations and adapted as well as we could.

In the meantime, a soldier I had met at the Overseas Club became my fiancée and we were planning to be married. You just couldn't decide to get married and go out and do it. Oh no! The soldier had to apply to his commanding officer for permission, and then the woman had to be investigated and fill out applications, etc. We were given permission and were planning to be married in June of 1944, but the army had other ideas.

My husband to be was in the infantry and he landed on Juno Beach at 11:00 a.m. on June 6 – D-Day. He was on the front line from then on. Leave was granted to these men on a "need to rest" basis. He was given leave in January 1945. He came back to where I was stationed and we travelled home to be married. We did not have a white wedding because we had not known in advance and could not book into a restaurant for a meal. So our wedding dinner was fish and chips with as many people crowded into our living room as we could manage. Also, every hotel was booked solid, so we had to spend our "honeymoon" in my parents' home. Still, we were just glad to be together. We had 10 days leave, and then he returned to action and I went back to camp.

War brides were returned to Canada by the government. Women with children came first naturally. I came to Canada in March of 1945. We were packed in six and eight to a cabin. I was unfortunate in that I was seasick most of the way across. The strange thing was that when I was finally able to go up on deck, one of the first people I came across was the Sergeant Major I had served under during my last posting in the army, and that was the only time I ever saw her. We were amazed at the food we were served; all the things we had done without all through the war were suddenly available. Some of the women made themselves sick overeating.

We landed at Halifax, and I never realized what a big country I was coming to until we started travelling on the train to Ontario. I thought I would never get off that train. I came to Napanee and the conductor didn't let anyone leave the train until he made sure someone was there to meet us. It was 2:00 a.m. and it was pitch-black when we arrived. At first it seemed that there was no one there. But then he came out of the dark, this strange man I had travelled over 3,000 miles to be with. I had never seen him in anything but his uniform and now he was in civilian clothes. That first night we stayed in a hotel near the station. In the early hours of the morning I heard a siren, grabbed my clothes and was heading for the stairway when my husband caught hold of me. He comforted and reminded me that I was in Canada and that it was only a train whistle I was hearing.

The next morning, we started the drive back to my husband's farm. We kept going and going and going, so it seemed. Just about when I was beginning to wonder what I had gotten myself into, we came to a village and I said, "Oh, are we here?" But we still had another three miles to go. We did eventually get home. I came from the large city of Glasgow to a farm with no water, no electricity and a woodstove, and we were a mile from the nearest neighbour. People accepted us and were helpful and understanding of the long way we had come to make new lives with our men. We lived each day as it came, a lesson that has been forgotten in the complacency of the peaceful years.

🍁 Kay de Vos

Pop! Pop! Pop! Those were the sounds my sister and I woke up to on the morning of May 10, 1940. While we were trying to figure out where they came from, our mother burst into our bedroom and announced that this was war. After only five days of active fighting in Holland the Dutch Army surrendered to the superior firepower of the Germans. World War II lasted six long years, an eternity for a 12-year-old girl. My family's immediate concern was for my two brothers who were mobilized into the army. One brother never experienced anything dangerous, but the other one was in an actual battle. Luckily, they both got home safely.

It is amazing how soon you get used to an altered state of affairs. I took the German occupation of our country in stride and made the best of it. Actually, life after a while went on pretty much as it had before, with only minor changes at first. Not long after starting high school, the students were evacuated for a couple of months. The German soldiers wanted to occupy it because of its close proximity to the coast from where they shot their infamous V-2s off to England. This meant we had to double up with another school in The Hague, alternating five hours in the morning one week and five hours in the afternoon the next. Since our actual school hours were shorter than normal, we were loaded down with homework every day.

At first I would ride my bike to school, but as time went on, the Germans were in need of rubber and everybody had to surrender their rubber bike tires. I tried, as did everybody else, to get along with wooden tires. In the end it was better to walk the half an hour or so. Since our school did not give any instruction in typing and shorthand, I decided to take evening courses at a special institute. This was in the winter and because of night bombers going over our country on their way to German cities, there was no street lighting.

One night while on my way to the Study House somebody stepped out from the shadows of a house, put an arm around my shoulders and addressed me in German. My heart almost stopped. A German soldier! I could feel his gun holster pressing against my side. Noticing my distress, he asked me, "Hast du Angst? (Are you afraid?)" "Y-y-ess," I answered, trembling all over. He answered, "Hab doch kein Angst, du bist doch meine liebe, eigene Frau? (Have no fear, you are my dear, own woman.)" The poor man was lonely no doubt. He asked me where I was going and I told him I was on my way to a night school. He accompanied me there and asked me what time I would be back. He did nothing to coerce me and it was a rather touching situation, but the last thing I wanted was to become involved with a German soldier. So I told him I would be coming back an hour later than I actually would be. Thank God he wasn't there when I came out of the school. Just to be sure I would not run into him again, I took an alternate route home.

Girls that went out with German soldiers were given a bad time. Some people were so incensed they dragged these girls out into the street, shaved their heads, painted them with orange paint and left them tied to lampposts for a while. I happened across one of these scenes where people were jeering and spitting at this girl. While I could understand their frustration, I could not bear to watch it. It seemed so barbaric!

At first, there were food coupons for things like sugar and meat, etc., but as the war dragged on more and more products became scarce. The winter of 1944 to 1945 was the worst. Railroad employees went on strike, ostensibly for the disruption of supplies to the German Army, but it also meant that no food came through for the people in the western regions. My younger sister was lucky enough to be sent to a farm in the east by an organization that took care of children up to 14 years of age in order to give them a better chance for survival. For the first time in my life I experienced real hunger, as did so many others, especially in the big cities.

People organized tours to farms in the country to find food, mostly vegetables, but they kept us alive. At one time, my older brother worked for a food distribution centre. When a shipment of potatoes came in we were allowed two 60-pound sacks of potatoes, but we had to get them home by our own means. The distribution centre was at the other side of the city, a good one-hour walk. So my brother somehow fashioned a crude cart, which the two of us dragged across the city and back again with the potatoes. All the while we had to keep a sharp eye out for the so-called "food inspectors," who made sure people did not sneak such luxuries as two sacks of potatoes past them. Somehow we made it home with our loot. My mother was overjoyed at the sight of us, and especially the potatoes. Those potatoes lasted us for the rest of that winter and to the end of the war, which came in May.

There were razzias to contend with toward the end of that winter. These were frequent raids by the Germans to look for young men to ship off to Germany to work in the wartime factories. A truck with German soldiers would come roaring up a street and screech to a halt. The soldiers would storm through the street, ringing all the bells and going through every house to find young men. But we were prepared for that, too. My brother had a hiding place above the ceiling in the bathroom with just enough room to crouch for a short time. As soon as we heard the word razzia, and that went through the neighbourhood like wildfire, he would quickly climb into his hiding place. One time a young soldier came to our door and went cursorily through the house; you could see the job was distasteful to him, but he had to do it. He engaged my mother and I in conversation right in front of the bathroom door. My brother could hear every word!

War is ugly and it brings out the worst in people. And it sometimes creates a solidarity that you do not always find in peacetime.

🍁 Jean Drake

On Labour Day of 1939, my first love was at our place for the whole weekend. I had met him that summer; we lived nearly 200 miles apart, so we wrote many letters. That weekend we heard the news on the radio from our Prime Minister McKenzie King that war was declared and Canada would help Britain against the Nazis of Germany and the Communists of Italy. I was 17 and he was 21. At the time, he was helping his uncle build houses. He said he would enlist, get this over with and have peace once more. He joined the Royal Canadian Air Force (RCAF) and was stationed in Toronto for a few months, so he was at our place most weekends.

In December he discussed my engagement ring with my father, and my parents said he could meet someone overseas and I would be left here at home. Instead, at Christmas he bought me a gold wristwatch from Birks. I remember one neighbour saying, "I hope he comes back to see you wearing it." I thought to myself, what a thing to say. But she had lost a son in World War I.

My sister, who was 10 years older than I, was teaching at a one-room school for $400 a year. She already had her diamond and planned to marry the following year. When Canadian Industries Ltd. (CIL), an ammunitions factory, opened up in Ajax, Ontario, she quit teaching and we both worked there on the cordite line. The pay was so much better and some of it was set aside each pay to purchase War Savings Bonds.

My sister and I had to pass medical tests before we were accepted. We were sent to the makeshift hospital where we had to strip and place two towels, fastened together at one end with two safety pins, over our heads. I grabbed two bath towels, so I felt quite covered. All that was left for my sister were two hand towels, so she made me exchange one long bath towel for a shorter one. We passed our medical and were glad to pass the towels on to the next embarrassed group.

There were three shifts at CIL - the midnight shift was the worst. By 3:00 a.m. I would be so sleepy and I often felt sick to my stomach. I could sleep through the day, but still not be rested enough for that midnight shift. One night there was a severe thunderstorm. My sister and I were tugging over a tray; I let go so the tray triggered off the alarm system. Everyone made for the exit in the pouring rain and mud. We didn't move. Finally, a big wrestler-type picked each of us up under his arms like a sack of potatoes and took us out into the rain. We told him what happened and he said, "You keep your mouth shut!" You see, cordite if contaminated with dirt could explode. So everyone was jammed into a railway car and taken back to another line and issued new shoes and a new uniform. An investigation said it must have been lightening. Our lips were sealed, until now!

By this time letters were flying back and forth overseas. My friend was stationed in England. A lot of his letters were like

German plane bearing swastika.

49

picture frames. So much had been cut out, but they would reseal and forward them on to me anyway. One letter that wasn't censored included a snapshot of one of Hitler's planes bearing the swastika that had been shot down. We used to send parcels every month or so. My mother was a great knitter of air force blue socks and sweaters; we also sent candy and salmon. When my boyfriend knew he was leaving for overseas, he told me that on his return he would build me a new house, with a pond for all the little ducks.

Then the dreadful news came. He had paid the supreme sacrifice with five others in an airplane crash over England on February 26, 1943. I was pleased that his mother asked me what I would like engraved on his marker. I replied JOHN 15:13, "Greater love had no man than this, that he lay down his life for his friends." She thought it would be too much, but sent it in as requested. It was engraved, every word, and he was buried in Selby, England.

I came out of church one sunny spring day and there was his older brother. This is the man I married and together we had a family. He built us a home, as his brother had once promised, but without the pond!

❧ Anne Dreer

The first six years of my life, until 1944, I lived in Croatia, which at that time was a province of Yugoslavia. I had two brothers, one two years older and one five years younger, the baby. My parents farmed; our house and barn were in a village and the land and vineyard in the outlying area.

Until 1944 our daily lives were not much affected by the war. We were Danube Swabians living side-by-side with our Croatian neighbours. Our ancestors had settled in that area in the seventeen hundreds. Because Croatia was part of the Austro-Hungarian Empire, we retained our German language and customs. Half of the population of our village was German and the other half was Croatian. The Germans were bilingual and got along well with their Croatian speaking neighbours.

When Germany occupied Yugoslavia in 1941, German schools and customs were encouraged. My older brother started school in 1942, together with the Croat children. In 1943, it was decided that the German children should have German classes.

By 1943, the partisans – a communist underground organization – were trying to overthrow the pro-German Yugoslav government. Nobody knew who was a secret member of the partisan group; it could have been your next door neighbour. Being German, we were afraid. Some German men disappeared and were later found murdered. At Christmastime 1943, heavily armed partisans came to our house in the middle of the night and demanded that my dad hand over his rifle. He complied and they left. Some time later, Dad bought another rifle. The partisans came back.

Dad and a Croat friend had planned to go hunting early one morning. His friend knocked on the window and called his name. Without lighting the lamp, my dad put on his clothes and when he opened the door there were a lot of men in the courtyard. Because it was still dark, they did not see him and he was able to sneak into one of the spare bedrooms and hide under a bed. They came into the house looking for him and the gun they knew he had bought. Mother gave them the gun, hoping they would go away.

They also wanted money. We had just had a new well dug and the money to pay for that was under the mattress. They took it. They went through all of the rooms looking for Dad. I can still remember one man standing in the middle of the room with a hand grenade. "If he doesn't give himself up, I'll blow the place up," he said. Mother was pleading and crying; my baby brother was in the cradle and I was crying. By this time it was beginning to get light out and to our relief they left. After this episode, my dad feared for his life. That same night they had taken another German man, gouged his eyes out and then shot him in the back. His crime? This man usually bought eggs from farmwomen and sold them at an out-of-town market; the partisans begrudged him his profit.

The German Army wanted my dad to put together a hometown watch to protect the town against the partisans. He refused. The young German men had all been drafted and the older men were too old to fight. They would have been targets for the partisans. Dad was going to be brought before a military tribunal for refusing, but was called to the railroad watch in a nearby city. A number of men had to be on duty to watch for fighter planes and sound the alarm sirens. Mother was left alone with us and had all the farmwork to do. She had to hire a young Croatian man to help with the chores and a young woman came to help as well.

From that point on, there was a shadow over my life. I was not carefree anymore. I spent most of the summer of 1944 at my maternal grandparents in a neighbouring village. That village had a larger population of Germans and was able to put together a home watch. I attended a German nursery school and started Grade 1 in September.

In late October, we received orders from the German Army that the German families were to be evacuated. That meant leaving our house and land and livestock. We had to prepare to journey to Germany. Relatives gathered at my grandparents' place. As well as my mother and my two brothers aged 8 and 1, there was my teenage aunt, my mother's widowed sister and her sons, aged 4 and 6. Although I did not know it at the time, my mother was in the early stages of pregnancy.

In preparation for the journey several pigs were butchered. The meat was roasted, put in large tins and covered with rendered lard. Many loaves of bread were baked. Grandfather also took a big keg of brandy along. Bedding, clothing and household utensils were loaded on a tarp-covered wagon. We took as much food as space allowed. A smaller wagon was hooked on and loaded with more supplies. I had to give my doll and doll bed that I got for Christmas to the neighbour's children.

On October 22, 1944, the horses were hitched to the wagon and we all piled on top. There were approximately a hundred wagons. The first few days of the trip were not too bad. The weather was still dry and we had food. It was not too cold to sleep on the wagon out in the open. We crossed the border from Yugoslavia into Hungary. Grandfather used the brandy to pay for feed for the horses. If we were fortunate, the Hungarian farmers let us sleep in their barns with the animals. Occasionally, some let us stay in their homes and gave us food. Their reluctance to help us was understandable since we were German and considered enemies. Eventually the brandy ran out and our money was worthless and from then on it was hard to get shelter at night.

When it started to rain, the road became muddy. If the roads went uphill, we had to get off and walk to make the wagon lighter. Every night when we stopped, Grandfather took a piece of rope and stretched it across the spokes of the wagon wheels to clean off the mud that was caked on. The mud made the wagon so much heavier. By morning it would have hardened and been impossible to get off. Our shoes and clothes became soggy and muddy. There was no place to dry them at night; there was no place to wash and dry the baby's diapers.

When we crossed the border from Hungary into Austria, extremely cold weather set in. The horses were weak and emaciated. To make the wagons lighter, we had to walk most of the time. Sometimes the route we took was on the outskirts of a city under air attack. Then, we had to stop and run to the nearest woods. It was frightening to see bombs dropped and smoke rising from the fallen buildings. We were always hungry. One night we were in a city when the air raid sirens came on. We all had to go down into the air raid bunkers. It was dark. Children lost their mothers and were screaming.

Eventually it became too difficult for my mother and aunt to continue on the wagon with my grandparents. We were in Upper Austria. We were put on a train with a group of other women and children and continued travelling. One night we were stationed in a big building, it might have been a school or a hospital. There, we all had baths and they gave us dry clothes. The next day, we moved by bus to Engelhartszell, a small town across the River Inn from Passau. That was near the end of November. We had been on the road for over four weeks.

We were stationed in a school with about 40 women, children and old people. There were piles of straw along the outside walls, which were spread over the floor at night to sleep on. My aunt had a blanket but we didn't have one. Mother couldn't bring one because she had to carry my little brother. At night all of the windows had to be darkened with black paper blinds because of air attacks. All the light bulbs had to be painted blue. Every day several people had to go to get food from a local hospital.

Maybe it was a convent because there were nuns there too. We usually got a pot of potatoes and cabbage or sauerkraut. I don't remember any meat. One time there was pudding. That was a treat! Once in a while, a woman came, maybe from the Red Cross or the Health Department, who gave all of the children a calcium and vitamin pill.

After some time we found out my grandparents were only about 80 kilometres away in Tarsdorf, near Braunau. They had a room in a farmhouse. We were able to find a room about 5 kilometres away in the upstairs of an older couple's home. They had no family and were kind to us. The man was a cobbler. From this point on my mother and aunt had to buy food for us with food stamps. We seldom had enough. There were three beds, a table, some chairs and a wood cookstove. The old couple gave us firewood and sometimes gave us food. They even let us children play dress up with the old clothes in the attic.

Christmas 1944 came, but we got no presents. We hadn't really expected any. We did not know where my father was, or even if he were still alive. Some weeks later, he found us. His unit was moved to Austria, but the Russians were advancing and my father's group was told to disband. For us, it was a reunion with mixed emotions. We were far from home, penniless and uncertain of our future. The war was not over but it was obvious that Germany was losing.

Our immediate concern was finding accommodation for our own family. My aunt and her boys stayed at the cobbler's and we moved into a room on a farm. It had three beds and a wood cookstove. From scrap wood my father was able to make a table and bench. We had the few pots and dishes and some bedding which my grandparents had brought on the wagon. We lived, cooked and slept in that room for five and a half years. My father started to work on the farm. He got no pay, just his meals, and we did not have to pay for the room. He usually shared the plate of food he got with us as we sat around the table watching him eat. All food was expensive and most of it rationed. The social assistance we got allowed us to get a pound of meat a week. Often, we just had boiled potatoes for our meals.

The stores had no clothes, fabrics or other manufactured goods because all of the factories had been bombed. Our shoes were in bad shape. The cobbler could have made shoes but he had no leather. The farmers had enough meat, eggs and butter but were reluctant to sell any because the money had no value and there was nothing to buy in the stores anyway.

In 1946, my mother and aunt discovered that 50 kilometres away in Salzburg, there was a large number of Jewish people who had been released from a concentration camp. They were waiting to emigrate to Palestine. Mother convinced a farmer to sell her some eggs and butter and she and my aunt got a ride to Salzburg in the back of a brick truck. They found the camp where the Jewish people were stationed. They were getting all their food from the American military; they gladly traded their American wool army blankets for fresh eggs and butter. They also had good cotton and flannelette sheets. From then on, my mother and aunt made weekly trips to Salzburg. The farmers gladly traded butter and eggs to get textiles. And we got winter coats from the wool blankets and clothing and underwear from the sheets. We also had butter and eggs for ourselves.

In the spring of 1945, the war was over and in the fall we had to start school. There were about 70 school-aged children in that township. Our workbooks were made of what looked like newspaper. We had what we called ink pencils; if they got wet they bled like purple ink. We didn't have slates like the Austrian children. We had two refugee teachers, a husband and his wife. The man taught the lower grades and his wife taught Grade 4 and up. They were both liberal with the cane. If you did not know an answer from the times table, you got hit twice on each hand. Those teachers thought their main job was to discipline us. We were all afraid of them.

When I was in Grade 3, there was a skinny little girl in Grade 1. She had been in a concentration camp and always looked frightened. That teacher sometimes bent her over the desk and whipped her for not knowing an answer. The whole refugee community was so afraid of any authority that no one spoke up and put a stop to these beatings. When you are in a strange country, are not wanted and have no status as a citizen, you are silent.

The Austrians spoke a different German dialect. In order to not be discriminated against, we quickly picked up their form of speech. To this day, when I am with German speaking people other than refugees from our area, I will not speak my own dialect. I am not ashamed of it, but having been intimidated, put down and made to feel inferior because of it, I cannot bring myself to speak my own mother tongue.

Austria had many refugees after the war. This put a lot of strain on the country. Officially, the Austrian Government accepted us. In everyday life, it was different. We were often told, "Why don't you go back where you came from?" Some called us gypsies and didn't believe that we ever owned anything. We did not start the war. We did not want to be in Austria. It was ironic; Hitler was Austrian and his birthplace was only 30 kilometres away in Braunau.

🍁 Edna Drummond

At the start of the war, I was living at home on a farm outside of Almonte, Ontario. I had been working in home care, but when the war started my brothers enlisted and I felt that I should also do something to assist the war effort. My oldest brother was overseas with the army and I wrote to him asking which service he thought I should join. He said, "Definitely the air force!" It was 1943 and all the Forces were open to women by that time.

My mother didn't think too much about it and she wouldn't let me enlist, so instead I went to Toronto to work in an ammunition factory for three months. It was scary working there. I made tracer bullets that were used in airplanes. You manually filled them with gunpowder. If you didn't do it right, they could explode and blow up your finger or hand. The big bombs were made there too. Some of the people who worked on those bombs had their hair turn green. I don't know why that happened, but I decided I didn't want to work on the bombs!

There weren't many safety precautions. We wore white uniforms and each shift we were required to rub against a "gold thing" stuck on the door, which was meant to take the static electricity out of our body before we entered the factory. We couldn't have any bobby pins in our hair or wear anything metal.

When December finally arrived, I joined the air force. Basic training at Rockcliffe was not what I expected. We had to do so much marching! We had to do everything perfectly and make no mistakes. Living in barracks was also quite different. I quickly learned to take the top bunk so others wouldn't sit on your bed after you had it made up. If your bed wasn't perfect, you had to remake it. My mother and father were able to visit since they lived so close. I was also allowed to invite them to visit during basic training. At our graduation ceremony, we got diplomas. I graduated up to Leading Air Woman (LAW).

From Rockcliffe I was sent to Guelph for six weeks training to become a chef. Although we wore white uniforms when we were cooking, we were also issued regular uniforms. I really enjoyed our training there. We made a variety of foods and then we had to eat what we made. We had to try some of everything that was made, whether the results were good or bad. Luckily, I knew how to cook, so I did not find the course difficult.

In Guelph, we worked with dieticians who showed us how to prepare our menus. This was especially helpful for those people who had never cooked before. I made it through the class and I was sent to Moncton, New Brunswick. One of my brothers was also there at that time, serving with the air force. There were two stations in New Brunswick. I was located out in the country and my brother was in the city.

I worked with six other chefs and we had to cook for 2,000 people in the Airmens' Mess, and they all poured in at once at mealtime! The personnel formed a long line and it took an hour or more to serve them. Then the men and women would seat themselves separately. Can you imagine cooking steak for 2,000 people? We hired civilians from Moncton to do the dishwashing. The chefs never washed the dishes or pots and pans.

When I first started cooking there I was asked to make a cake and when I inquired as to where the equipment was, I was told, "Right there, use your hands!" So I had to make this big cake and mix it with my hands. We used such huge bowls! Later, I went to work in the Officers' Mess. It was more like a restaurant because officers ordered their food individually and the chefs prepared what they requested. Also, they had to pay for their food. I liked working at the Airmens' Mess the best because of the casual atmosphere.

I had many people working with me. Each of us had a job to do and we did whatever we were told to do that day. We switched duties every day. We had an officer who was in charge of the kitchen and she would put up a sheet of daily assignments. One day I made a pie for the Officers' Mess and an officer had asked, "Who made the pie today?" I thought, "Oh no, what did I do?" He relieved my anxiety when he said that it was the best pie he had ever tasted in a restaurant or anywhere. The other girl working with me was a bit envious and tongue-in-cheek said to me, "Well, you aren't making the pies tomorrow!" Overall, it was definitely a team and I learned teamwork.

The main difference between the messes was the quality of food. The different ranks had access to different foods. I found it amusing one time when an officer ordered poached eggs on toast, which he called an "Adam and Eve on a raft." I had no idea what he was talking about! He had to explain it to me. We couldn't cater to anyone's special dietary needs, except for officers.

Our kitchen was big and we served good meals. My brother would often call and he would ask what we were having for dinner and I would tell him, "Steak, french fries, vegetables and dessert." He would say he was having macaroni and cheese, again. He would then ask if he could come over and eat at our base. Shortly after I said, "Okay," he would be coming in the back door.

There were a few of us sent to Prince Edward Island and the quarters were an improvement over Moncton. I liked it better because it was a smaller place and people were friendly. There were also fewer people to feed! I was in PEI for a year. At the end of the war I couldn't do anything to celebrate. There was no party or days off for the chefs; it was just another day.

Chefs didn't get to go home until all the other people had left the service because they had to keep feeding them. The war ended in August 1945 and I didn't go home until January 1946. You knew a base was closing when the cooks left!

I found adjusting to civilian life difficult. I had enjoyed being with so many people and being part of a group. I really missed that about being in the military. I went to work cooking at the Almonte General Hospital from May until August when my boyfriend returned from England and we were married. I discovered that I didn't know how to cook for just two people anymore!

My mother never understood my decision. She didn't think that women should be in the services. I went because I felt that I should go serve my country and that was my part to play. I was proud to receive my three medals for serving.

🍁 Hermina Dunnewold

I was born in Holland in 1927 and lived there until March 1954, when I emigrated to Canada with my husband. Over the years I always had a great admiration for the men who liberated us. Whenever I met someone who served in the war, particularly in Holland, I always said, "Thank you for what you did." Then, on the occasion of the 50th anniversary of the liberation of my native country, I thought about how to reach more people to say thank you. So I just sat down and wrote a letter for the paper. I wrote this message for our local daily newspapers, *The Sentinel Review* in Woodstock, Ontario, and the weekly *Ingersoll Times*, in Ingersoll.

Those who were liberated remember
Dear Sir:
I would like to take this opportunity to say thank you to so many veterans who liberated Holland, my native country, 50 years ago, and to all those other men and women who fought for freedom at that time. Watching the coverage on TV of liberation festivities in Holland brought back so many memories of oppression and sadness. But especially memories of the unspeakable joy we felt when the Canadian liberators came to free us from Hitler's tyranny.

I was so impressed with how much the Canadians gave of themselves, the men who went overseas and their families who let them go, especially the ones who paid the price with their lives. I was deeply moved when I saw all those graves on TV. So many gave so much.

Many Jews and those who helped them died in concentration camps, along with those who worked for the Resistance Movement and were caught and never heard from again. My grandmother and her family successfully hid five Jews during the war.

We give thanks to God who made it all possible.

Thanks again fellow Canadians. I am proud to be a Canadian.

Hermina Dunnewold

❧ Enid Durand

I was born and raised in the town of Bournemouth, England, a popular seaside and holiday resort. Sunday, September 3, 1939, we all heard the words of Neville Chamberlain tell us we were in a state of war. Somehow we had all expected it. My father had been building an air raid shelter at the end of our garden away from the house. Everyone was busy blacking out the doors and windows and even putting special covers on the car headlights. We were all issued with gas masks, packed in square cardboard boxes with a shoulder strap, which had to be carried at all times.

My family remarked how thankful they were that I was a girl and still a teenager, so the war would not affect me. My father, in his forties, would not be called up. But wanting to do his part, he joined the Home Guard. At first they paraded and drilled in civilian clothes with broomsticks for rifles. Eventually, the Home Guard got army-type uniforms and one night a week they went on duty on top of high buildings to watch for enemy planes.

One of my memories is of Dunkirk in May 1940, when all those little boats crossed the English Channel to bring back the British and Allied troops. Being on the south coast, our town received troops and our church was informed that its hall would be used to accommodate French troops. The Guides and Scouts canvassed the neighbourhood for blankets, boots, shoes, socks, bowls, towels and soap. When the troops arrived, they were in a sorry state, with worn boots or bare feet. As an Assistant Guide Leader, I helped serve hot food and tried to make conversation with the soldiers in my schoolgirl French.

Not long after, the famous Battle of Britain began in July of 1940. At that time, we were still able to use our petrol ration for pleasure and one Sunday we went to our favourite spot to pick blackberries, the highest point in the County of Dorset on the south coast. There, we watched the Spitfires and Hurricanes fighting the German planes overhead.

During the Blitz my hometown was not considered a target area, but we had children from Southampton evacuated and billeted with us. We were close enough to the Southampton and Portsmouth docks that we could see a glow of fires and hear the gunfire during raids on these cities. At first when the sirens went in the night, we would get up and go to the shelter. But as the winter wore on, the sirens would go off after supper and stay on all night because we were a town in the flight path of the bombers. We could tell what cities they were headed to, whether it was London, Bristol or the Midlands. One of the longest raids was the night they bombed Coventry, after that my father put bunks in the shelter and we slept there every night.

Meanwhile, I finished school. I had planned to go to university for a domestic science course. But because it was in London I changed my plans and took an apprenticeship in photography and learned shorthand and

Enid in uniform.

typing. The war raged on and rations got smaller. Now we could only use cars for business and lots of people stored them for the duration. My father's petrol ration allowed him to drive back and forth to work as he had a garage and serviced trucks used for carrying groceries and essential supplies, but he didn't dare drive anywhere else.

By late 1943, it appeared the war was going to go on for quite a while longer. It looked as though I would be called up after all, so I decided to volunteer with the Women's Royal Naval Service (WRENS). After several interviews and tests, I was accepted. All I had to do was wait to be called up. But before that day came, I went to a Red Cross dance in Bournemouth, where a group of Canadian airmen had just arrived and decided to attend. That decision certainly changed my life.

Two of the Sergeant pilots insisted upon walking a friend and I home, four miles out of town. We had to walk because the buses stopped running after 9:00 p.m. Although everything was blacked out, these two insisted they could navigate their way back. I guess they did as the one called John turned up for a date and movie the next day. He was waiting to be sent for bomber training, so in the meantime we spent time together. Finally, John was posted to a squadron for bomber training and a day or so later I was called up.

I spent two weeks scrubbing floors, cleaning bathrooms and toilets, marching and doing squad drill and learning all about the Royal Navy and the Wrens. During this time the navy decided if you were the person they wanted, and if the navy was really for you. I was accepted and became a Signal Rating. I was sent to the Portsmouth dockyard, the HMS *Victory*. However, I was billeted in a big naval training camp outside of Portsmouth. I worked a watch system, three days on and three days off, slept in a big, cold Nissen hut and ate in a huge mess.

I was bused to our place of work located in a ridge of hills overlooking Portsmouth Harbour, known as Fort Southwick. This Fort was one of three that had been built for defense during the Napoleonic wars. This one had been preserved and a series of buildings connected by tunnels had been added. I had to climb about 200 stairs to reach the place where I actually worked. I became a Signal Distribution Rating, receiving, sending and distributing signals. I was attached to the headquarters of the Supreme Headquarters Allied Expeditionary Force (SHAEF), Southwick House, where General Eisenhower and staff planned the D-Day invasion.

More and more Allied troops arrived along the south coast and the harbour below was filled with ships and landing craft. Bombing raids had been stepped up, so we all knew the big day would be soon. My watch went off duty on June 5 in the pouring rain and strong winds, but when we were riding the bus back up the hill on June 6, the harbour was empty. The invasion had begun. After several months of working underground in pretty grim conditions, many of us were posted away. I went to an officer's training ship, the HMS *King Alfred*. I was still on the south coast, billeted in a small pre-war hotel on the sea front. I worked with only 24 Wrens - a real luxury - as opposed to hundreds of men and women.

During this time, John finished his bomber training, received his commission and was sent to his operational squadron in Yorkshire to fly Halifax Bombers. We had managed to have a few weekends together and decided we wanted to be engaged, much to my parents' consternation. However, we won and while on leave together just before Christmas 1944, we became engaged. At that time we were experiencing doodlebug and V-1 rocket raids. I was transferred to HMS *Boscowan* at Weymouth, about an hour from home by train or hitchhiking.

John and I talked about being married in September, but that was "iffy." In April 1944, John flew a raid and received damage to his plane. Because he was at the end of his first tour, John thought he might be sent back to Canada. But then VE Day altered our plans. He was sent to the Repatriation Department in Torquay on the south coast. It seemed as if John would not be leaving for a while, so we took a chance and planned to be married on July 9, 1945.

Then after VJ Day, they started to demobilize all married Wrens, and I was out fairly quickly. John was still waiting to return to Canada, so I joined him in Torquay. In October John returned to Canada, but had agreed to return to England to join my father's business, which he did early in 1946. But rationing was still imposed in England and there was no hope of a place of our own. So we decided to emigrate to Canada with our son Alan, despite all the dire predictions from my family and friends that I would be back in six months.

🍁 Muriel Elms

At the outbreak of World War II, I was living in India with my parents and still at school. My father, who was in the British Army, had been stationed in India since 1933. We were all due to return to England in November 1939. Due to unforeseen circumstances, my father was posted to Singapore in July 1939. My mother and I then joined him in February 1940. I attended a Commercial College and led quite a hectic social life. During this time I met Leslie, who was also in the British Army. We became great friends and later on we were engaged. It was a happy time, but what butterflies we were, flitting from one social event to the other. England and the war seemed far away.

In December 1941, I was a bridesmaid at a friend's wedding. During the festivities a message was sent through from an army office stating that the Japanese had invaded Malaya. At that point we were made aware just what war meant. British soldiers were sent to Malaya to obstruct the Japanese invasion. Many of our soldiers lost their lives. The Japanese continued their relentless march down the wasteland of Malaya, destroying and pillaging as they advanced towards the island of Singapore.

Then during January 1942, the bombing of Singapore began. Army, navy and air force bases were the targets at first, followed by indiscriminate bombing of commercial docks and their residential areas. It was frightening. As the days slipped by, the Japanese were but five miles from where we were living. Eventually, the Governor and senior military personnel decided to evacuate all British and European women and children, either to Australia or England. Obviously transportation by ship became difficult. Various shipping companies were eager to help and several vessels were offered for the mass evacuation.

We were told to bring what we wore, plus a change of clothes and anything that could be carried in small hand luggage. My parents, like many other people, lost their home. Mother and I boarded a ship bound for England on February 13, 1942, amid a lot of sorrow and tears. The Japanese invaded Singapore on February 15, 1942, and all the military and many, many civilians were captured and made prisoners of war. My father spent the next three and a half years in a prison camp on the island of Singapore. Leslie, together with hundreds of other prisoners, was sent by rail cattle-car to Malaya. They were put into makeshift prison camps and spent the next three and a half years working on the infamous Burma-Thailand Railway. It was a horrifying experience for all of them, and many of them died.

Our journey back to England took my mother and me three long, harrowing months. The ship made stops along the way, for five days in Ceylon, for two weeks in Durban, and then ten days in Capetown. We finally arrived in Liverpool early in May 1942. From there we made our way to a small town in Yorkshire where we lived with my grandparents.

At that time Winston Churchill was Prime Minister with a coalition government in power. He really was a "British Bulldog" and boosted everyone's morale. It was a different England than the one my parents and I had left in 1933. Rationing was in force and continued until well after the war had ended. Air raid sirens that signalled the German bombers seemed a way of life and we spent many nights in air raid shelters. The general outlook of the civilian population seemed to be, "We have a job to do, so let's get on with it." It was a job well done too, and with a smile and lots of humour.

Women played an important part in the war effort. As the men went off to the various theatres of war, women took their place in both civilian life and the Armed Forces. I found this out all too soon. Men and women of certain ages were either conscripted into the Forces or into work considered of national importance by the Ministry of Labour. Rather than be directed into the Armed Forces, I volunteered for the Women's Land Army (WLA) and signed up for market gardening. We all needed our veggies! Some weeks later my documents arrived and I was told I had the choice of working in a munitions factory in Sheffield or going with the WLA to work on a farm. I chose farming and was sent to a farm in Derbyshire some 50 miles or so from where my grandparents lived. This was November 1942, and I was there until September 1945.

During those years, my thoughts were constantly of Leslie and my father. Communication with them was almost non-existent. My mother received five cards from my father via the Red Cross with ready-printed messages. The POWs were allowed to choose from one of two cards stating something like "I am well," or something similar. These cards were supplied by the Japanese and prompted by the Geneva Convention. My future mother-in-law received four cards, which she always sent on to me. In turn, we wrote letters via the Red Cross, but Leslie or my father did not receive them. We never gave up the thought that they would return to us one day and they were always in our prayers.

Life on the farm was a whole new experience for a city girl. It was hard work, but there were some laughable moments. I lived together on the farm with another Land Girl, Kathleen, who had been there since 1940. We were treated like part of the family, which made life bearable. Kathleen and I had replaced two men and were expected to learn most things about farming - driving a tractor, haymaking, corn harvesting and planting acres of potatoes, cabbages and turnips by hand! It was a dairy farm and I learned to milk cows by hand. I soon learned to tie their tails to their hind legs with a string. It was no fun being flicked in the face every few minutes.

Apart from the hard work, we had some fun. Every once in a while, we cycled to the movies four miles away. We met up with other Land Girls once a month, an occasion organized by our local health and welfare representative, who would also listen to any "moans and groans" and sort things out. Our uniforms were provided, so if any replacements were needed they were ordered for us at this time. We listened to a battery-powered radio every evening and followed the progress of the war on the news broadcasts. Sundays were usually spent doing the usual chores and in the evenings we would have a singsong around the piano.

After my first year on the farm, Mr. Howard, our boss, bought a milking machine and a generator. So life was made easier, though it was something new to learn. About this time I learned to drive the tractor and also a van. I then got a new job delivering milk in bottles to a small, nearby market town. Kathleen had delivered the milk previously. It made a nice change for me, especially meeting the residents of this small town. We bottled the milk at the farm, so there was a dairy to keep immaculately clean and sterilized and this job fell to me. As well, I did a small amount of bookkeeping. Our day began at 4:00 a.m.

Life flowed on for us and the war was never far from our thoughts. Even living in such a remote area affected us. The Ministry of Agriculture had a big say in which crops were grown. Every farm had to be self-sufficient and corn feed for cattle was governed by milk production. The figures for milk production were sent to the Ministry each month and coupons were issued to enable farmers to buy their feed. Big brother was really looking over the farmers' shoulders. It was good for the war effort and we all felt as if we were doing our bit.

Finally, VE Day came in June 1945. There were street parties and there was much rejoicing. Church bells rang once again; they had been silent for six years, only to be rung if we had been invaded. But there was still the war in the Far East, which continued until September when Japan capitulated. The news that the atom bombs had been dropped and the ensuing results filled me with horror. The devastation, the lives lost and the far-reaching consequences were beyond my comprehension. But how could I not be glad?

My beloved Leslie and my father would be coming home; the waiting and the worrying for my mother and me were over. They were both released on October 16, 1945, and arrived back in England at the end of the month. After a short stay in the hospital, our beloved men were on their way home. Leslie and I married in December 1945.

Memories come back of my life as a Land Girl and Kathleen and I still keep in touch - a long letter now, once a year. When we reminisce, Kathleen sometimes reminds me of the night I fell into the "muck midden." "Ugh!" Or as we say in Canada, the manure pit. But that is another story!

🍁 Maureen Emmerson

I was 13-years-old, living on the northeast coast of England, when war was declared on September 3, 1939. It was a Sunday morning – the streets were hushed and free of traffic. Everyone was hunched over their radios to listen to our Prime Minister Neville Chamberlain's fateful news. Shortly after that news bulletin, the air raid sirens sounded all over the country. I had been sent out to the dairy across the street for a gill of milk, which I was carrying home, carefully. My mother was waving frantically from the front of the door as I ran, slopping milk from the jug all the way. I was ushered unceremoniously to join the family under the kitchen table with cushions on our heads!

We found out later that a single unidentified plane had crossed the south coast and, in our jittery state, expecting the worst, the whole country had been alerted. By the end of the war we were quite blasé and sirens were used sparingly! At first, I can't say that I realized the true horror of war. We watched the small boats leave the Tyne for the Dunkirk rescue mission and cheered those who returned safely. We listened intently to the radio reports of the Battle of Britain, but it seemed unreal and far away.

Little change was apparent. We lost our beloved beach to rolls of barbed wire and land mines, as well as our links to an army training field. Food and clothes were rationed, but not severely until later in the conflict. We were declared a neutral zone, which meant that we were neither evacuated, nor received evacuees. In those early days we laughed at the Home Guard and the National Servicemen who trained with wooden rifles and makeshift uniforms. We only realized later, that they indicated the dangerous state of our unpreparedness.

Gas masks in cardboard boxes were issued, with strict instructions to carry them with you at all times. Heaven help us if we ever had to use them! The boxes became the depositories for all kinds of paraphernalia – lipsticks, handkerchiefs, cookies, precious pebbles and marbles, even a live frog once!

If properties had a garden, air raid shelters were built half underground, otherwise they were made of brick and concrete. I remember helping to dig the hole for our Anderson shelter. It was a construction of arched galvanized steel about 8 feet wide by 6 feet, 3 inches high. Workmen, often volunteers, erected the steel and then everyone pitched in to pile the dirt over it. We were lucky to have the only dry shelter in our section of the street. It was quite crowded some nights with 12 to 15 adults and children squashed inside on the upper and lower bunks. We kept it warm with a lit candle in an earthenware plant pot, with another pot upside down over it.

Each one in the family had a specific duty if the siren sounded. I took the cookie box and the ever-ready thermos of tea. My brother was in charge of the blankets and pillows, while Mom grabbed the case of important papers and the pepper pot. The latter she declared was to repel invaders. I've no doubt she would have used it!

My brother was always last down the stairs because he insisted on wearing his tie! One night the siren sounded shortly before we heard the scream of the first bomb. My brother arrived at the shelter looking pale and dishevelled. He had thrown the pillows and blankets down the stairs and jumped down on top of them. His tie was not tied that night!

We were spared too many close calls, although we spent many long nights in the shelter listening to the dull throb of the German bombers from Norwegian bases on their way to hammer Glasgow and Manchester. It was after one such night that a lone bomber, on its way home, jettisoned its load before it was clear of the coast. One bomb landed behind our house, blowing the roof off and shattering the windows.

Another bomb landed down the street but fortunately did not explode. We were all evacuated for five days to a nearby school, while we waited for the bomb to be defused and makeshift repairs to be done to our house. I was most worried about our canary, which we had not been allowed to bring out. My mother, along with other members of the Women's Voluntary Service (WVS) worked tirelessly at the school to feed 300 people who had to leave their homes. It was dark in the house when we returned to boarded up windows – and a very hungry canary! It was some time before the boards were replaced with wartime glass, which let in the light but was almost opaque.

This particular bombing incident brought me, finally, to the realization of the true horror of war. We were told at high school the next day that one of our classmates and three others from her family were killed in that raid.

Students at my high school were actively involved in helping the war effort. Air raid shelters, a pig-rearing operation, rabbit hutches and allotment vegetable gardens occupied our playing fields. All students were involved in one way or another with rotating farm chores, under the supervision of teachers or volunteers. The worst job was boiling up rejected small potatoes and kitchen waste, which had been carefully saved. The result was a foul smelling swill which the pigs enjoyed immensely and thrived accordingly. We seemed to spend an inordinate amount of time trying to corral hordes of little piglets that always found a way out of their pens. Our family, now reduced to my mother and me, as my brother was in the army, also had an allotment garden in a field close to home.

In October of each year, teams of students were sent out into the fields to help with the potato harvest. In November, we had a week off to bring in the sugar beets; a cold, wet, muddy and thoroughly uncomfortable job. In summer, we collected rose hips and blackberries for Vitamin C (since there was no citrus fruit for the duration of the war), nettles and male fern root for cattle medicine, and silver paper and aluminum pans as scrap metal. Even tramlines and garden railings were sacrificed. Nothing was wasted or taken for granted.

All students over the age of 14 were enrolled in some kind of training corps. For girls it was the Girl's Training Corps (GTC) or Guides, for boys it was the Army, Navy or Air Force Cadets or Scouts. I was in the GTC. We thought we were smart in navy skirts, white shirts and navy forage caps. We were taught first aid and rescue techniques, how to deal with incendiary bombs with stirrup pumps and how to identify airplanes, which we never used because all the planes seemed to fly at night! We learned Morse code and semaphore, though I'm not sure why. Mostly I remember parading with all the other organizations for War Bond days and desperately trying to keep in step with the band in front of us!

I would have liked to join one of the services when I was of age, but I started work at 16 in a structural engineer's office in a reserved occupation. This is when the war had a major impact on my life. In those days, women were not expected to have abilities or ambitions in engineering beyond copying the engineer's drawings in ink; "lady tracers" they were called.

With the shortage of men, however, I was encouraged to advance as far as possible. I had a good head for figures, so I began with simple designs for reinforced concrete buildings, air raid shelters and airdrome runways and facilities. I eventually became a graduate of the Institute of Structural Engineers, one of only two women graduates at that time. I am sure other women can recall the same kind of wartime opportunities. It seems ironic that we needed a war to further the emancipation of women and to recognize their potential.

I value the learning of those wartime years - frugality, teamwork, community togetherness and appreciation for small luxuries. And I am grateful for having had the opportunity and the chance to use all my abilities. However, I would gladly forego all those positive experiences if it meant we would have been spared the loss of life, the waste, the violence and cruelty, the hardship and all the lasting negative effects of war. May God grant that we never again have to face those horrors.

🍁 Alta Engstrom

When war was declared in September of 1939, I was one month away from my eighteenth birthday. My younger sister was to marry in October of 1939 and we were more concerned about getting ready for her wedding than we were about the war. There were no boys in the family, so war seemed far away and would, we thought, soon be over.

I was working half days and staying at my sisters in Timmins in 1940. I married that same year, and because my husband believed that women should not work out after marriage, I had to quit. We sorely needed the money. My husband had just got a job in a local gold mine. Rent was $20 a month and the car payment was $20 a month, so there was little left over. It was the day before payday and we needed a loaf of bread to make my husband's lunch for work the next day. Bread was 10 cents a loaf and we had 9 cents. So we walked along the street to see if someone had dropped a penny and came to a bakeshop – the sign said, "Day old bread, 8 cents." We had a penny to spare!

By 1940, people were leaving the farms and towns to go into the army, air force or navy, or to go to work in the war factories. In 1941, my husband joined the army and left for England. He made me promise to stay home with his parents, or with mine, and not go to work. Perhaps he was afraid I would meet someone to take his place? All the young people were away making money; I was very unhappy.

I joined the Canadian Women's Army Corp (CWAC) and started basic training in Kitchener in March 1943. I learned to tie a tie, make a square knot and precision march. It was not long before I was sent to cooking school. After finishing the course, I worked for a while cooking for the

Alta (far left), with friends, 1943.

women officers in Kitchener. They had few complaints and seemed to appreciate us. However, it wasn't long before I was moved to an army camp in Orillia.

Orillia was a training camp for new recruits from all over Canada who were sent there for two months for basic training. The women had one hut and the rest were for the men. Our hut was out of bounds to them. We worked five and a half days a week, from 6:00 a.m. to 6:00 p.m. on most days, and until 9:00 p.m. on Thursday. There was a male cook and waiter who were Corporals, three waitresses who belonged to CWAC, plus myself. We were young and work did not seem hard. The men on basic training came in daily to wash dishes. This all changed, however, when the two Corporals got transferred.

Suddenly, I was the only cook with three waitresses. The officers in charge refused to send in dishwashers. I had no help. Days were now from 6:00 a.m. to 6:00 p.m., seven days a week, and til 9:00 p.m. on Thursday. This state of affairs went on for about three or four weeks. It seems that the CWACs were required to work under a person with stripes. But, it was a man's army, so I did not get my stripes. One day the Mess Officer brought me some liver at 10:00 a.m. and demanded it for dinner at noon. I told him I could not have it ready for noon, it usually took me three and a half to four hours to prepare it for a hundred people. An argument followed. However, he won the argument and the officers got raw liver at noon. Two days later I was returned to the barracks in Toronto. When the officer in charge learned of the conditions we were working under she was appalled. I remained at the barracks in Toronto and she sent four girls to augment the staff. Again, I was the only cook, but had lots of help from the CWACs.

One day I learned of a note on an officer's desk that stated they were to be sending girls overseas. I immediately asked to be put on the draft. When she asked why, I told her that while I was in Orillia, I received a letter from my husband in England saying he had another lady in his life. I wanted to go over to see for myself what was going on. I was devastated when I received his letter because I was a true-blue wife. I was raised naive and innocent. It never occurred to me that men had other women. I had many rude awakenings after I joined the army. I had a lot to learn.

I was on draft and left for England. We were 14 days zig-zagging our way in a large armada of ships. As long as a ship could float, it was used during wartime. The one I was on had 99 passengers, including the crew. It was a pleasure craft. There were 48 CWACs and one female officer and 50 male officers on board. It was June 1944 and halfway to England, a steward woke us early one morning to tell us the Allies had landed in Normandy.

On landing in Scotland, the dock was not built for ships, so we were loaded onto a flat barge. We were an hour from ship to shore. On landing on the dock, we filled our water bottles, were given a sandwich of dark bread and boarded the train for London. This was a sad time. When we arrived at camp, girls started to look for brothers, husbands or boyfriends. Some had already left for England and some were dead on the beaches of Normandy. My husband was still in England.

The house where we were billeted was three stories, plus a basement where the cooking was done. I had a Corporal Cook who had been born and raised in Scotland and appeared to know how to cook mutton. We had not learned this in cooking school. I never saw such terrible stew or dishes made with this meat. Lamb chops were placed in a dish, covered with water and placed in the oven. I decided the best way was to sear them on both sides before placing them in the oven. The Corporal would be on the top floor and smell them cooking. When I'd hear her coming down the stairs, I'd quickly hide the frying pan, put water on the chops and pop them into the oven.

I did not know at the time why the Corporal disliked me. But it seemed that when I made porridge, it was not lumpy. Also, her method of making pancakes was to mix the batter the night before, so the next morning they were flat. To overcome this, I put the baking powder in one cup of flour and added it to the batter the next morning. No one caught on. The girls would ask who made the meal. If I made the porridge or pancakes, they would eat it. Eventually, the cook staff told me the Corporal was jealous. This was all news to me. So the Corporal decided the officers could have me, and I got moved again, three doors down the street to the Marble Arch. The three waitresses and myself cooked for the officers and were glad to have to cook for so few. This was my third kitchen in which I was the only cook. However, I had lots of help, and if I went on a weekend leave, the waitresses took over the cooking. I got my Corporal stripes here!

On one of my 72-hour passes, I went with another girl to Stratford-on-Avon to visit Shakespeare's home. At the Waterloo train station we were told that there would not be a train to that destination. So we asked for the closest station and decided we could walk from there. When we arrived it was midnight, raining and so dark because of the blackout. The station agent said, "And where are you girls going?" He told us there was no way we could see in the dark and he was closing as soon as the mail truck came. Then, in walked an English air force officer. He said the same thing: "What are you girls doing here? My goodness, you can't get there tonight. But, I'll tell you what, I live there and I usually get a ride with the mail lorry. We shall ask him if he has room for you." The mailman was not too happy, but agreed to give us a ride. We never even asked the Captain his name. Such was wartime!

He took us home with him, settled us in the parlour and said, "I'll go ask Mama what to do." When he came back, he told us his mama said to give us a cup of tea and a biscuit and then take us to the guest room. The next morning at 5:00 a.m., Mama woke us up and said: "Girls, get up and come downstairs. I've made you breakfast. And then you must leave before anyone sees you. My son has always brought home birds with broken wings, dogs run over by cars and stray cats, but never has he brought girls before, and today is his wedding day!"

While in England, I travelled a lot on the underground. The English used it as a bomb shelter at night and it was sad to see whole families spread their quilts and sleep in the noise and the dust. At Christmas, the girls in our barracks gathered all the sweets we could to deliver to the children who slept there. The same ones came every night, so with the help of the station agent we knew how many were there. Wrapping paper was scarce, so we saved every scrap from parcels we received from home. Two of our girls delivered them on Christmas Eve.

When the war was over, we prepared to go home. We were told our building at Marble Arch was being remodelled to house war brides and their children, so we were moved to Aldershot to await transfer to boats. We packed our kit bags and said goodbye to London. I had a tear in my eye because I had grown fond of England. When we arrived at camp, we were shown into a typical army hut, one that had stood empty, according to the soldiers we talked to, during the entire war. There was the usual round coal stove in the centre and army bunks lined up on both sides. There was a half

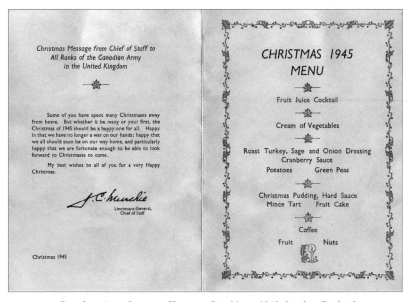

Canadian Army Overseas Christmas Day Menu, 1945, London, England.

an inch of dust covering everything, including the beds. The beds had one army blanket and a pillow. When the time came to go to bed, we wrapped the filthy pillow with our towel, spread our housecoat for a sheet and covered up with our great coat. We were allowed one skuttle of coal, but after talking to the soldiers some of the girls were told to go at midnight and steal coal from the coal pile. This was in the fall of the year in an unused building; naturally, we were not a happy group!

At Southhampton, we boarded the *Ile de France*, a French ship; there were hundreds of soldiers and one platoon of girls. It was one of many ships brought into service for the war and afterwards was sent to be scrapped. The *Ile de France* had taken on all its supplies in South Africa, so they had nothing that appealed to us. I had been missed on the pay parade before we left, so I had to borrow five pounds from a friend. I bought a pack of cigarettes and took them home and my father smoked the tobacco from them in his pipe. They were as strong as cigars. Coming home was only a matter of four days. My mother-in-law met me at Union Station, so I stayed with her for a few days before going home. My husband went with me to meet my family and friends. I had not yet signed my divorce papers. We thought we would get together to see if there was any way to resolve things. There wasn't! We parted a few days later, never to meet again. He returned to England to bring his new wife and two children back to Canada.

🍁 Myra D. Ennis

I was 13 and getting ready to go into my second year of high school in 1939 when war began. Galashiels, our quiet little Scottish tweed-manufacturing town, was transformed almost at once. Young men and women we had known all of our lives left to join the army, navy or air force and new people appeared to work in the mills that were busy day and night weaving cloth for uniforms. We became a garrison town and soon our streets were filled with marching men. Bren gun carriers, tanks and big army trucks became as familiar as the milkman's cart or the baker's van of pre-wartime.

When the blackout came into force, all windows had to be covered as soon as darkness fell, not a chink of light could show. Air Raid Wardens patrolled the streets to make sure that nothing shone through the heavy black curtains that covered every window. We were issued identity cards that had to be carried with us at all times. I still remember my number - SDMA16-3. Next came the gas masks, terrible rubber-smelling things that we would need should there be a poison gas attack. The masks came in a heavy cardboard box with a strap to hang over one's shoulder. We faced a fine if we did not carry them at all times.

Rationing of both food and clothing began. It must have been difficult for mothers who had families to feed and clothe. We had a big garden, so there were always lots of vegetables, but meat, butter, fats, sugar, eggs and tea were in short supply. Bread became a heavy, grey lump filled with husks. Oranges and orange juice were only for pregnant women or babies and bananas disappeared for the duration of the war.

We were issued coupons twice a year for clothing. We had to be careful how we used them because once they were gone we couldn't buy anything, not even a pair of socks, until the next issue came around. Government regulated clothing came into being. Only a certain amount of cloth could be used for each garment. No excess pleats in skirts, no excess cloth in coats or jackets. "Make Do and Mend" was everyone's motto and we became quite inventive making clothes over - altering, dying, changing things around - so that we would appear to have new outfits.

In 1940, when our Army was driven onto the beaches at Dunkirk and Winston Churchill made his "We shall never surrender" speech, things were pretty grim. We lived with the threat of invasion and we became used to the bone chilling wail of air raid sirens as enemy planes flew overhead on their way to bomb larger cities.

The boys in my class were joining Air Cadets, Navy Cadets or the Army Training Corps in order to prepare for the time when they would be old enough to fight. Two of my uncles and my three oldest cousins were in uniform; one uncle had been at Dunkirk. I vowed that at aged 18, I would join one of the services. In the meantime, the best I could do to help was work at our church canteen serving tea and sandwiches to hungry soldiers and washing mountains of dishes.

In 1941 so many ships carrying supplies were sunk in the Atlantic that rations had to be cut again. Factories were working night and day to build equipment to replace what had been left behind at Dunkirk. The country was filled with soldiers from many countries - Canada, Poland, United States, Australia and France. I joined the Girl's Training Corps and went to classes to learn first aid, Morse code and how to use a stirrup pump to put out fires from incendiary bombs, among other things. I left school in 1942 and went to work for an electric supply company. The war seemed to speed everything up. We grew up fast.

In 1943, when I was 17, a unit of Canadian soldiers was garrisoned in Galashiels. Other than serving cups of tea and sandwiches at our church canteen, I had never met any of the soldiers who came and went in our town over the years. But now things changed. I met a young Canadian at the bus stop on my way home from work one day. He chatted to me as we waited and asked if I would like to go to the movies with him. At first I said no, but he had such nice brown eyes and such a fascinating accent that finally I consented. I didn't tell my mother of course!

Myra, spring, 1944.

After the movie we walked through the park and he told me all about his home and his family. He said the first thing he wanted when he got back to Canada was a cold glass of milk and a great big piece of chocolate cake. We were having a family picnic the next day. I knew there wouldn't be any cold milk or chocolate cake, but I asked him if he would like to join us. When I told my mother that I had invited a Canadian soldier to our picnic, she didn't look pleased. But when she met Orwell, she liked him at once. We began going together and I soon knew that he was the one I would marry when the war was over. When his unit left to fight in Italy, I wrote to him every day and he wrote back whenever he could. In those letters, we planned our life together.

Right after my eighteenth birthday in February 1944, I fulfilled the vow I had made and volunteered for the air force. I was proud to be in uniform and felt I was really helping out. I trained as a Radar Mechanic. I enjoyed what I did and learned how to get along with people from all walks of life. It was an experience that taught me a lot. There were happy times working together with good friends. Then there were sad times when planes didn't come back and boys we had laughed with the day before were suddenly gone. After the Normandy invasion, D-Day, June 6, 1944, there were tragic losses and many hearts were broken. But the tide of war had turned and it seemed that peace was coming closer.

I was 19 in May of 1945 when the war in Europe ended. The Pacific conflict was drawing to a close and one day I received a wonderful phone call. After fighting through Italy and into Holland, Orwell was on leave in London and would be in Scotland the next day. I wangled a leave and on July 16, 1945, we had a wonderful wedding and two-day honeymoon. I got out of the service in August and we spent many weekend leaves together until Orwell was repatriated to Canada in January 1946. I followed in May of that year, a war bride, sailing on the *Aquitania* with hundreds of other war brides to a new life in a new country. I was homesick at first. I missed my parents and my sister, but I soon came to love my new country and the village of Elora.

The war encompassed all of my growing-up years from 13 to 19, from a "just turned teenager" to a married woman. Someone once said that it must have been a drag to grow up in these circumstances, but it wasn't. It was a time when people cared for one another, helped each other in any way they could and worked together for the common good. And after all, it was when I met "my Canadian," and that is something I never regretted.

🍁 E. Maxine Erb

My father was trained by his father and grandfather to be a watchmaker and a jeweller. Dad and Mother were married in March 1929, when the world, as they knew it, collapsed. After 10 years of scraping and scrimping to keep the wolf from the door, the war started. I was 8-years-old and my sister was 6. My world consisted of school, dolls, reading, roller skating and skipping. Life took another twist, but in lots of ways it was easier. We had more money and food rationing didn't bother us. Mom could make do with very little and soon we were trading sugar coupons for meat coupons. Tea rationing caused the most hardship, but we were used to making two cups of tea with the same bag.

Dad tried to join the air force. He felt that his experience in watchmaking and precision instruments would be an asset as a member of the ground crew that built planes. A car accident in 1933 shattered his kneecap and he walked with a pronounced limp. He was desolate when the air force refused him. Mom wasn't! A sympathetic Recruiting Officer suggested he apply at National Steel Car in Malton, later renamed Victory Aircraft Ltd. (VAL), to help build airplanes.

A few weeks later we moved from St. Catharines to West York Township. Dad settled into his new job quickly. We changed schools again and Mom had to get acquainted with new neighbours and new shops. Dad's hours were long, but he was happy with his new challenges. We had a telephone! First time ever! Few were available, but calls came in for Dad during the evening and the night, sometimes necessitating quick trips to Malton. Because of Dad's work, we had a B gas ration allotment, and although our '37 Dodge needed much tinkering with, it survived until 1947.

Eventually, the National Steel Car at Malton held a grand reception for its employees and their families. There, in a hangar, was the biggest plane I had ever seen; it may have been the first plane I had seen on the ground. The Lancaster Bomber! Dad was so proud as he showed us about - taking particular pride in the instrument panel. Most of the explanation of the modifications he had made from the British designs went over my head, but clearly this was his baby! Dad stayed with VAL until the end of the war. Then, along with thousands of others, he joined the ranks of the unemployed, making room for returning soldiers.

Mother was of Germanic background, but we just kept quiet about it. After all, it was her grandfather who emigrated and left Germany because of the wars at the time. Mom's contribution to the war effort was different. She became a Foster Mother, working with the Infants Home, a branch of the Children's Aid Society. Nine months after a troop train left Manning Pool, there were usually three to four babies that came into Mom's care. The clothesline was full of flapping diapers, the fridge was loaded with 18 to 24 bottles of formula, the dining room was lined with three or four cribs and the front hall of our two-bedroom house was crammed with two carriages, along with our coats and boots.

Mom's life consisted of babies - sleeping, crying and wakeful. We were never done with washing and formula making. We had a washing machine but soap was scarce, so she reverted to making her own. Formula was made from cans of Farmers Wife No. 2, dextro-maltose, measured carefully with the water adjusted as the babies grew. Before school there were babies to be fed and changed; and after school, there were babies to be fed, changed and walked.

As kids, we didn't know a lot about what was going on. Harry Bloor, who lived two doors down the street, joined the British Navy as soon as he turned 18. He was killed in the Battle of the River Platte, his first battle. I think he was aboard the *Ajax*. We shared our precious tea ration with his parents. Of their five sons that went to war, only Harry failed to come home.

During the war, curfews were imposed on kids - so the school compensated by holding "Tea Dances" from 3:30 to 5:30 p.m. on school days. Chaperoned by teachers, we danced to records of the big bands. By now I was 13 and in my first year of high school. French was compulsory and German had been removed from the curriculum. Knitting for the Red Cross took up most of our spare time.

When VE Day came we had a special assembly at school. We were dismissed to go home to attend special, hastily arranged, services at the churches. Later on, a huge 2,000-voice choir sang "Hallelujah Chorus" at the Canadian National Exhibition (CNE) grounds. Street dances were held, but we weren't allowed to attend any of these. When VJ Day came, Aunt Kay was visiting and took us girls downtown to Shea's Theatre. The show was stopped, the lights turned on, the announcement made and we were invited to leave. Outside, it was pandemonium. Aunt Kay hurried us against the crowd, surging downtown. I think we might have walked two miles before we found a streetcar that was moving!

🍁 Margaret Everett

World War II had a profound effect on my life. To supplement the depleted work force, too many young people were allowed to cut short their education. In fact, they were encouraged to seek employment to

Margaret, May, 1944.

help the war effort. Much to my everlasting regret, I left high school early.

In my last year of public school, I worked on a farm during summer vacation. If students had good marks at Christmas and maintained them until Easter, they could graduate early to do farmwork. That was a good experience. In the summer of 1942, I started delivering messages for Canadian National Telegraphs on my bicycle. Their office was at Bay and Bloor Streets in Toronto. Later, I was transferred to the grain exchange in the Royal Bank building on King Street.

It was while I was working in that mid-town branch that I began to deliver numerous messages and report deliveries. These were important and signatures had to be obtained from the designated. Those deliveries all seemed to be "death or missing in action" reports being sent to Canadian wives and mothers.

After August 19, 1942, I delivered so many more. This was after the disastrous British-Canadian raid on Dieppe, France. There were so many report deliveries that I cannot recall when they stopped! It was a difficult task. I recall thinking that I was likely more understanding and sympathetic than were the young boys who delivered, but there were so many I could not possibly do it alone. I delivered messages all over central and north Toronto, from the poorest cottages of Cabbagetown to the rich mansions of Rosedale and Forest Hill.

🍁 Dolores Ferguson

Evidently, my life was not very upset by the war because my diary lists a lot of movies and dances, some of which were Air Cadet dances where we went to meet boys of course! We were thrilled to see the good news and moving pictures of the war activities which came ahead of the main feature. We went to the movies frequently at 10 cents a matinee, and I was upset when it went up to 11 cents. Many of the movies were romantic adventures. We were so naive to think war was thrilling!

My stay-at-home mom went to work in a grocery store. I remember that it was hard for her to lie, denying the presence of bags of sugar under the counter. They were reserved for regular customers.

The boys who went off to war were our heroes, of course. We were lucky that our relatives all came home, except for a young cousin from out West. We didn't know him well, but after that we kept in touch with his twin brother. They joined the air force at the age of 17. The one died at 19 years of age. He was a tail gunner whose plane didn't make it back to the base.

While at high school in Blenheim, a town of about 3,000 at the time, we had Japanese students in our classes. We had no idea of the politics of that shameful time in our history. We just knew that these families had been moved from the West coast and were working on farms nearby. These students and classmates were just "one of us;" we enjoyed them all.

❧ Jean Ferrier

I was 5-years-old when the war began. I remember being frightened, especially when we had to blackout our house. From our darkened house I would watch the Air Raid Wardens practice putting out fires in the park across the road. I remember the sheer terror I felt when the air raid sirens went off unexpectedly. One time there was a fighter plane on display in the park. How thrilled I was to get up close to it and to talk to "real airmen."

My strongest memory, however, revolved around my favourite doll. Someone came to school and really impressed upon me the need for toys for children overseas. So I decided to give them Betsy Linn. She was a cloth doll dressed in a spring green and yellow Swiss dot dress and bonnet. My mother tried to talk me out of giving her away and I cried a lot of tears on parting with her. I just hoped that some other little girl loved her as much as I did!

❧ Ruby G. Fletcher

When war was declared in September of 1939, I was still a schoolgirl in Devon with two years of school left. There was a lot we had to get used to, but one of the hardest things to adjust to were the blackouts. No lights were allowed to show from any doors or windows and there were no street lights. It was unimaginably dark!

Food rations varied from month to month and from area to area; they were also affected by how much and what was being imported from overseas at the time. A weekly ration for one adult was comprised of two ounces of tea, four ounces of butter or margarine, two ounces of cooking fat, eight ounces of jam, honey or marmalade, eight ounces of sugar, two ounces of cheese, four ounces of bacon or ham, two and a half pints of milk and a meat allowance of two small chops or half a pound of stewing beef. There was also a points system for tin goods, like spam, baked beans or powdered eggs. Vegetables, bread, fruit and fish were not rationed, but were so rarely available that their non-rationed status was almost meaningless.

In 1941, I went to work as a housemaid for a while, and then as an usherette in a cinema in my hometown. My elder brother Roland joined the Royal Navy; my elder sister Margaret became a member of the Auxiliary Territorial Service (ATS), and I joined the Women's Royal Naval Service (WRENS) as soon as I was old enough. My two younger siblings were too young to sign up. After basic training I was sent to Plymouth, Devon, and attached to the HMS *Drake* in Davenport. This was a dryland ship and any incoming ship's first duty was to report there.

On May 8, 1945, the war ended in Europe; it was VE Day and the blackout was lifted. You can't begin to imagine how wonderful it felt after five years of darkness. The lights were wonderful. They shone out of every door and window and on every street corner. Everything was lit once more. The streets were full. Everyone was celebrating, horns blaring and people singing. As soon as we were off duty we joined in the celebration with Americans, Canadians and anyone else who cared to join in. I had been given two days victory leave and went home to celebrate with my family.

One of the Canadians was an Engine Room Artificer (ERA) from the HMCS *Minas* with the Royal Canadian Volunteer Naval Reserve (RCVNR). His name was Kenneth Fletcher. Even though I had paired up with another gent, Ken made a point of coming around and making a date with me for the following day. Unfortunately, neither of us could keep the

Ken and Ruby, September, 1945.

date as his ship, a bangor minesweeper, was under orders to sweep for mines around the Channel Islands, as the Germans had not yet surrendered there. As it happens, his ship was fired upon and Ken was wounded.

Ken wrote to me and we corresponded for a while. When the *Minas* came into port once again, we dated. I took Ken home with me on my next leave and he asked my mother's permission to marry me. She took a liking to him and said yes. I had to borrow my wedding dress, as clothing was still on points; I was the seventh bride to wear it. We were married on September 20, 1945, my mother's birthday, just four months after we met.

Of course, I was anxiously awaiting news from the government as to when I would be able to leave for Canada. Finally, I received papers from the government offices saying I was to leave from Liverpool early in June 1946. The ship I was to board had been a hospital ship during the war. It had gone through several name changes, but was now known as the *Letitia*. I slept in an upper bunk, as the lower bunks had cots attached for women with children. I well remember the night we had to have all engines full stop due to the threat of icebergs. To sit out in the middle of the ocean, in the pitch dark once again, was nerve-racking.

Near the end of June 1946, we arrived in Canada. We were in Halifax, Nova Scotia. We were taken through a large warehouse-type building, now named Pier 21. Each of us was met by a Canadian military personnel who helped us gather our belongings together and got us to the train to continue our trip. It took me two days by train to reach Hamilton, Ontario, where I was to meet Ken and his family.

🍁 Joan Folkard

When war broke out I was 15-years-old and was finishing my schooling and completing my Associate degree at the Royal College of Music (ARCM) in London, England. At the age of 16, I had 22 pupils and played the violin and viola in the Bournemouth Symphony Orchestra under many famous conductors, one being Sir Thomas Beecham. My father was in the same orchestra when he was 16 under Sir Dan Godfrey. My brother and I entertained the Forces because my father composed the music. One piece was called "Hurricanes and Spitfires," all pizzicato (plucking the strings). The troops loved it! Another was called the "Merry Sergeant," and there were many others.

One evening, in the middle of a performance, my panties fell to the ground; they were French knickers with a button to hold them up. My father had always said, do not stop playing for anything! So I finished playing, picked up my panties, bowed and walked off the stage to catcalls!

My parents had a bomb shelter built in part of the dining room and the music room. My brother and I had bunk beds in the smaller half of the shelter; my parents had a double bed in the other half. We were in the flight path of the enemy planes returning home after their raids and they dropped the remaining bombs before crossing the Channel. My father would always wake us to tell us the air raid siren had sounded; then we listened for the sound of the bombers engines, then the explosions. This went on every night and it was very frightening!

Many of the high school students in nearby Southampton were evacuated to our area. One student was an excellent pianist, another was a composer,

Joan with her father, mother and brother modelling their gas masks, 1940.

and because they were musical they were invited to our home. The pianist's name was Brian and the composer was called "Mousy" because his ears stuck out. I did not like him, but Daddy thought he was wonderful. "Mousy" invited me to his home in Southampton for a weekend. My parents said yes! His family ate dandelion salad, which I had never heard of before.

I joined the Entertainments' National Service Association (ENSA) because my parents would not let me join the Forces; they thought I might meet men! But I could join ENSA because that was music, which is all my father cared about. He did not seem to realize that I would meet many more men travelling with ENSA. I stayed with a lady called Lorna who lived in Dorchester and had a huge house that had been built in the 1800s. It had 14 bedrooms and was full of antiques. Lorna had a library van full of books, plus a gramophone and records. During the day we went to the army camps. The men would return the books they had read and choose more. They liked to hear music and always asked if they could dance.

Some of the officers were billeted in the most beautiful squires' homes with fresh salmon streams running through the grounds. Sometimes they invited us to dinner and afterwards we would go fresh salmon fishing. This was fun, but it was not the normal thing that happened! I always had my violin with me and there was usually someone who could play the piano.

Lorna used to give dinner parties for the air force who had just come off "ops." This is where I met my husband Bill; a nickname given to him by his father. His real name was Michael Charles Folkard. He was a fighter pilot in the Battle of Britain, No. 609 Squadron. After that, he was sent to Amada Road in the State of Orissa, India, where he trained fighter and bomber squadrons from the Burma front. He then joined No. 152 Squadron at Tulihall in the Imphal Valley in Burma. He said the "Japs" were far worse than the "Huns" or Germans.

Bill was sent back to England with terrible skin trouble, which originated from the parachute straps when flying. Unfit for tropical service, he looked like a sight from Belsen, all skin and bones. He was 6'4" and only weighed 120 pounds. He had horror stories to tell. It was not easy for him to talk about those days, so he always made light of them. Bill was then posted to

Warnwell Dorset, which was close to Dorchester.

On VE Day we went to Weymouth Harbour because the German boats were supposed to be there. It was a false alarm. Bill and I became engaged shortly afterwards. We married on August 20, 1945. Bill was posted to Hawkinge Kent. He found us a house in Folkstone, which was close to the base. From there, he was posted to Charterhall, Scotland. There we had a squires' summer home, stone floors, five kitchens, six bedrooms and a baronial hall with bear skins hanging on the wall. At the far end of the hall was a vestibule with a telephone. This was our only convenience; there was no hydro, just oil lamps. Bill used to bring the oil from the air base; it was my job to clean the lamps every day. No heat, just fireplaces. I used to go to bed with a Harris Tweed suit on! Boy was it cold. Our only neighbours taught me how to make butter. When we went on leave, we would take butter home to our parents. It was all a great experience!

🍁 Patricia Forget

I was born on the Island of Jersey, located in the Channel Islands, and was living there when war broke out in 1939. I was 6-years-old and this is my story of the German occupation. Many people, including the doctors, had evacuated our Island before the Germans attacked. My aunt, uncle and cousins managed to catch the last boat. We planned to leave, but didn't make it. There was a lot of confusion at the time. People destroyed their house pets and left most of their possessions behind.

The Island was attacked from the air because Germany saw potato and tomato trucks moving toward the harbour and they mistook them for army trucks. Ten people were killed and others injured. The German soldiers arrived in good spirits, thinking they would soon take England. They marched through the streets singing happily. Their uniforms were so smart with shiny boots. The first thing they did was to have their swastikas flown from the airport and public buildings. The Reichmark was introduced, yet English currency was still accepted. Signs were posted with orders for civilians to follow.

My first encounter with the enemy was shortly after they had taken over all the hotels for billets. We lived close to one of the hotels, so my two sisters, both older than I, and a friend decided to have a look. I was dared to deliver a note written by my friend that stated, "Will you meet me later?" My sisters cried, "Don't go! They will shoot you!" I went regardless. The German soldiers just laughed and looked confused. They probably couldn't read the note anyway!

The days that followed were quite different. We had been cut off immediately from England. Gas masks were issued, rationing and blackouts were enforced. I remember the day I was fitted for my gas mask. What an unpleasant business. I went with my older sister Barbara and we kicked up quite a fuss. The mask smelled of rubber and we thought we'd suffocate. Both of us screamed, refusing to try one on. Eventually, they had to guess at our size. Fortunately gas was not used during the war.

In July 1940, we were given an ultimatum to surrender. We had to fly the white flag; we had no choice. Jersey and the other Channel Islands were in a good strategic location for war. Under a direct order from Hitler, the Island was turned into a fortress. The work was done by slave labour, mostly Russian prisoners. At the end of the war, we found out they had been ill-treated. Many had died without a trace. Among the things constructed on the Island was an underground German hospital. The full purpose of this hospital was uncertain.

The greatest hardship for the people of Jersey was starvation. Food, clothing, shoes and coal and wood for fuel was rationed, so much per household. The same with tobacco, but because my father didn't smoke, he used it for bartering. Electricity and gas for homes was limited. Petrol for cars was only available to doctors.

We went through happy and sad times, always hungry in the latter years. About a year after war broke out, we moved to a bigger house. I met my close friend Margo, who lived up the street. We would spend the hot days of summer at the beach or in the nearby valley. Sometimes mines would wash up on the beaches. But I was happy and oblivious of the troubles of the world. However, we didn't have the unrelenting bombing, although anti-aircraft guns would sometimes go off during the night. Life was a surreal reality.

Whole milk was becoming scarce. There were as many as 11,000 German soldiers consuming gallons of milk per day. We were given a free half-pint bottle of milk a day at school. People would queue up for skim milk. Queuing up for everything seemed to be a way of life. Matches and soap were hard to get. The soap from France was of poor quality, as they were also occupied by Germany. Soap became really difficult to obtain. It mainly went to the hospitals. France was our only supplier of food, clothing and shoes. Eventually, we could only get wooden soles.

By 1942, food was severely rationed. The Germans ate our pork and veal. We only had worn out dairy cows from France to eat. A community kitchen, run by our cookery teacher from school, was opened. We used to go for vegetable and tomato soup. It cost six pence a bowl. You could get a small dessert like tapioca for a penny or two extra.

I was surprised one day when my mother gathered us around her to tell us she was expecting a baby. I had mixed feelings at the time, thinking she was too old, but she was only in her thirties. On Christmas Day of that year, my mother shocked us all, giving birth to twin girls, Christine and Marilyn. There was a big celebration in the maternity ward. She was away for two weeks and we missed her terribly. My father hadn't been too well and found it difficult to cope. That was the beginning of the bad times for us.

When my mother returned home we thought everything would return to normal. Our life, of course, was not the same. Christine always seemed to cry, while Marilyn was such an angelic baby. We borrowed a twin pram for the baby girls. People used to stop us on the streets to look at them. Everyone favoured Marilyn. Due to the lack of food, my father's health became worse and he was hospitalized. The babies had a ration of French gruel. They were doing well, but my mother was not. I didn't even notice until she almost collapsed. The doctor came to our home and said she would have to go back in the hospital. This was the worst time in my life. My whole world fell apart.

Our neighbour tried to help us, but we were paid a visit by the Island's Welfare Nurse. The babies were already staying in a créche, but we were alone without anyone to look after us. It was the summer of 1943, and I was 9-years-old. My eldest sister was only 12. It was announced that we had to be placed in an institution. My oldest sister Margaret was to stay at a friend's house, but the rest of us weren't as lucky. My sister Barbara and I went to a girls' home. This home was like a prison. It was the only girls' home on the Island. It was used as a correctional place for unmanageable girls. There were prostitutes, thieves and homeless girls like us.

The day we arrived, my sister and I kicked up a big fuss, screaming and crying for a long time. We eventually calmed down. We were issued with plain clothing for school and a pretty frock and shoes for Sunday. We were only permitted to wear our shoes to church. During the week, we went barefooted. The food was the worst. It was terrible and badly cooked by the senior girls at the home. For breakfast, we had porridge – a grey watery substance with huge lumps. Lunchtime wasn't any better – potatoes in their skins served in the water they were cooked in. The best meal was suppertime – two slices of bread with margarine and a glass of milk. Once we had stewed cherries from the garden because the States Committee came for an inspection. We were so unhappy there!

The worst part was the thought that we might never go home. We hadn't heard from our mother; there was no mail anyway. I still remember the feeling of despair. I think this affected me in future years. We were there nine weeks altogether. During that time I had a bout of tonsillitis, which was the only time I had good food. Then one day Margo's mother came to visit. She wasn't permitted in the home, so she waited outside the school by the fence and spoke to us. We were so relieved to know we hadn't been forgotten. She had walked many miles barefooted to see; there were no buses and shoes were difficult to find. She saw how unhappy we were and immediately told my mother.

My mother signed herself out of the hospital and sent for us. We were so happy to go home. We knew everything would be all right now that Mom was there. My poor brother David had been in a boys' home, but he never really spoke about it. My mother wanted to bring the twins home, but was so weak after being in bed for so long. Her friends encouraged her to wait until she was stronger to bring them home.

A week passed, then a messenger came to the door to tell my mother that Marilyn was sent to the hospital with gastroenteritis. She died that night with my mother at her bedside. It was a sad and difficult time for all of us. I was not at the funeral, but heard the church bell toll. My father was still not home. The days that followed were so sad. My mother brought Christine home immediately. Our whole life changed. My mother felt consumed with guilt. As time wore on, we took up our lives again.

There was little fuel for bakery ovens, so people got together and pooled their resources, only using the ovens when they were full. We did this because our gas for cooking was cut off during certain times of the day. As well, electricity was only on for a short time each day. Coal and wood were rationed. I remember being cold all the time. When my cousins evacuated, they left us their gabardine raincoats. That was my one and only coat during the war, which became rather threadbare. We had heavy rainfalls in Jersey and my coat would get soaked through. Many days I had to put on my coat, soaking wet. My feet were so cold and my ankles were covered in chilblains.

In 1944 my whole family contracted a skin complaint. Mine was the worst because it became infected. The rest of my family went home from the hospital after a week. The condition of my health was such that my hands wouldn't heal. They were red and swollen with huge poison spots. The nurse used to cut the spots open every morning, but they were up again the next day. While I was in the hospital I had a sore throat, so they took a swab. The next thing I knew, screens were put up around my bed and I was carried out on a stretcher into an ambulance. I was sent to Overdale, an isolation hospital for fever and TB patients. I had contracted diphtheria. The nurses and Matron were so kind, much nicer than the General Hospital.

I had to have injections to remove the infection from my throat. They used special feeders for some foods because I was not allowed to have a pillow or sit up. After a number of weeks, I was given a pillow, then two, until I could sit up. I was in the hospital nine weeks, even over Christmas, but the food was really good. On Christmas morning I had the best surprise of my life. Two of my teachers had obtained an egg for me. It was presented to me in an egg cup, soft boiled. It had a painted face and Santa cap on. I hadn't tasted an egg in years. Even though I had good food, I didn't gain any weight because I kept getting tonsillitis. The Matron asked the health doctor if I could have my tonsils out to stop the infection. The doctor refused stating that there wasn't enough anesthetic, only enough for serious operations.

Our Bailiff had drafted an urgent message to the German Command for transmission to the Allies. It stated that many drug supplies were exhausted and the anesthetics were practically gone. The Red Cross ship, the SS *Vega*, was indeed a welcome sight. It was now 1945 and the end of the war was near. The Red Cross parcels arrived, some from Canada and New Zealand.

Patricia with her brother David (who is wearing a Liberation Medal), 1946.

The Canadian parcels had a can of Maple Leaf butter, Klim dried milk and Kam luncheon meat. When I was discharged from the hospital, they sent my parcel home because they felt I needed the food. With the arrival of new supplies I went back in the hospital to have my tonsils out. After that my health improved steadily.

For the most part, the war years were really quiet for me, except for the occasional guns firing in the middle of the night. We had an air raid shelter, although I never had to use it. My parents were in a constant state of anxiety, wondering what was going to happen next. We had been cut off from France due to the dangers in the English Channel. Even though we did not have bombings, there was a grim reminder that a war was going on. Bodies of naval seamen and airmen would wash up on the beaches. They were given a proper burial in a rose garden in a park where we had often played. There were German graves as well, on another side of the Island.

Liberation day came on May 8, 1945, when Churchill's speech came over loudspeakers, "… and our dear Channel Islands are to be freed today." What a joyous occasion. All school children were given liberation medals. On May 9, the German Forces surrendered. I remember seeing them; they were thin and their uniforms looked worn and shabby. They were short of food as well. One thing that stuck in my mind was an inscription on the belt buckle worn by a German soldier that read, "God is with us" in German. I thought, even the enemy thinks they are right and that God is on their side.

🍁 Ida Gatien

I was born in Denmark in 1923. When I was four, my family moved to Canada. We returned to Denmark in 1938, but had to leave for Canada again as the danger of war increased. We were aboard the last ship of civilians to leave Denmark. When the war started, we lived in Saskatchewan. I was 17-years-old. We moved to Winnipeg, and then to Port Arthur to farm. Along with my mother and sister, we milked 60 cows a day by hand. Once the war started, it was difficult for small farmers to buy the equipment they needed to continue their business. The farmers had to form a dairy cooperative.

In 1942, when all the men had enlisted, I was able to get a job in the cooler at the cooperative. There were 12 glass bottles in a case and I had to stack the cases 12 high. I wasn't tall, but I was strong from the physical labour of working on the farm. I could handle the heavy lifting.

I worked seven days a week, eight hours a day and earned $7 a day. The wages were good for a girl in those days because if you worked in a store you only made a couple of dollars a day. I realized the guys driving the horse and wagons making deliveries were making much more than I was working in the cooler. Eventually, I was given a milk wagon and doubled my wages overnight. I also had to join the Teamsters' Union. I was the first female in the local and I remember thinking, "How can I go to a meeting with all those men?" But most of the other drivers were older men and they were all good to me.

Since I had grown up on a farm, I knew how to drive a horse. We had to harness our own horses in the morning and load our own wagons. We also collected the money, which people left in the empty bottles. My horse knew the route and he walked along from house to house while I ran in with the milk. In the summer, I would leave Port Arthur about 4:00 a.m. to go to Loon Lake with a truck full of ice cream and milk. By 8:00 a.m. I was back in Port Arthur and would then do my regular milk route.

It was a good job for me, as I had left school in Grade 7 to work on the farm. I delivered for about two years and then the war ended. When the men returned, I lost my job to them.

🍁 Alberta Gaunt

The day war was declared on Germany, I was a 14-year-old schoolgirl, living with my mother and sister in a third floor apartment in Holborn, London, England. During the following weeks the schools proceeded to evacuate their pupils out of the London area. Some parents chose to keep their children at home with them – it was optional. I had my spare uniform and other essentials in a small suitcase, plus a gas mask in a cardboard box with a string holder strap; I was dispatched by train to Luton, in Bedfordshire, a small town 30 miles north of London.

My classmate Irene and I were billeted with Fred and Bertha Pipkin and their 3-year-old, Joy. Irene and I shared a double bed in one of their small bedrooms. There was an outside toilet and we considered ourselves lucky. The Pipkins were kind and treated us well. With the influx of evacuees, it was a daunting task to schedule all of us into the rural schools. I attended two schools daily, one in the morning, another in the afternoon. This involved a lot of walking and I promptly lost all my puppy fat!

My sister evacuated with her firm, which had rented a large manor house, and she generously mailed me a six-penny postal order every week for pocket money. Every person 18 and over had to register under the Essential Works Order. My sister was transferred to a government job in the Civil Service on Baker Street in the heart of London.

I was completely oblivious to the Germans invading the Netherlands, Belgium and France and the terrible evacuation of our troops at Dunkirk. In 1940 I decided to leave school at the end of the term in August and go home. Little did I know that I was heading into the Battle of Britain and the 86 nights of the bombing of London and other large cities. I was hired as a Junior Clerk with Burroughs Wellcome, a pharmaceutical company at Snow Hill, near The Old Bailey and not too far from St. Paul's Cathedral.

Some of the ground floor apartments in our area had been shored up and were used for air raid shelters. When the bombing began, we would take a pillow and blanket and sleep on the shelter floor. We were like sardines in a can! The teenage boys were wonderful. They helped extinguish fires and smother incendiary bombs with sand bags. They also rescued elderly people with bleeding faces cut by the flying glass and brought them to safety in shelters. A 16-year-old neighbour was killed while sand bagging an incendiary bomb. Eventually, my mother, sister and I decided to stay in our apartment at night. The three of us slept on a bed chesterfield in an alcove, thinking that whatever happened the three of us would be together.

On my way to work, I would step over fire hoses. The firemen, red-eyed and weary, were still up the ladders spraying water on the smouldering buildings. Tanks filled with water were installed on various streets, so that the firemen could access them if the water mains were hit. Sometimes we heard another siren, and it was the brave men of the Bomb Disposal Squad warning people that they had an unexploded bomb on their truck. They were taking it to an open area, where it could be detonated. Sometimes they didn't make it. We were surrounded by death and unsung heroes.

After one heavy raid I went to work and my building was no longer there. We were told to go home and await instructions by mail. When I arrived home, my mother and two cousins were there. All our offices had been bombed. I received my instructions to report to our Head Office, the Wellcome Research Institute on Euston Road in another part of London, which involved a long bus ride. My mother's firm relocated to Colindale, a northern suburb of London, which she had to use the subway to reach.

The government invented a cartoon character named Billy Brown of London Town to issue advice or warnings. The subway windows were covered with a protecting mesh to stop the glass from shattering. It made it difficult for people to see what station they were at, and so someone had started to pull some of the mesh away. There were captions featuring Billy above the windows saying, "I trust you'll pardon my correction, this stuff is here for your protection." Someone had replied, "We thank you for the information, but we can't see the ruddy station." Similar captions were posted at the bus stops. "Face the driver, raise your hand, you'll find that he will understand." The reply to that was, "Of course he'll understand, the cuss, but will he stop the ruddy bus."

One night my mother got up to have a peak out of the side window when there was a heavy explosion and our windows came crashing in. I saw a crumpled shape and cried out thinking it was my mother, but it was the torn black material blown in with the breaking glass. How we escaped getting cut was a miracle. We grabbed our flashlights and decided to go down to the shelter. There was glass in our shoes and my sister had a large sliver right by her head on the pillow. The glass was embedded like darts in our furniture. My cousin who lived in Edgeware, a northern suburb of London, invited us to stay in her house; we stored our furniture in one of her rooms and gladly accepted the offer. It was closer for my mother to travel to work, but my sister and I travelled farther.

Under the Essential Works Order, it was impossible to change jobs without permission from the authorities in the shape of a release form. I saw a job advertised for a Junior Ledger Clerk in Cricklewood, closer to where I was living. I applied and got the job. When I handed in my notice at the Wellcome Research Institute I was informed that I could not leave. Fortunately for me, I had a friend in the local Labour Exchange and was advised how to circumvent the issue. I was able to get my release and start the new job. I was now 16.

Taking this job had an impact on the rest of my life. My new firm made the landing assault crafts, like the ones used in the D-Day landings. I worked in the Accounts Office and became friends with a fellow worker named Rose. It was 1942 and Rose was introduced to a Canadian soldier named Oscar. I was introduced to a Welshman, a Corporal in the Royal Air Force (RAF) named Ken. I had known him three months when he was posted to India. He asked me to wait for him, which I did.

There was a shortage of housing and my mother, ever fearful that we would not find accommodation if the war ended, took three rooms on the third floor of a tenement house in Kentishtown, back in London. My mother and sister had to do fire watch duty after work. I was still too young. So when the raids were on, they would be patrolling the streets, while I went into the Anderson shelter in the garden with a retired couple, Mr. and Mrs. Hughes who occupied the basement apartment.

In 1943, Rose married Oscar, her Canadian. He was stationed in a small village called Billingshurst. She sometimes asked me along, and I spent many a happy hour dancing with Canadians in the small village hall. They introduced us to the jitterbug! We were thrilled when D-Day arrived - our troops and Oscar landed in France.

Ten days later, the Germans sent over their latest weapon, the V-1s, a pilotless winged aircraft, which we called the doodlebug. It was most nerve wracking. When it passed over, the house and ground would shake. We waited to see if the engine cut out, and when it did, we knew that it was coming down. We would heave a sigh of relief when we heard the explosion elsewhere. We had survived, but someone else had not. During one of these raids, Rose, who was pregnant, had the ceiling fall on her when a V-1 explosion blasted the house. Six weeks later, she delivered twins who only lived a few hours. I cried when I read her letter and I thought of Oscar receiving the news amidst the fighting in Europe.

Then the Germans launched V-2 rockets and there was no defence against them. You could not hear or see them coming; you would only know after hearing the explosion. Gradually, our troops gained ground in Europe, overran the launch sites and the bombing ceased.

When peace was declared in Europe, we turned on all our lights. Rose and I joined the dancing crowds in Piccadilly Circus. Everyone was so happy. We had survived a terrible experience, but we were fortunate that we had not been occupied like our Allies in Europe and Russia. Later, the war ended with Japan, and the world was at peace.

In 1946, Rose sailed on a Canadian war brides ship to Canada. Ken returned and was "demobbed" and we were married. But like a lot of wartime marriages, it ended within a few years, leaving me with my daughter Susan. World War II made me a stronger person. I face my problems head on.

🍁 Janet M. Gibson

An entry in my mother's diary on August 31, 1939, read, "A terrible week of suspense with the threat of war." This was followed on September 3 with, "Britain declared war on Germany."

At this time, I was in Grade 3 in a one-room rural school in Perth County, Ontario. Within days the chap who worked as hired man on the farm beside us and the one who worked on the farm across the road, both being natives of England, had enlisted for active military service. Other young men in the community soon followed. My brother, who was then 17, went to Hamilton to work in the steel mills until he enlisted in the 16/22 Saskatchewan Horse Regiment in June 1941.

Shortly after the start of the war there was a movement in the community to organize a branch of the Red Cross. My mother was the treasurer and very active in this work. She made many trips as a member of the Buying Committee to purchase yarn and material for the members to make quilts, pyjamas, socks, sweaters and other articles for the servicemen. Meetings and bees were held and the ladies of the community worked diligently on projects to bring warmth and comfort to the boys. The Red Cross Society provided a neat and valuable little yellow book called *Knitting Instructions for the Armed Forces*, which was published compliments of the Yellow

Pages of the local telephone directory. This included directions for socks, mitts, sweaters, helmets, gloves and even knickers for the Women's Services.

Private money was raised for the war effort through Victory Bond campaigns, usually twice a year. A local person canvassed the residents selling the Bonds. My parents subscribed to each campaign. There was also a War Savings Stamps Program for children. Each Friday the pupils brought their contributions to school for the stamps they were buying that week. At noon the teacher took the money to the local general store, bought the stamps and gave them to the students in the afternoon. It took $4 worth of stamps to fill a book and in five years time each book was worth $5.

We were a patriotic school with a very patriotic teacher. We learned war songs, "There'll Always be an England," "The White Cliffs of Dover," and several others. Every day for a short time after lunch, we marched around the classroom to the strains of the marching bands, which were played on the little portable windup record player. Every Christmas concert included a patriotic drill and songs. Often another concert in the spring was in aid of the war effort. We always stopped outdoor activities at noon and recess in order to watch a training plane in the sky.

News on the radio was a steady diet at our home. My father had emigrated from Scotland as a teenager, but his family remained. When the days looked black for the British Isles and invasion by the Nazis was a strong possibility, news was so important to us. Speeches by Winston Churchill, Franklin D. Roosevelt and Mackenzie King and broadcasts from the Royal Family at Christmas were never missed. On December 7, 1941, we had a visitor from Kitchener, who was also a native of the same town in Scotland, and when word was received of the Japanese attack on Pearl Harbour, he and my dad sat all afternoon glued to the radio.

For his early training in Canada, my brother was stationed at various sites, including Sherbrooke, Quebec, Debert and Sydney, Nova Scotia, and at Thorold and Camp Borden, Ontario. While at Camp Borden, he became a trooper in the tank regiment and was home on leave for a few days each month. Then, on May 19, 1943, he was home on his last leave. We all wondered quietly if this would be the last time we would see him, but we had to think positively and have confidence that he would return.

Whenever he came home on leave, I was amazed at the amount of time he spent shining his boots and polishing the brass buttons on his uniform. The army certainly demanded an immaculate appearance. This was evident in any one you saw in uniform. They were a handsome group of young men. When my brother went overseas in 1943, he added many more courses to the ones he had already taken during his training in Canada, each one reported in a letter. While stationed in England he visited my father's family in Scotland while he was on leave.

My mother's diary records on June 6, 1944, "The great and long looked for invasion of Europe commenced this morning. The radio gave news of it all day - no other programs." Of course, we expected my brother had been part of this landing while driving his Sherman Tank. We learned later that he was not in the initial landing, but arrived on the Normandy beaches three days later. News of the invasion and the liberation of Western Europe filled our days. While freeing Holland, troops were billeted in homes.

While my brother was overseas there was a box of goodies sent to him each month. It took a month to gather up enough chewing gum, candy, chocolate bars, etc., as these items were scarce and limited in the stores. I knit a turtleneck sweater to send. Things were packed in a sturdy cardboard box, wrapped in brown paper, then wrapped in a piece of cotton cloth, usually a flour or sugar sack, and sewed with strong cord. The address was written in purple indelible pencil. Letters were written frequently and also received, with as much news as could pass the censors.

Over the years there were the reports of servicemen who had lost their lives, were wounded in action or missing. Everyone felt so bad to hear this news. It was wonderful news on May 7, 1945, to hear that after five and a half years the European war was over. I was in Grade 9 at high school. The news was announced at a gathering in the assembly hall and school was cancelled for the rest of the day. What celebrations there were for VE Day, all over the nation! In our community a service was held with the church being packed by people who gathered to give thanks for the end of the conflict.

The servicemen began to return home. My brother had signed up for duty in the Far East and was one of the first to arrive back in order to prepare. However, the war with Japan was over before he had to take part. Another church service was held to celebrate the victory over Japan. My brother was discharged in September and after devoting over four years of his life to his country, it was time to get on with his own future. When all the servicemen had returned home, they were honoured at a presentation night at the church. Sincere tribute was paid to those who did not return. Honour Roll Plaques were prepared and hung in each church bearing the names of all who served. Finally those years of the terrible threat to the world's peace were at an end, and families, the country and the world could start to recover and rebuild.

🍁 Shanna B. Gimbert

Shanna

I'll start with my graduation as an M.B., Ch.B. from Glasgow University in October 1938. War was imminent, but I wasn't really worried. I went straight to Glasgow Sick Children's Hospital to do my Surgical Internship.

I finished my six months and when our family doctor said he could get me a job with the city's Outdoor Medical Service, I jumped at the chance. The weekly salary was the princely sum of seven guineas a week, the equivalent of about $30 dollars at that time. That's what I was doing when war was declared. My patients in the clinics seemed to be mainly old men with chronic bronchitis or emphysema. But there were house calls to some of the worst slums in Glasgow, only exceeded by the slums in Dublin where I had done my training in obstetrics.

I eventually arranged to work nights and take the Diploma of Public Health Course at the University. The work was entirely house calls, but I had a room in the head office of the Department of Public Health. Fortunately my parents had given me a car as a graduation present. Sometimes there would be no calls and I would be able to sleep all night and not fall asleep the next day in the lectures. At other times, I might have to make a call somewhere on the outskirts of the city, which could be quite difficult in the blackout.

I remember one call I had to make. It was to a Police Box at Govan Cross. A Police Box is a really small cement structure, about four feet by four feet. I couldn't understand why I had to go there. But soon all was made clear. There was a woman lying on the cement floor of the Police Box who had just given birth. All I could do was tie off the cord and get the police to call an ambulance.

Scotland had not been greatly affected by the war, except for rationing - mainly food, clothing and petrol. I was now at the Royal Maternity Hospital, otherwise known as the Mat or the Rottenrow, the street it was on. This time, unlike Sick Kids, I thoroughly enjoyed the nine months I spent there. The food wasn't great, but we didn't have to worry about shopping. All the interns, about 12 or so, ate in our private dining room at one large table and the senior resident sat at the top and served us. Often on a Saturday the evening meal was tripe, and I can still see the senior resident and hear him say, "Any one for stewed knitting?" Needless to say, it wasn't popular.

I think it was about this time that the London Blitz started. It was really a terrible time with dreadful air raids over London every night and many casualties and horrible destruction of property. Eventually raids died down and things were relatively quiet, so I decided to work in London. It was something I had always wanted to do. I had a cousin in Goodmayes, Essex, in General Practice so I did a locum for him for a short time. Then I got myself a job as senior doctor in a small maternity hospital at Parsons Green, Fulham, in London. It was a small, relatively new hospital with about 20 patients. It was situated on the edge of a green space called Parsons Green, about two minutes away from the local underground station. This was important since I had laid up my car a year or two before because of the shortage of petrol.

The Matron, the other doctor and I each had a little flat on the third floor.

The wards and the delivery and operating rooms were on the second floor, and the prenatal and baby clinics, along with a large waiting area, were on ground level. There was an Air Raid Precaution Station (ARP) in the basement. Dr. Anne Gibson-Hill and I took turns being on call in the ARP unit. I remember we were given a uniform consisting of a navy blue jacket and pants of the most ghastly rough material. Just down the road from the hospital there was a fairly large house, which was called the Babies Hospital. That was where we sent the newborns that were having problems. Two sweet old lady nurses ran it and they did a marvellous job.

I remember one incident when we were called out in the middle of the night. We went into a damaged house and heard a faint voice from under the staircase. When we opened the door to the cupboard, there was a little old lady crouched on a stool holding a metal basin over her head like a helmet and murmuring, "Is it over yet?"

It was shortly after coming to Parsons Green that the V-1s started. They were nasty! You could hear them coming, hence the name "Buzz Bombs," and when the sound stopped, you knew they were about to land and explode. One day after I had done my rounds at the hospital, I went down to the Babies Hospital to do rounds. While I was there, a buzz bomb went over, which fortunately passed over us and exploded. I was off duty after that, so I went to the hairdresser's and another bomb passed over. I then took the underground to Bond Street and joined a friend for lunch in one of the nice little restaurants in Mayfair. Believe it or not, we spent quite a bit of time under our table as buzz bombs flew over. Never a dull moment!

At some time during my stay at Parsons Green all our patients were evacuated to the country and Dr. Gibson-Hill and I were left to do the outpatient clinics. We also had to do our own food shopping and cooking. Food was still rationed, but we could still get dried eggs. I remember we even got a rabbit once. Ann was even less of a cook than I, having been used to lots of servants in Singapore.

By the fall of 1944, there were fewer bombings using V-2s and the ARP posts were gradually being closed down. Ours was due to close in the middle of December and a farewell party was being planned. Some of the ARP fellows got to know a Royal Canadian Air Force (RCAF) Flight Sergeant, who was also in charge of the photographic section on the top floor of Harrods Department Store. So they asked him if he could get some film and take some photographs at the party. He said he would try.

The evening of the party I was entertaining my friend Margot in my apartment. After dinner, I apologized to her and said, "Look, I've got to put in an appearance at this party, but I won't stay too long." I went downstairs and stood around talking for a little while, when someone came over and said there's someone here who would like to take your picture. I turned around and saw a tall, handsome, Canadian airman. He took my picture, he asked me for a dance and then he asked me for a date. That's how it all began!

I was born in Warsaw, Poland. I was 9-years-old when on September 1, 1939, war was declared between Germany and Poland. We lived on the outskirts of Warsaw. My mom thought that we would be safer in the country, so we left the city and went to a friend's farm. We gathered what we could carry and walked. It was a slow walk because my grandmother was on crutches because she had lost a leg. Our friends welcomed us. My dad stayed in the city because of his work. Within days, other people fled the city and our friends took in as many as could stay in their barn.

We could hear airplanes roaming above us and shooting. It was a frightening time. With so many people, food was running out. One day Mom decided to go to town to see if she could get some bread and other necessary items, but in the meantime the German Army invaded the countryside. Mom could not get back. We cried and prayed for Mom's safety and wondered if we would see her again. After a few days, Mom was determined to run through the front lines. She knew some German and just kept calling out that she had to get back to her children. She was stepping over dead bodies as she walked through the crossfire. She made it back to us. Our prayers were answered.

The army moved on several weeks later. We walked back to our home only to find it burned down. We left my grandmother with my uncle and we stayed with my dad's mother. During the German occupation, Jewish people suffered. Most were segregated into a ghetto and then taken to a concentration camp. As well, lots of Polish people were taken to labour camps. Due to overcrowded living conditions, we had to make another move. So we went by boat to my aunt's in another city in Poland. Eventually, we found a place to live.

Early in 1945, the Russian Army invaded Poland and the Germans retreated. That was another bad time, as Russian soldiers were raping women and girls. My school friend and her mother were raped; my friend was only 15. My mom spoke a little Russian, so she was respected, but we were always in fear. By August 1945, Mom decided that we would try to get to Germany. Mom's German language and our Protestant religion helped us to get back into East Germany. It took two weeks. We travelled by train on top of coal. We also had to walk a lot since train tracks were being bombed, but we made the journey and stayed in a refugee camp.

We were placed with a farmer's family and we stayed there for three years. Although we received shelter during this period, food was not available. Mom had to go out into the forest and the fields and gather mushrooms, potato skins and other greens. After three years, we left East Germany and crossed the border to West Germany. There we found a Polish transit camp, which was established through the General Andrews II Corps of the British Army. Mom applied for a visa to Britain and within a few months, it was granted. Finally, we found peace in 1948.

🍁 Laura M. Haferkorn

I don't remember a thing about the first official day of the conflict known as World War II. I guess I was too busy looking forward to my fourth birthday, which fell a few days later. At the time, I was living in Centralia, a tiny village in the western part of Ontario where my father was a United Church Minister. When Dad decided it was his patriotic duty to enlist, it wasn't long before he was called up for active service. This meant we had to leave the manse and move to Toronto to live with my mother's elderly parents. What a shock it was to be engulfed by the traffic noise in the bustling city streets after the tranquility of village life.

I have many memories of those war years. I remember being thoroughly alarmed when Mother, who seldom showed her feelings, burst into tears when Dad's first letter arrived. Every night I scanned the newspaper for familiar names among those listed under "Killed," "Wounded" or "Missing in Action." I was fascinated by the scary, thick, black headlines. Each morning, I ate my porridge to the faraway sounds of the 1:00 p.m. news from the BBC World Service, which was invariably preceded by a solemn military march.

At school we packed ditty bags, which included a washcloth, a cake of soap, a tube of toothpaste, a chocolate bar and some chewing gum. I would tuck in a note that said, "From your little friend, Laura Marie." I would come home after school to find Mother and her friends drinking tea and knitting, surrounded by piles of socks, scarves and those odd head coverings called balaclavas. I remember meeting a group of shy British children who were introduced to us as "war guests."

I struggled to write the weekly letter to Dad, in response to his sent from "somewhere in England" or "somewhere in Italy" that was decorated with funny little drawings. I prayed every night for the war to be over and for Dad to come home.

VE Day is my strongest memory. By then I was nine and a half years old. On the morning of May 8, 1945, I was sitting in my Grade 5 classroom, only half listening to the teacher and looking forward to what I considered a special treat. Mother had gone downtown shopping for the day and had sent me off with a packed lunch. This was the first time I'd been allowed to take my lunch to school. Mother liked us to come home for a hot lunch of vegetable soup or macaroni and cheese.

Suddenly the teacher was interrupted by the buzz from the PA system. From far off, a deep voice could be heard repeating, "The war in Europe is

Laura with her brother and father, January, 1946.

over! The war in Europe is over!" There was stunned silence in the classroom and then pandemonium. The teacher sat down heavily at her desk and put her face in her hands. My classmates started screaming and jumping on the tops of desks, all except for Johnny whose Father had been killed the previous winter. Johnny and I were the only ones in the room still sitting frozen in our seats.

The school was closed for the rest of the day and we were sent home. On the way, I met my mother coming back from downtown. Her face was white. She told me that while she'd been in Simpsons, someone had come running into the store with the news. Sales clerks and customers dropped what they had been doing and rushed into the street. The crowds frightened Mother, so she caught the first streetcar that was going her way.

After lunch, my brother Jimmy and I decorated our bicycles with crepe paper and rode them down to St. Clair Avenue, where we joined a mob of people, cheering and laughing as they paraded up and down the sidewalks. It felt like a holiday. At suppertime, Mother couldn't stop crying. I remember being nervous and excited at the same time. Dad had been gone for nearly four years. I knew my prayers would be answered. Now he would be coming home. I peppered Mother with questions. Would Dad be wearing his uniform? Would he remember me? Or would we be like strangers? What would we say to each other? Would he even like me?

Dad did not come home until just before Christmas of 1945. He was kept in England in his role as pastor to help ease our returning soldiers back into civilian life, "Civie Street" I think they called it. The initial joy at his return soon turned to disappointment. Dad wasn't used to children and said we got on his nerves. Nothing we could say suited him. Sadly, we were never able to make up for the gap caused by his prolonged absence. Dad decided to leave the church and go back to university to study social work on a Department of Veterans Affairs allowance. We stayed on in Toronto in my grandparents' house.

How did the war affect my adult life? Well, in 1954 I married a German immigrant who got out of Germany and took his Canadian citizenship as soon as he could. We built a good life together and raised four daughters.

Over the years, the girls asked us many questions about the war. We both worked to instill tolerance for other nationalities and other religious beliefs. But they never really knew a grandfather, or the rest of my husband's family. My husband's father was killed in the closing days of the war; his mother was eventually trapped behind the infamous Iron Curtain when the Russians occupied that part of Germany. And my own family was never the same. After years of unhappiness, Dad and Mother separated and Dad went back to England to live.

🍁 Jean Hall

During the war years, life in England for my family was one of being ready and alert for any eventuality. Fear of being attacked by the enemy was always on our minds. People carried gas masks to be prepared if bombs were dropped. Food was rationed and lineups were prevalent at stores when word spread that scarce food items were available. People were required to hang black blinds on all of the windows in their homes, and these had to be lowered every night. Cities and towns had to remain in darkness so that enemy planes overhead could not detect where there was a heavily populated area.

Running for cover to the air raid shelters was a frequent occurrence, but the sirens mostly went off in the evenings. The sirens at the airdromes let off shrill ominous sounds and residents were told to always heed the warnings of possible air attack by enemy aircraft. When the alert was over, the all-clear siren emitted a different sound and life went back to normal until the next warning. Some air raid shelters were made out of cement blocks and each home had a small one in its backyard, while larger ones were built at the airdromes.

In 1942, when I was 20, I received a formal letter from the government telling me that I was being conscripted to serve in the war effort. Unfortunately, I was in a hospital bed recuperating from an appendectomy when the notice arrived at my parents' home. The doctor assured me that he would take care of the matter, but was informed that I would only be allowed six months to recover. As forewarned, my second conscription notice arrived in exactly six months time. There was no other choice, I left my hairdressing job and reported for duty at a specified depot.

New recruits to the Women's Auxiliary Air Force (WAAF) were issued two uniforms; the dress uniform had a skirt, while the "battle dress" uniform had slacks to wear when driving trucks or ambulances. Recruits, however, were not allowed to try on the uniforms for size. The person in charge of supplies simply looked at each new person and decided if they needed a small, medium or large uniform.

Wearing my small clothing, I began the month-long basic training at

Gloucester, England. Training consisted mainly of marching, lectures and learning how to salute, etc. In the hangars at the airdromes the recruits listened to the daily lectures, which always ended with singing "war" songs. Those singsongs were a highlight of the day and helped greatly to keep up spirits.

At that particular time, the women in our group were given two options - to be a cook or a driver. I chose the MT or Motor Transport Division. I was taught how to drive trucks and cars and also learned how to operate vehicles in convoys during blackouts at night. One of my jobs was to pick up truckloads of rations and take them to the cookhouse. An airman went with me to assist in the loading and unloading. I also transported mailbags from the railway station to the airdromes and hospitals, etc.

Later, as an ambulance driver, accompanied by a medical orderly, I transferred patients from one hospital to another or delivered them from a train station to a hospital. While the air raid sirens sounded frequently, as time passed they became so routine that fear of being attacked eased somewhat.

For my friends and I, life in the military during the war was not all work. One popular form of entertainment was joining in singsongs around pianos in the pubs. There always seemed to be a pianist among the crowd and everyone loved to sing the popular, as well as the war, songs of the day. Another favourite activity was going to the various airdromes on weekends where live bands played at the many dances. The young women were always watching for handsome airmen to ask them to dance.

While at Acklington, I met a Canadian airman, Corporal John Dalton Hall, from Navan, Ontario. Later, I was posted to Northallerton Hospital, some 10 miles away from Leeming. There, our chances of meeting were not as often as we wished. Meanwhile, John's twin brother Delmer was stationed in administration at the Leeming Airdrome. When he learned of an opening for a driver at his base, he asked John if he was interested. So Delmer arranged for John's transfer to Leeming, which allowed us to spend more time together.

Transportation to the big dances at the airdromes was in the back of a lorry, which was a canvass-covered truck. The women and airmen sat on wooden benches in the back. John often volunteered to be the duty driver to transport his comrades to the dances, and while there we were able to enjoy some quality time together.

John and I fell in love and following a two-year courtship, I married my Canadian airman in a quiet church ceremony on February 17, 1945. A small reception was held afterwards in my parents' home in Ashington, Northumberland, with family members and a few friends present. Adding to the happy occasion was a wedding cake, baked and shipped to England by John's Aunt Elda Bradley from Navan, a member of the Navan Women's Institute in Ontario. Mrs. Bradley lovingly baked the fruitcake knowing that the ingredients for such a cake and its icing would not be available in

England due to the strict food rationing.

When the war ended in 1945, John returned to Ottawa and I came to Canada in March the following year. With so many families to be transported, couples with children were given priority and were shipped to Canada first.

🍁 Mary Belle Hambly

I was born in 1941, and had three uncles and one aunt in the military service. When I was quite small, I remember going with members of my family to the village of Marlbank, where there was an effigy of a man named Hitler. Coveralls filled with straw, with a hat and boots attached, hung from a sign at a gas station that was no longer used. A large group of people gathered to watch someone set Hitler on fire. He burned really fast and everyone seemed really happy and gave three cheers - "Hip, Hip, Hurrah!" - three times with their arms extended in the air. I thought these people were cruel.

🍁 Iris Hawker

Prior to the declaration of war in 1939, my parents owned a pub in southeast London, after moving from a country hotel in Surrey. After September 1939, all the children were evacuated from London into the country for safety. My twin brother Peter and I were only 8-years-old, and although we did not want to leave our home and family, we had to go along with all the thousands of other London children. I'll never forget standing on the Plumstead Railway Station with our gas masks and nametags waiting for the train to take us to the south country of Devon.

At first, Peter and I were billeted together. But later we were separated into different homes for the first time ever. Peter was in a nice country pub and I was in a small house not far away. We started school there, and I remember the London kids would compete against the country kids at games like skipping and ball.

When the bombing of London started, we feared for the safety of our family. My family's pub was in a dangerous spot, opposite an entrance gate to the eight square mile Woolwich Arsenal where ammunitions were manufactured. Apparently, the Germans knew this was adjacent to the River Thames and would target this area constantly with their bombs by following the reflection of the river.

We knew there were constant air raids over London, as well as other big cities, killing many brave citizens and destroying so many homes and historic buildings. The King and Queen were loved and admired for their devotion to the country and citizens during the hardships caused by the bombing. They toured the devastation after the air raids, giving hope and heart to the people.

Occasionally, our parents would come to visit us in the country when they could get away from the business. These visits were reassuring to us. One time, Mother came to see us and her leg was in a cast after having fallen down in the blackout and breaking her leg.

The worst time was during the Blitz of 1940 to1941, when hundreds of German bombing planes came over London continually causing destruction, with fires burning everywhere. As soon as the worst of the bombing was over, we were allowed to return home to London and experienced the last years of the war there. We slept downstairs in the big cellar underneath the pub. Our father always slept upstairs in the second floor in his bedroom. He had served as a Captain in the British Army during World War I and wasn't afraid.

We were so lucky not to have been bombed. So many homes and business buildings were hit, including many factories in the arsenal, killing many war workers. The air raid warning sirens would sound off with a high and low pitch. When the raid was over, the all-clear siren sounded off in a high even pitch. This was a welcome sound. I will always remember the sound of the pilotless bombing planes that came over London. Their engines screeched, then suddenly stopped before they fell, exploding on impact. We called them doodlebugs.

My brother Billy had enlisted in the Royal Air Force (RAF) when he was

Victory Party, Lenten Street, London, England, June 30, 1945.

18-years-old. He was in training, but unfortunately became ill. It was discovered that he had TB, a serious lung disease. Although they operated, Billy never recovered from the surgery and he died in 1942. Because he was in the air force, they draped a Union Jack flag over his coffin the day of his funeral.

Later during the war, a young cousin, 21-years-old, also in the RAF, was a commissioned pilot. During a raid over Germany, Bobby Axton was shot down over France. He was buried there in a cemetery with thousands of other servicemen. Billy and Bobby are my heroes and I always buy two poppies each year.

The war lasted for six long years. Eventually our Allied troops began to win battle after battle - on land, at sea and in the air. When, at last, we beat the enemies and peace was declared in 1945, there were great celebrations everywhere. Each street had a big party and there were tables and chairs down the middle of streets for all the children, and all the mothers and grandmothers brought us goodies to eat. There were pony rides for the children and music and singing. It was a great time to celebrate our victory.

🍁 Dorothy Hemstra

During the night of May 9, 1940, we heard the horrible sound of thousands of planes crossing over our province of Friesland. To me, it was an eerie sound without end. I was 11 at the time and I knew little about war. There was talk about Hitler invading Poland and Czechoslovakia, but that was far away. After that particular night I knew life had changed, literally overnight.

We heard the bad news the next morning. Germany had bombed London, England, and the German Forces had overrun our Low Countries of Belgium and the Netherlands. Our country was ill-prepared. For five days, they fought man-to-man, but had to give up having lost a lot of brave men. That's when a five-year occupation started, which took an unbelievable toll on the Dutch people.

Long lines of German foot soldiers passed our house. We were so afraid that planes would come over and start shooting at them. My dad was not an outspoken man, but I never forgot the moment that he prayed out loud for our safety. It made a lasting impression on me. Scary days and nights followed. At night, the Royal Air Force (RAF) bombers would fly over our area to Germany to destroy factories where they manufactured planes and weapons. And vice versa, the German Air Force bombed England. We lived near a military base where they would shoot at airplanes, often with terrible results.

The Wehrmacht, the German Armed Forces, took everything away from the citizens, bikes, tires and horses, whatever they needed. Most of the time they did not pay for it. Needless to say, we hated and were afraid of German soldiers. A group of officers were stationed in our town. One day, I had gone to school alone on my bike and another biker came up behind me. Afraid as I was, I did not dare to look at the soldier. He spoke to me in German. I could understand him a little. He asked me where I came from and how old I was. I whispered, "Twelve," and then looked at him. He said something to me I had never expected an enemy to say. "I have a little girl like you at home." Completely surprised, I did not know what to say, but was thinking that this soldier is a father, he has children, he is like us, a human being.

Another effect of the war was food rationing. Food stamps really made it hard to have a normal meal. My mother was pregnant with my sister and she ate oatmeal porridge twice a day. She was sick of it, but there was not much variety. My dad was a hired man on a dairy farm, so we did have milk. But not everybody had milk, unless a farmer had a cow that was not registered. Meat was hard to come by. Once in a while there would be a message from the town crier that meat was available; an old cow or horse had been butchered and we could get two pounds per family. We had a small garden, which supplied us with fresh vegetables.

In 1942, we did not have much fuel for the winter. We had some coal and wood, but the winters were so cold and there was lots of snow. We walked to school in "Klompen," wooden shoes. My brother and I would take a rope with us and gather old tree branches and pieces of wood to bring home. Mom could burn them to cook supper. We lived seven kilometres from our school and we didn't have warm clothing. I remember putting newspaper under our clothing to keep the wind out. We wore hand knit stockings, which the wind blew through. My mother had an awful time washing our clothes; sometimes there was no soap.

People were really brave in those days. Young women brought secret messages to an underground resistance network. Some people had a radio hidden so that they could listen to the English news. From this news, our people would know what to do to undermine the German Regime.

Surviving through 1943 and 1944 was difficult. People walked for days to get milk from farmers and whatever food they could lay their hands on in order to bring it home to their starving families. The big cities were worse off. They told us stories of people dropping in the streets from hunger. People were burning furniture to cook cats, dogs and tulip bulbs for a meal. That was unbelievable to our ears. It taught us to never waste food and to be thrifty. In our area, a soup kitchen had started. The soup always consisted of mashed potatoes and canned vegetables, with some fat in it. It filled our stomachs. Pea soup seemed to be the best, but it was a good thing that we didn't know what was in it!

Another political danger was among our own people. We had traitors, members of the National-Socialistische Beweging der Nederlands (NSB), who would secretly serve the German Gestapo for money. During the winter of 1944, my boyfriend helped his Dad pick up milk twice a day from many farmers, bringing it by boat to the cheese factory. He was the age to be taken away to the labour camps, but he kept on working. One evening, a member of the Secret Police came to our village to pick up young men. This traitor wore a balaclava and went to my boyfriend's home to collect him, but fortunately he was at my house. Several German soldiers walked into his parents' living room without asking any questions, looked under everything, even under the blankets where his sister lay ill. My boyfriend was lucky, but others were not. Some of his friends were transported to the German labour camps.

Toward the last year of the war, I was 16 and had started working as a maid for a farm family. The long hours I had to work were worth it because of the food that was served. Early in 1945, we heard rumours of heavy fighting between the Allies and the Germans in the south of Holland. Our province of Friesland was set free in April 1945. Without too much resistance, we were free.

We welcomed the Canadian soldiers who came into our town with rumbling tanks. What an unbelievable freedom they brought. There are no words to describe it. To this day, I am thankful for their valiant efforts and to their families and loved ones who suffered so much loss. At that time, we did not know what the future held for us. But we would meet some of these brave men again, in our new country named Canada. I am truly grateful to them.

🍁 Willy Herweyer

Our family of eight consisted of my parents, five girls and one boy. I was 12-years-old when the war started. The morning of May 10, 1940, we woke up early from the noise of airplanes flying over. We ran downstairs and asked our mother what was going on. She told us the Germans invaded Holland, and that meant there was a war. I can still see her standing in the kitchen slicing bread. No matter what, we had to eat.

After breakfast we went outside. We saw hundreds of parachutists jumping out of airplanes about 10 minutes from our house. Later on, they marched past us. We lived about 30 minutes from Rotterdam. On May 14 they bombed the whole inner city. It was terrible. Hundreds of people were killed. The streets were jammed with people fleeing. Our beloved St. Lauren's Church stood with part of its tower in the midst of ruin. People had to live in basements and attics or with relatives. Thousands were homeless.

Soon after, we were ordered to blacken all the windows. Our house had wooden blinds, so that was easy. We also had a curfew and nobody could be out after 8:00 p.m. Radios were confiscated, so that we could not listen to the BBC. That summer the Germans set up a campaign for everyone to get a card, with their photo, address, age and fingerprints on it. The Jews had a capital "J" on theirs and we had a "B."

The Jews were deprived of their livelihood. The businesses were sold to the Nazis for a fraction of what they were worth. The Jews were also isolated from the rest of the population. They were excluded from hotels, restaurants, parks, theatres, libraries and recreational facilities. The Dutch were informed through an illegal paper what was going on in Holland and the rest of the world. If you were caught with this paper, you were arrested.

My brother was a member of the underground. He did a lot of daring things. Some of his friends told him the Germans were trying to capture him, so he had to disappear. On a dark night a farmer hid a rowboat in the bulrushes for him and a friend. They waded into the river just as the German Army trucks, artillery and soldiers were coming down the road. It was November and they were wet and cold. But they made it across.

The underground placed thousands of Jews in safety. If you were caught hiding them, they sent you to concentration camps too. Some people made double walls in their homes with standing space for several people. They had to be quiet when the Germans were searching a house so they wouldn't be heard. There was always a cabinet hiding the revolving door. They also made holes in closets, where two people would fit.

The Germans had to eat too, so everything became scarce. I ended up working on a farm, so I had enough to eat. People from the cities came with carts, bikes, even baby carriages, to ask farmers for food. They walked for hours. Near the end of the war, thousands died of starvation. The Germans opened the dikes and flooded the land. One thing was a blessing. There were a lot of fish to catch. After the war, my husband never ate fish for a long time. The war affected me for life. I still can't throw food away.

🍁 Jessie Hill

My memories of the war years are mostly happy, romantic and fun. Certainly, there were sad times. September 3, 1939, was a truly sad day. That was the day war was declared. It was also the end of my wonderful, fun-filled summer. We lived in Port Carling, Muskoka, one of the best tourist resorts of the time. Many of our tourists that season were young men already in uniform. What young woman didn't love a man in uniform, with his jaunty air, freshly pressed trousers, shiny shoes and hat at a rakish angle? All wartime music was happy. Songs, such as "Don't Sit Under the Apple Tree," "Rosie the Riveter," "Alexander's Ragtime Band" and "Elmer's Tunes," were sung by Vera Lynn.

At the beginning of the war, I worked for an elderly couple and their son, who were German sympathizers. Mrs. Schreiber always listened to their short-wave radio to Lord Haw-Haw, an Englishman who defected to Germany. She would clap and cheer for him during his speeches. Mr. Schreiber would draw pictures of Britain's Prime Ministers - Chamberlain and Churchill - in the snow, belittling them and praising Hitler. Their son, a wealthy and smart man, had a lot of electronic equipment. It was rumoured that he sent and received messages from Germany. One day, the Royal Canadian Mounted Police (RCMP) came to our house to talk to me. My dad allowed the questioning, but only with him in the room. I didn't know anything to prove that the Schreibers were in contact with Germany and no charges were laid.

The Muskoka Sands tourist resort was used as a prisoner of war camp. The steamships sailing the Muskoka Lakes during the war years passed close to the fenced, high rock wall of The Sands. The largest ship at the time, the *Sagamo*, had a live band on board for entertaining its passengers. When passing The Sands' enclosure, they played "There'll always be an England." The prisoners gathered at the fences to watch and listen. Whether or not they knew the tune, they would always cheer and clap for the band.

On Christmas Eve in 1940, I was in London with my husband Jack attending a show. When we came out of the theatre, there was a carnival atmosphere in the streets. It was a beautiful winter evening; the street lights were twinkling. Young men in uniform hugged and kissed any girl on the street. It is a wonderful memory for me. The Military Police were also present with MP on a band on their sleeves; they were always in twos, keeping the peace. I don't remember any violence, just a happy, fun-filled atmosphere.

At the age of 23, my brother went overseas, landing in Sicily. He was a mechanic, so he was not on the front line. Jack was in the army for a few months before being discharged due to a hernia. A Dr. Curts, who many of you will remember, learned to repair hernias during the war. After moving to Thorndale in the late 1940s, Jack was the first civilian patient he operated on to correct his condition.

A boy I went to school with, Bob Pridday, was awarded the Victorian Cross - the highest award given by Great Britain for bravery. The wing of his airplane was hit by the enemy and caught fire. Bob climbed onto the wing in mid-air and put out the fire, thus saving the lives of all on board. Our friend Jack Drover was in a plane that was shot down over France. As the plane fell, Jack was thrown into the front, kicked out the nose and the entire crew parachuted to safety. They were rescued by the French underground and stayed with French families until the end of war.

On May 8, 1945 – VE-Day – the war was over, that wonderful day when everyone went to London to party in the streets. All the businesses were closed; the church bells were ringing; tickertape was thrown; everyone was celebrating. We went to a movie, where the news of the day included pictures of Belsen Concentration Camp with the horrible images of open pits of bodies of men, women and children. The natural instinct was to look away. I can clearly remember the voice of the announcer saying, "No, don't cover your eyes. Look, so you will know of the terrible atrocities that the Germans have done." Later, the troop trains brought the boys home. The last one we went to see was in May 1946 when my brother came home.

🍁 Mona Hill

My parents were anxious that we three girls receive an education. My two sisters chose teaching. My choice was to be a nurse. I did housework for our family doctor and with his support I found myself training as a nurse at the Cornwall General Hospital in September 1939. War had just been declared, so I spent the war years nursing in various places and circumstances. Because I always lived in residence, I had no experience with rationing of any kind.

While training, I worked 12-hour days, six and a half days a week, in addition to classes and studying. I was hardly aware there was a war on, except that a basic training army camp was set up within site of the hospital. Many of the young men from our area trained there and would come to the hospital. When they no longer came, I realized they were probably on their way overseas.

I graduated from nursing in September of 1942 and went to work at Smith Falls Cottage Hospital. While there, my desire to join the army grew. My co-workers tried to discourage me, but while I was home the next summer helping with the harvest, I went ahead and applied. I received word that the army would not accept me until I was 25-years-old.

In February 1944, I received my call to report to the Kingston Military Hospital for officer's basic training. I was kept busy with full-time nursing duties and assembling my officer's uniform and overseas supplies, so I had little time for military training. The poor Sergeant Major had his hands full trying to teach us to march and salute. The need for our nursing services was greater, so in spite of our lack of military training, we found ourselves bound for overseas by the end of May. We spent 10 days in an army camp near Halifax. Then, in the cover of darkness, we were put aboard a ship and by morning we were out of sight of land.

There were 125 of us aboard a banana ship, which had been appropriated by the British Army for use during the war. It was one of about 100 ships in the convoy. We never did see the other ships during our 11-day crossing. We carried our life jackets at all times and slept with our clothes on, but never seemed to worry about safety. We spent the time whale watching, reading, having singsongs around the piano and enjoying the "cruise."

We landed in Scotland and were greeted by the Red Cross ladies who served tea and scones. We were put aboard a train bound for London. This

Patients ready to leave for home by hospital ship, 1945.

was our first experience with wartime restrictions in England. There was no heat, water or food on the train and we found it cold and damp. From London, we were sent to various destinations.

My new-found friend Barb Green and I were fortunate to be assigned to #13 Hospital, not far from Brighton on the south coast. It was an old, civilian hospital, which had been taken over by the Canadians and enlarged by adding Nissen huts. We arrived shortly after D-Day, so many of our patients were wounded at Normandy. We also received many patients who had been given first aid on the frontline and were then flown back to England. They appreciated clean beds and hot food!

We each cared for a 40-bed ward with the aid of an orderly. Many of the orderlies were men, no longer fit for active duty. They adapted themselves well to an orderly's duties and were excellent at it. Any of the patients who were mobile at all, helped in any way they could. It was excellent teamwork. We worked 11-hour days and 13-hour nights, six days a week. Penicillin was used extensively. It was given by injection every four hours, day and night and was a wonder drug!

This hospital had a compound that housed about 150 German prisoners of war. They were mostly cared for by their comrades, but if we were needed, we went in under escort. These men seemed no different than our own men. They enlisted to defend their homeland, not because they wanted to fight a war.

In April of 1945, Barb and I were moved to Basingstoke Hospital. Prisoners of war being released from the Far East were sent to Basingstoke to begin their recuperation. These men will always live in my memory. They were emaciated from starvation, as well as mentally abused. At first, they could only take fluids. Gradually their diet was increased until they would devour plates full of food. They seldom spoke and were afraid of open spaces. They were slowly persuaded to go outside, as long as two of us went with them. I wondered how they ever adjusted to civilian life and what became of them.

Thank goodness the war ended in May. We did not feel like any big celebrations. The ex-prisoners were too recent a reminder of the horrors of war. I did, however, have the opportunity to watch the victory parade in front of Buckingham Palace. There were troops from the army, navy and air force representing every country in the British Empire. The Royal Family was on their balcony and even Winston Churchill drove by with his famous cigar.

War wasn't over for many of the troops. There were cleanup duties. My friend Barb went home due to family illness, but I was sent to # 2 Hospital at Hazelmere. This was a large hospital and would be one of the last to close. This was a stressful time, as people were frequently given leave with nowhere to go and no money to spend.

It was, however, a more relaxed time in the hospital, as patients were often just waiting for room on a hospital ship, or we were dealing with the usual every day illnesses. We had more time to spend with patients. Occasionally, there would be entertainment in the Mess Hall. The Red Cross and Salvation Army did what they could to help; the "Sally Ann" helped with their canteen and the Red Cross helped the men who had married in England and had families to take home.

While in England, I was given leave every three months, plus a rail pass to anywhere. I had the opportunity to visit my father's old home near Belfast, Ireland, and meet some relatives. I toured all parts of Scotland and England and visited London's historic sites. I could not go to the beaches because of the land mines. I bought a bicycle and enjoyed the countryside. I attended local dances and enjoyed popularity because I was a Canadian girl.

After peace was declared, I was able to travel to the continent. I had the good fortune to have a trip to Paris and one to Switzerland. In July of 1946, I sailed for home aboard the *Queen Elizabeth*, along with war brides. It took only four days, compared to the 11 days going over. I came home to a different life than the one I left in 1939.

I was soon back nursing, this time at the Renfrew Victoria Hospital. A year later, I married Arnell Hill and went to live on his home farm near Cobden, Ontario. I am grateful that I trained as a nurse and had the experiences that I did. I learned a lot from the comradery we all shared and hoped I had helped, in some small way, those less fortunate than myself.

🍁 Joyce Hodgson

I was a girl of 18, living in Twickenham, Middlesex, England, 11 miles from the city of London when the war started. I was employed at MacFarland and Langs Biscuit Factory. Inside the factory on the wall, there were three lights, amber, red and green, like the traffic lights. When it was peaceful the light stayed green. When the German bombers crossed the Channel the amber light shone, and when the fighters were overhead, we would get the red light. When this happened we had to run across a field and over the railway tracks to the shelter, with the planes fighting overhead. Some of the girls would scream and refuse to go. We had to stay at the shelter until the all-clear was issued.

In November 1940, the Germans dropped incendiary bombs on Pouparts Jam Factory and blew up the sugar. The Germans had mistaken it for an ammunition dump. Living only a few blocks away, we had bombs drop on our house. The Air Raid Precaution (ARP) man was killed in our attic trying to put out the bombs. We were evacuated for three days. Six months later, we had to evacuate again for a delayed time bomb. When my parents went out at night, they would walk on opposite sides of the street, so they both wouldn't get killed in the event of a bombing.

I was conscripted on August 19, 1941. I was sent to training school in November for four months to become an electrician. The class consisted of four girls and sixteen men. The men were mostly wounded men from Dunkirk. On March 25, 1942, one other girl and I were posted to the Clifton York Fighter Squadron. We were to stay with the local vicar and his family. However, his children came down with the chickenpox, so our first night away from home was spent in the Guard House. Needless to say, we were nervous!

The first day on the job, we were sent out to the runways to repair the lights, which were red, green and white. We did not know there was a special way to install the lights. That night an Australian Fighter Squadron landed and they wondered what was going on when they came in to land. The lights shone in all directions. Of course, the next day we were up on the carpet, but nobody knew whether to laugh or be angry.

We stayed at the Fighter Squadron for one year, and then on April 4, 1944, we were posted to the Royal Canadian Air Force (RCAF) Bomber Squadron at Leeming, Yorkshire. One day a week, we worked at the military hospital changing light bulbs and fixing plugs and wiring. We were billeted with the Land Army girls and one ENSA girl on the Women's Auxiliary Air Force (WAAF) site. We were included in all their activities on camp. There, I met my husband, who was an air gunner in the No. 429 Squadron. I arrived in Canada on May 21, 1946, on the HMS *Aquitania*. We docked at Pier 6 Halifax, Nova Scotia.

🍁 Marjorie Holt

On September 3, 1939, my mum and dad, brother and sister and myself sat around our kitchen table in Copthorne, Sussex, to listen to the Prime Minister tell us we were at war with Germany. My parents were upset, as they had lived through World War I, my dad in the army and my mum in war work. My brother and sister who were only 12 wondered what was going to happen, but I knew life in our village was going to change so much. Most of us were in war work and the boys we went to school with were in the Forces – either as soldiers, sailors or airmen.

The village where I grew up was only four miles from Gatwick Airport, so I applied for a job at the airport hoping I could help the war effort. I got attached to the air force repairing bombers. We worked in gangs of about seven girls doing repairs. We all got along so well. We shared good news and sad news with each other. The first bombers we worked on had large Whitney engines, and for about three years we worked on Wellington and Lancaster planes. I worked at Gatwick from 1940 to 1946.

There were troops stationed everywhere and my mum and some of the ladies decided to put on dances three nights a week. The village hall was packed on these nights. I worked from seven in the morning until seven at night, rushed home and got ready to go dancing. It was so much better than sitting home wondering where the bombs would drop that night.

In 1941, I went to a dance at the village hall and met a tall Canadian soldier. He was in the Canadian Engineers stationed about three miles away. He asked me to go to the movies the next night. He got along well with my family and he liked going out in the evening with my dad to the pub to have a pint of beer.

Doug and I were married on October 19, 1943, and three days after we were married his outfit was sent to Italy for a year. Then, he was brought back to England before being sent to France, Holland and into Germany.

When the war ended in 1945 the celebrations were something I will never forget. We burned all the blackout curtains. I don't think anybody went to bed that night or the next. I don't think we thought that we would ever see the end, but we fought tough and won. It was the most wonderful feeling.

My husband left England in November 1945 for Canada and I followed in March 1946. I came over on a troopship, *Ile de France*. There were about 50 war brides. I was upset saying goodbye to my family and friends, but my dad made sure I had enough money in my bank account if things didn't turn out right. The trip across the Atlantic in March was rough and cold.

Finally, we arrived in Halifax in a snowstorm. I had never seen snow blow around like that before. They put us on a train to Toronto, but it went via Maine and all we saw was lakes, rocks and trees. It got a lot better as we neared Toronto. Doug met me at Union Station and we stayed in Toronto for a few days and then went to Waverley to meet his family. He heard there was a farm for sale in Wyevale, so we bought it. I was lonely and homesick for a while, but the people in Wyevale were so good to me and made me feel so welcome. Life began to come together.

🍁 Narda Hoogkamp

On April 10, 1940, German soldiers marched west into the Netherlands. They had good maps with details of important places. For a year or so, many spies disguised as nannies and cleaning ladies had infiltrated the labour force and easily mapped out roads and items of interest to the invaders.

For a 6-year-old girl who had just started school in April, there was not much change at first, except the adults were fearful of the future. Things started changing over time. All of our cattle, horses, pigs and chickens had to be accounted for on our mixed farming operation and the numbers submitted to the new regime. We were now told how much milk and how many eggs to ship and how many bushels of grain were expected of the fields, which had been evaluated during the growing season.

Rationing was also begun and we got coupons for necessary items - sugar, tea, coffee and citrus fruits were seldom seen. I remember getting a colouring book and asking what colour a lemon and banana were. We were fortunate to have an inspector, who asked us, "How much is this pig supposed to weigh?" As there were eight of us in the family, we were allowed to kill pigs for our consumption up to a certain weight per year.

Like most farmers, we had an illegal churn to make our own butter. It consisted of two round wooden planks, one to fit the top of the milk can and the other with some holes attached to a stem. It worked pretty well. We skimmed some of the milk for our own use before shipping. We traded the butter we made for coupons for wool and textiles. The churn, except when in use, was never in the house. It was hidden in a big hedge several feet away from the farm. You never knew when you would get an inspection, and it was better if the numbers agreed with the German's count.

We grew a bit of rapeseed (or canola) and we had a little machine, also illegal, to press the oil from it. The oil was used to light the house and barn in the evening. It was my job to turn the handle for pressing the seed. These little machines were homemade and the ingenuity of people was surprising.

I remember one time that one of our heifers was hit in the lungs by a bullet, so my uncle and I had to walk her over to the butcher to be slaughtered. The next morning there was a long line up for meat because people were allowed to buy two extra pounds since it was a casualty.

The west part of the country was really desperate for food. We did custom thrashing in our area, usually two or three times a year. The fellow with the tractor and thrasher hoped there was enough gas to run it. People from the west walked and biked for hours; they would come for food. My grandfather would give everyone a scoop of grain, all that he could spare. He never overcharged. He treated everybody fairly and did not get rich like many others did.

Early during the occupation, our hydro was cut. Shutters had to be closed, so that the Allied planes flying over on their way to bomb German cities and factories could not see the light. We stood outside watching the Lancasters fly over, hoping they would not get caught in the searchlights. There was one searchlight stationed at the end of our field and, usually, if two lights got a bomber in focus, it would be shot down.

The Germans had their own weapons. The V-1 rocket made a lot of noise. We had to listen for when the noise stopped, which meant it was coming down. Many of these rockets came down in our area. The V-2 improved rocket was noiseless; many came down in Belgium, the North Sea and England.

We lived five kilometres away from Doesburg, the bridge over the Ysel River was the link between east and west. In 1944, when the Germans were losing the war and the Allied Forces were stronger in the air, we watched many times as they shot the bridge to pieces, stopping all traffic until it was repaired. Germans only travelled at night under cover of darkness, especially on the main roads as the Spitfire planes shot everything.

German soldiers would notify us a few hours before they came with their horses and one or two trucks. We had to supply food for their animals and they would kill a calf for their own use. Early one morning they came yelling for us to open our barn doors. A gas truck drove into the barn with a plane right above him. The pilot pulled up and did not shoot. Thanks to that pilot, we were not blown up.

In September 1944, the Allied Forces had infiltrated the southern provinces and were marching north. September 17 was a bright day. The bridge had been shot down in our area, not too far from the house. Later, we watched Canadian paratroopers come down in the distance. It was near Arnhem, just north of the Rhine. The Allied Forces did not get far enough, having trouble with rain-drenched roads that could not support all the heavy equipment. So they were stuck in the mud. Some of the paratroopers got back over the river, some were captured and there were many casualties.

A family from the south could not get back and stayed in one of our pigpens. At least they had a roof over their head and some food. The Christmas of 1944, we had three more men staying who could not get back to the city. I don't know how many people were hiding in the woods surrounding our home. Like everybody, I had a sack right by my bed, packed with a few personal belongings, so if we had to go, I could grab the bag and at least have some clothes.

There was a lot of sabotage, especially during the last months of the war. Doesburg, an old city with a moat, took two weeks to be conquered. In the middle of April, Canadians liberated us and set up station at the park. The cook gave us white bread, sugar, tea and coffee; they just wanted some fresh eggs in exchange.

🍁 Margaret Howden

My first recollection of war was when I was about 5-years-old. My uncle died and they said it was because he had been gassed in World War I. Of course, I didn't know what "war" was, but my cousin, a year younger than I, no longer had a father. That I remember! We lived near Hamilton and every year on November 11 at 11:00 a.m. the factory whistles blew and we heard them at our farm. My mother always stopped work and observed a period of silence. I didn't understand why, but I did the same.

When I was 9, my eldest brother enlisted in the Royal Canadian Air Force (RCAF). He thumbed his way to Ottawa; servicemen had no trouble getting a ride. He left for England in 1940. His last night at home, he left me a doll whose eyes opened and closed. I still didn't know what "war" was, but my brother was no longer at home. We wrote letters, sent parcels and eagerly waited for his letters home.

The next year, another brother enlisted in the army. His letters home told us about his life in England, Scotland, Holland, Africa, Italy and other countries. I remember one letter in particular to Mother with a sprig of heather in it. But I still didn't understand about war.

The news from the front didn't reach home as quickly, so we were always wondering! Cigarettes, chocolate bars, gum, toothbrushes, toothpaste, hand soap and hankies were some of the articles requested. While in Holland, the servicemen gave the children chocolate bars and they were so happy to get them. When on leave in Holland, my brother was welcomed into their homes.

When my brothers returned home, I was no longer a child, but a teenager, and we were so happy to see them. One came home with an English war bride.

I finally understood what war was all about when I went to the movie theatre and saw the news clips of the war. In the Warplane Museum at the Mount Hope Airport, there is a memorial book on display with the names of the young men and women who gave their lives that we may have our freedom. That was what war was all about – freedom!

🍁 Muriel Hurst

I was 15-years-old when the war started. I lived in Middlesbrough, North Yorkshire, in England. With war in the offing, my dad did not wish me to leave home to go to Newcastle to continue my education to become a Children's Nurse. On September 3, 1939, the sirens sounded for the first time. It was the most chilling sound I have ever heard.

It was not long before the Town Council came and dug a hole in our garden to allow an Anderson shelter to be installed. It was about six feet deep and was made of corrugated iron sheets; the two feet that was above ground was covered with sand bags and sods of earth. A small entrance took us to the few steps down to the inside. It was fitted with bunks at both sides. At first whenever the sirens sounded, the whole family collected blankets, torches, drinks, etc., and rushed outside into the shelter. This was difficult to do as my 80-year-old grandma lived with us. So we tried to judge when we thought bombs were coming our way. Unfortunately, we weren't always right and one night I was still in bed when a huge explosion rocked the house. We were up and down into the shelter like rabbits. The next day we learned that a whole row of houses two blocks away had been destroyed.

My brother Jack, with whom I was very close, had been called to his army unit earlier in 1939. In 1940, he was in France and after Dunkirk we didn't hear from him or about him for three weeks. He did make it safely back to England. My other brother Ted stayed home for a while, until he enlisted in the Royal Air Force as an instrument repairer. However, his ears let him down and he went back to the foundry where he had worked before. I joined the Girl's Training Corp, which was a cadet force for the women's services, as I hoped to enlist one day. I rose to Staff Sergeant.

In the meantime, my dad, who was a railway fitter, had become ill as a result of long hours under dirty and dangerous conditions. After Middlesbrough Railway Station was destroyed, he stayed at work for three whole days. That was the way of his life until he eventually died from ulcers in 1944. The war killed him, just as much as it might a serving soldier. But like many other civilians, he didn't get any credit for his sacrifice.

It was due to my dad's illness that my call up for service was delayed for a year. That meant that I was "too old" for the women's services and was directed to Newcastle to be trained as a war worker, in my case as a grinder operator. The irony was that Newcastle was where my Dad had not wanted me to go for my academic training before the war. At the same time, my brother Jack was fighting in Africa with the Desert Rats. He went to Sicily, but was wounded and sent back to Africa for treatment. He came home in 1945.

At the Newcastle training centre, where I was for six months, I fell in with another four girls and we became a close group. Eventually, we were sent to an aircraft factory near Coventry. We worked grinding parts for Lancaster bombers to very fine tolerances using micrometers. My specialty was undercarriage pieces. We were about 200 miles from home and we were given free railway passes twice a year for holidays. It was annoying to me to find out that because I was not yet 21, my wages were lower than the other girls, although my work was identical. We worked 12-hour shifts, seven days or nights on a weekly rotation.

The five of us bought bicycles and rode to and from the factory, which had been built out in the country four miles from Coventry. We also biked

Muriel, 1943.

around exploring the local area. One time, we went to Warwick Castle and saw the famous peacocks. It was all so new to us, since we had not previously been far from home. When we went on leave, we were given ration books to use at home. I gave these to Mum, who lived alone with Grandma. Mum always managed to put on a good meal for me whenever I came home, and fish and chips were always available all over Britain.

The hostel where I lived had a central administration building, which included its offices, shop, post office, dining room, kitchens, dance hall and reading and writing rooms. The food was adequate. But Thursday's meal was the best, fried battered Spam and chips. We always looked forward to Thursday! This central complex was surrounded by rows of domestic huts, where we lived. We all had a single-room with a built-in wardrobe, bed, chair, drawers and a mirror. The room was about six feet wide. Showers and toilets were enclosed and private, but all together at one spot.

The Warden, Mrs. Pringle, was the housekeeper and looked after us like a mother. At one time we were moved into other quarters and one of the girls became covered in big red blotches all over her arms and legs. We asked Mrs. Pringle what it was and she told us it was bed bug bites. We protested so much that they moved us back with Mrs. Pringle.

When America came into the war, a lot of army hut camps were built in Britain for their soldiers before they moved on to the battlefronts. One of these camps was quite close to the hostel. We were encouraged to extend hospitality to them. There were dances and big band concerts, along with live shows. In return, they invited us to dances. But the cultures didn't blend and soon they were stopped from coming to the hostel because to some of them there were no rules. When you are in another country where there is no shortage of women, but a shortage of local men, it was thought that nylons could get you anyone you fancied. They broke windows to get into our huts, so it all ended.

VE Day came in May 1945, and we went into Coventry expecting celebration, but it was quiet and empty. I think people were glad it was over, but still too shocked and tired to do a "song and dance." I recall attending a service at the bombed out cathedral after it had been cleared of rubble. It had no roof and I remember seeing a big cross that had been made from the burnt timbers.

Of course, we still had Japan to deal with and lots of our lads were drafted to the Far East. But the end came quickly due to the bomb, after which there was no longer a need for aircraft parts. October 30 was my birthday and my brother Jack came to share it with me. I had a cake from Mum and cards from friends. I also had a letter from the authorities giving me my release from duty on November 5, one week later. On the way back home on the train I could see the November 5 bonfire celebrations of Guy Fawkes Day brightening up the skies. It was the best possible proof that the war was finally finished.

I had now to face the future – get myself a job and remake a life at home. The Job Centre had given me a card quoting me to employers as a machinist, but didn't say what kind. They sent me to a sail and tent maker. My experience sewing was on granny's treadle model. Nevertheless, I got the job because I managed to sew a straight seam for them.

If I was to comment on what those years did for or to me, I can say that my mind was broadened considerably and that I learned to get along with all kinds of people. The war years matured me quickly and made me more self-confident. They taught me the horrors of war and how much people suffer as a result of it.

🍁 Pat Isaacs

I was a young child when war broke out. We lived in Kent, England, not far from the Woolich Arsenal on the Thames. My first recollection was of our family being evacuated deep into the country for some months. Of course, all of the men, including my father, were called up; the whole population was mobilized. All of the women, once their children were school age, served in the munitions factories or other war jobs. My mother, along with the mothers of all my friends on the street, wore overalls and a turban on her head. They caught a bus at the end of the road. Teenage girls, like my sister, were sent to farms as Land Girls, milking cows and cleaning stables, etc. They took the place of the men and boys who enrolled in the army.

If you belonged to an organization as a young person, you had various duties. I know that Scouts ran messages and in London they helped dig out bomb rubble. I used to belong to the Junior Red Cross and we spent our weekly meetings rolling bandages. At school we were taught to knit. We knitted nose warmers and other items for men in the trenches. If you were older you unravelled old sweaters and knit balaclavas and mitts or gloves.

Everybody was issued gas masks, blue for children and beige for adults. We carried them with us at all times. We learned the difference between enemy aircraft and our own Spitfires, so you would know enough to run for cover. They built the first shelters in backyards. They were a large hole in the ground covered with corrugated steel that was then covered with soil. This was known as an Anderson shelter. We grew cucumbers or marrow over it. Mother would take us down there every time the air raid warning went off and you didn't come out until the all-clear was sounded. If we were down at the local shops or playground when it went off, there was a shelter under a paved rink. Everyone helped the children and the elderly take cover.

In school we had stone shelters with bunks. We did our lessons down there. Later, when V-1s, or buzz bombs, and V-2 rockets came along, they built what were known as Morrison shelters in homes. These consisted of large steel tables with wire mesh on all four sides. We slept underneath the table and we would unhook one side to come out to eat.

Ration books were issued to everybody, blue for kids, beige for adults. We were allowed a half an ounce of butter per week, one ounce of margarine and one ounce of lard. We had four sugar bowls on the table each with our own ration and if you ran out you used saccharin tablets. Dried egg was the norm, but if I had to do the shopping I knew to look out for cracked eggs and begged the shop owners to sell me one. Butcher shops would sell whale meat, which supplemented our meagre rations. Before bed at night the kids had slabs of bread with meat drippings. All the backyards were taken over with vegetable gardens, which mothers and their children dug and kept.

As children, we were evacuated without our parents. We were all loaded on buses at the schoolyard and unloaded deep in the country, where everybody had to take in one or more kids. I was lucky; I had a kind couple and my best friend was right across the road. We lived there a year and had a ball! I think the war turned us into tomboys, as we played army and collected shrapnel. We were self-reliant. I don't remember being homesick or missing my mother. Our mother continued to work, even after the war. We went to school, did our chores and played until our mother came home. We had no babysitters. I was luckier than most because I didn't lose my parents and siblings.

❧ Ruth E. Jennings

When WW II broke out, my husband and I were living in a small town in southern Saskatchewan, about 20 miles from the USA border. We had no family and decided on a change of scene. So after saying goodbye to relatives and friends, my husband Tom and his brother took off for Toronto in our Ford Coupe. I went later by CPR train; it was a lot more comfortable than the Coupe. I stayed behind to sell our furniture and the bits and pieces we had accumulated in our few years of marriage.

We all got employment in Toronto, the men in a rubber company where tires of all description were made, a busy place during wartime. Tom's brother Cecil was called up and off he went. My husband Tom was rejected due to a former injury to his arm. As for me, I landed up in an office typing.

Tom and Ruth,
VE Day, Toronto, May 8, 1945.

This firm manufactured walkie-talkies, small radios that could send and receive messages. I eventually got on the line with a group of other women. We wired and soldered our walkie-talkies, then passed it on to the next person and she did her bit. Quite a change from office work, but much better pay! Every once in a while, a siren would sound and up we would get and leave the building in an orderly fashion. It was a safety measure, just in case. We didn't mind the break.

I played the violin and was able to join a little group at work that played different instruments, and we would entertain now and then for soldiers stationed in Toronto. We could play just about anything, so were usually able to keep up with requests. Tom could keep time playing the spoons, so he went along.

🍁 Kathleen Jermey

Having already received my training as a nurse and midwife when the Second World War began, I applied and was accepted into the Queen Alexandra's Imperial Military Nursing Service in 1941. Our uniform was grey and red. I was proud of it. I was given the rank of Lieutenant with two pips on my shoulder. I was first posted to a military hospital near Glasgow. It held about 200 patients, many of them young men who had fought and been wounded at Dunkirk. At night, when the German planes flew over on their way to bomb the docks and shipyards in Glasgow, the sirens would start ringing. When we were plunged into darkness, some of those young boys, 18 and 19-years-old, would start screaming; Dunkirk had been too much for them.

In 1942, I got my overseas order. I was sent to Lichfield, near Manchester, England, to receive my training for active service. I was there for six months, when our unit - the 100th British General Hospital - was formed with surgeons, medical specialists, doctors, nurses and orderlies. The unit also had a kitchen staff. We were taught to respect our senior officers by saluting them each time we met. We were informed of all the hazards we might encounter in a warm climate. Of course, there were all kinds of needles to get for malaria, cholera, dysentery, etc. We were to be equipped only with our uniform, a canvas valise and a tin trunk to keep the bugs out. The valise rolled out holding a canvas cot and collapsible canvas tripod

*Kathleen in uniform,
circa 1942.*

stand, which held water for washing. We also carried a tin mug, tin plate and utensils.

After six months of waiting, the dreaded notice went up, "Confined to Barracks for 48 Hours." We were moving out. We were allowed only one phone call and told to tell no one we were going overseas. I telephoned the photographer who took this picture, asking him to send it to my mother, whom I had told that when she received my picture, I would have left the country.

We were transported to South Wales in one-ton trucks and at Avonmouth, boarded a hospital ship bearing the Red Cross. The unit of nurses who went ahead of us went by troopship, which was bombed and sunk at sea. Some of these nurses lost their lives.

Our voyage went well, until we reached the Bay of Biscay off the coast of Spain. Our little hospital boat just "rocked." We were all horribly seasick until we arrived in Gilbraltar. We spent six days and nights there, until it was safe to proceed. The water was like a millpond, so calm and beautiful. At last we pulled into Algiers, North Africa, which we were told was our destination for a while.

After boarding trucks, we were transported about 20 miles up into the mountains. When we arrived, we were astounded to see our unit was to perform completely under canvas. Two nurses shared a teepee tent. There was only room for our trunk, rollout cot and canvas tripod stand, to be used for washing our clothes and ourselves. We hung the wet clothes on the tent posts. The water had to be carried quite a distance.

The wards consisted of long tents with 25 beds on each side. The mess was also in a large tent. Although the meals were less than to be desired, we were hungry and ate everything in sight, even the dehydrated food that tasted like straw. Our work involved the care of our soldiers suffering from gunshot wounds, amputations, malaria and dysentery.

Then a sad day came. The Germans dive-bombed the ships docked in Naples Harbour, Italy. When the sailors jumped overboard into the sea from their flaming ships, the enemy poured oil on the water and set it alight with fire. Many of these men were horribly burned. Once rescued, they were shipped to Algiers for care. It took two nurses all day to go around changing the burn dressings on these poor men who suffered so much. When they were fit to travel, they were sent back home to Britain.

One kind soul asked if he could do anything to help me when he returned home in London, England. I asked him, when he was able, to visit my mother in Scotland and give her all the details about where I was and what I was doing. Most of my letters she received were obliterated, as were hers to me. I finally had a note from this boy and he said he was sitting in my mother's kitchen smelling roast duck in the oven. I felt homesick. I didn't hear from him again after I had written back. I finally got a letter from his sister saying he had been killed in the London Blitz. It was so sad that he had gone through so much, only to go home and die.

After a year in Algiers, the enemy was being driven north into Italy. Our whole unit was transferred to Italy to a small town called Afragola, about 10 miles from Naples and only 50 miles behind the enemy line at Casino. We were still in tents working many long hours.

Before I forget, I must tell you about our bathrooms. They consisted of long planks of wood built above a trench with holes to sit on. There was only a small partition between each "toilet hole," so privacy was absolutely nil. Thank goodness for a sense of humour. Every night disinfectant and lime were poured in the holes.

When it was time to move again, we were so excited to be moving into a building in a town called Bologna, previously occupied by Germans. The building had been used as a hospital. To our dismay, when we arrived there, we found the Germans had poured cement down all the drains so there was no water. You can imagine what it was like trying to nurse malaria patients, who were running fevers up to 105 degrees, with no water to drink or wash.

As time went on, I was posted to a Casualty Clearing Station close to the fighting front line. All we could do was resuscitate the casualties, clean them up a bit and send them down the line to the nearest hospital. This posting was in a place called Udini, just five miles from Venice. It was there in May 1945 that we heard the War was over. There was such rejoicing and fun on the canals in Venice. Crowds of us were cheering in the gondolas on the canals. The gondoliers must have thought we had gone mad!

Our unit was not disbanded for about six months. I deferred my release for a year to stay on as an Operating Room Nurse in Trieste, Northern Italy, near the Yugoslavia border. I was given 18 days leave to go home to Scotland from December 6 to 24 that year. We travelled by troop train to Milan and boarded another troop train going north through Switzerland and France. We had ration stops where we were issued enough food to last us a day. Running along the railway tracks were ragged, homeless, hungry children shouting for bread and chocolate. We gave them at least half of our rations.

After sitting upright crowded in a railway carriage for three days and three nights, we were all exhausted. At Calais, France, we boarded the boat to cross the English Channel to Dover; then we took a train to London. I lost no time finding out when the "Flying Scotsman" left for my hometown where I had phoned my brother to meet me. What a celebration when I got home. I slept for three days afterward.

My journey back to my unit was equally memorable. It was sad leaving my family just before Christmas. We arrived in Milan on December 23 to find there were no trains moving to our unit until after Christmas. So we were cooped up in a hotel room where all our meals were brought to us, as it was unsafe to go out. Mussolini had just been murdered causing a great deal of unrest. That was a Christmas I shall never forget.

I was released from the army in 1946, returning home to Scotland to nurse in a hospital in Edinburgh. I was walking along past Edinburgh Castle one day and noticed a huge sign: "Come to Canada ... George Drew needs you." So, I thought I would go in and see what they had to offer. When they told me that Canada was in dire need of Registered Nurses, I signed up to leave six weeks later. I arrived on a Thursday in April 1947 and began working at the Christie Street Veterans Hospital (which is now Sunnybrook Hospital) five days later.

🍁 Dorothy Kelly

On September 3, 1939, Prime Minister Chamberlain announced over the radio, "We are at war with Germany." The air raid siren sounded for the first time. That piercing wail sent shivers down one's spine. I thought to myself, "Was this a raid?" I expected to see enemy planes overhead. What was I supposed to do? I was off duty that Sunday morning and living in residence at the hospital. Our job was to take care of the patients – there was no place for us to run for shelter. When the all-clear siren sounded, I went outdoors. Everything seemed quiet and peaceful.

During the summer of 1940, raids became more frequent and it was no longer safe to sleep in the house. I was living in a private home at the time that I shared with two other nurses. Our nights were spent in the Anderson shelter. As soon as the wail of the air raid warning started, we would run for the shelter. The other two nurses always seemed to be on night duty, a 12-hour shift. I spent endless nights in the cold, damp shelter alone. Before it got dark and the night raids started, I prepared myself a sandwich to take with me to the shelter. The sandwich consisted of two pieces of bread, no butter, with Bovril extract spread on it. I always got a queer feeling in the pit of my stomach and thought it was hunger, when actually it was fear.

During the raids, our searchlights would criss-cross the night sky trying to intercept the enemy planes. Many times, I would look out of the shelter, which didn't have a door, and watch planes in battle in the sky. One night the raid started later than usual. Betty, one of the other nurses, and I were preparing for the night, hoping we could sleep in our own beds. That was not to be. The onslaught was so severe it was not safe to leave the house. Looking out the window, I saw parachutes descending and I screamed to Betty, "We are being invaded – look the enemy is landing." Thank God, I was wrong. A flare had been attached to each parachute, so that the bombers would have a clear view of their target.

Gas masks were issued to everyone and they had to be carried at all times. There was a heavy penalty if anyone was caught without a mask. Gas attacks were something we feared. Special courses were given to all hospital staff instructing them how to handle such an emergency.

Daylight raids started in September 1940. On one of my days off I went to visit my aunt and uncle living in another part of London. During the afternoon, the air raid warning sounded. We watched the balloons go up over London. Feeling safe, we stayed in the apartment and watched the battle in the sky. After the all-clear had sounded, we noticed heavy smoke in the distance. That evening, I returned by underground railway. As I walked from the station to the house, it looked as though all of London was on fire. As usual, I spent the night alone in the shelter. The noise of enemy planes overhead and the scream of bombs dropping all around is etched in my memory forever.

The next day we were told that the London docks had been bombed. Not satisfied with the daylight raid destruction, the enemy returned again and again, all night long, destroying many buildings and burning our already rationed food stored in the dockside warehouses.

I moved a few miles out of London the next day. I was doing my midwifery training, so I had to change hospitals. Delivering babies in homes in peacetime is quite an experience. But in wartime, trying to find the right house down a country road in a blackout was not easy. We still got all the London air raid warnings, but just the occasional bomb. A bike was our means of transportation. Our only light was a bike lamp covered with a black cloth with a hole in it about the size of a quarter. We were issued helmets, like the army wore. I felt safe with the helmet on my head and the gas mask over my shoulder.

During my time in the district, one case stands out in my mind. Late one night, the phone rang. The caller asked to have the midwife come to a certain house out in the country; the mother was in labour. I was assigned to go and took a student midwife with me. We packed our bags on the back of our bikes and off we went. There was no air raid that night, but in the pitch black we lost our way. At last we arrived at the house and walked into a dimly lit kitchen where four children and their father were seated around a small coal fire. He pointed to the next room. It took us a few minutes to get used to the poor light and shadows from the kerosene oil lamp.

The mother was lying on the bed and beside her there was a fine, healthy newborn. I checked the infant, then I handed the baby to Carol and I took care of the mother. Each time I walked around the bed, I caught my head on a clothesline strung across the room. In the dim light, I couldn't see it. After making Mother and baby as comfortable as possible in these poor surroundings, we noticed tucked away in a dark corner of the room, a little fellow in a cot. He looked about 2-years-old. Goodness knows how long he had been awake. The mother had her babies so quickly that no midwife had ever managed to get there on time.

❧ Eileen Kenney

The summer of 1939 was a time of worry in our small community of Elmvale, Ontario. The threat of war was in people's minds and the newspapers were full of the impending war. As two young girls – aged 9 and 11 - my sister and I were not really concerned until war was announced in September of 1939. Canada was at war!

I can still remember when we came home from school how anxious my mother was that my father might have to join the army. At 35 years of age, he was eligible to enlist, but with a business of his own to look after and a wife and family, he was not required to join the Forces. However, many of my relatives did join. My great Uncle Sam, a 48th Highlander, was one of the first to be sent overseas. My Uncle Albert was also sent overseas, so his 3-year-old son lived with us, while my aunt worked as a cook to supplement the army pay.

By 1943, as well as my father's garage, our family was operating the Four Corner Tea Room at the main intersection of our village. Highway 27 was the route taken by many convoys from Base Borden, some 35 miles away. These convoys would stop at our restaurant for refreshments. Many of these soldiers were French speaking. Imagine how delighted they were that my French Canadian mother was able to speak to them. They sure hated to leave what seemed to them like "a little bit of home." This was often their first time away from home, and they were surprised when we told them of the French community of Penetanguishene, another 18 miles north of Elmvale.

Rationing affected our business - ice cream and chocolate bars were "on quota." Ice cream normally came to Barrie by train packed in dry ice. But sometimes my dad would have to drive to Toronto, 75 miles away, to get ice cream. Customers flocked in after a shipment and there was never enough.

Prior to the war, it was not a common sight to see planes flying over Elmvale. Galt, a busy training centre for the British Commonwealth about 100 miles away, "as the crow flies," sent out planes on training manoeuvres. I particularly remember one incident while in high school. One of several planes out on manoeuvres flew level with the windows of our second floor classroom. Of course, the whole class was excited. Such a thrill!

Edenvale, about 25 miles away, had an airstrip and underground bunkers, but we never knew what that was all about. It was very "hush, hush" and high security. Eventually, we got used to seeing men in uniform. Our local boys, as well as strangers, were often seen on the streets. Eighteen-year-old boys who frequented our Tea Room were often heard to say, "I got my call today," or "I'm leaving for training soon."

When I was 15 or 16, I had a boyfriend in the air force stationed at Arnprior, near Ottawa. We missed each other, so letters were "a must" and "leave" was special and something to look forward to. My sister, now 14-years-old, corresponded with a couple of friends who were overseas. They wanted to get letters from anyone at home, as they were lonesome. One of these soldiers was in Italy, where one of the boys from our area was badly burned in a Sherman tank explosion. We were proud of "our boys," and even boasted of three enlisted girls from Elmvale.

The war was hard on everyone in one way or another. I knew several girls who had babies after their husbands were shipped overseas. Pictures became precious for these new fathers who would not see their child until the war was over. Some of these men did not return and we were all saddened and sympathized with their families. Fifteen men from our village and surrounding farms never returned to their families. What a great tragedy!

War movies were "the order of the day." They depicted the horrors of the war abroad. The newsreels at the theatre were our only visual connection with our fighting boys. The cost of a movie was about 50 cents and was often a double feature. *Mrs. Minniver* with Greer Garson and Walter Pidgeon made us realize what England was going through and touched us deeply.

War songs were popular on the radio. Some were World War I songs and some were World War II. Of course, we knew them all, like "I'll be Seeing You" and "White Cliffs of Dover." Singer Vera Lynn was heard continually.

Finally in May 1945, after what seemed to us like an eternity, the war officially ended. Gradually "our boys" came home after being discharged. I recollect a trip to Toronto with my dad and my aunt and uncle to pick up my cousin who was coming home from overseas. The soldiers were paraded and drilled while families sat in the stands trying to pick out their own son or spouse from the many platoons of soldiers. Imagine the pandemonium when they were finally dismissed. There was much kissing and hugging and tears as loved ones were reunited. I still get emotional, after all these years, when I think about that special homecoming.

🍁 Lynn Korbyn

The world was turned upside down for me on May 10, 1940. I was 10-years-old and a farmer's daughter living not too far from Rotterdam, Holland. On that fateful day, early in the morning, bombs fell on the inner city of Rotterdam. When I got up that morning, my father and mother pointed to the north. All I could see was a big black smoke plume. In my village later in the day, a bomb was dropped on the post office, limiting communication with relatives. Another bomb was intended for our town hall, but missed its target. It fell on a butcher shop and killed a little girl. Her parents and a brother were injured.

Germany had declared war on Holland, Belgium, France and England. It only took five days for the Dutch Government to declare defeat. Many Dutch soldiers lost their lives on the Grebbeberg. The German Military Forces occupied Holland, an unexpected situation. People were scared. From that point on, we had to obey new rules. After a couple of days people went back to work. Children went back to school. In our village, there were German soldiers at the Police Station and Town Hall, but things were, somewhat, back to normal.

I finished public school in 1942, and then went to high school. By that time, things like coffee, tea, flour, rice and coal were getting scarce, as were clothing and shoes. I got hand-me-downs from relatives. I grew out of my clothes, so my sister made one dress out of two smaller ones. We got coupons from the government to buy one towel, one shirt, one coat or a textile once every three months. My mother exchanged her coupons with a lady who had babies. She needed soap and textile coupons to wash and make diapers. In exchange, my mother got her coffee and tea coupons. We all learned to do without.

In 1944, France and Belgium were liberated, along with the southern part of Holland. The German Army still occupied the northern part of the country. The Meuse and Rhine Rivers were frozen and the Allies could not get through. I lived in the south of Holland on an island called Hoeksche Waard, which became a buffer zone. The Germans broke the dikes and we were inundated. That meant our family and the whole village had to evacuate.

We were given three days in the middle of the winter to pack up and move out. There were not enough trucks and not much gasoline anyway, so most

Family farm, Holland, 1939. Nine-year-old Lynn is sitting on the bench; her sister is standing.

people relied on horse and wagon. I don't know how my dad moved cows, chickens, cats, a dog, hay, straw and food for all the animals, in addition to our furniture and most of our belongings. Nobody knew for how long we would have to go. We all hoped for a short time!

We went to stay with an aunt and uncle on their farm. At first they felt sorry for us and treated us nicely. After a couple of months, it became a drag for them, I guess. Nobody knew how long this situation was going to last. My dad had no income and food was scarce. The country was going broke. There was no freedom of speech. You had to watch out for spies. Even our uncle and aunt put us in a bad position. We got on their nerves, I suspect. We were all under pressure.

One day I was chartered by a German Lieutenant to come with him. I was told to clean the house where he had his headquarters. It took all day. What a mess I had to cleanup. I tried to talk German to the officers. They did give me food and drink, but no money! Once night fell, my parents got worried. My dad found out where I was and told the officers that I had to come home. They let me go, but it was quite an ordeal for my parents. They thought they had lost me. To a 15-year-old girl, it was an adventure!

During the war, German soldiers occupied different houses, or they were billeted in part of a house. They took over the living room at my uncle's and, of course, the furniture got a lot of wear and tear. So from then on we sat in the kitchen, which we had to share with my uncle and aunt. My two cousins, my sister and me were locked in the bedroom at night because the German soldiers were around day and night. During the night we heard the squadrons move in trucks, or sometimes marching. We also heard the drone of the Lancaster bombers of the Allied Forces overhead on their way to Germany to drop bombs. We could not always sleep because we were so scared.

Finally the war was over on May 8, 1945. The dikes got repaired. But we could not go back to the farm. The windows were broken, the doors removed, the floors ripped up and the wood ceilings taken out. The soldiers made bunkers from our wood. The cellar was full of water; there was an inch of mud all over everything. Our house and barn had to be made liveable. We had been evacuated for 18 months. We had to start all over. The Dutch Government and the Marshall Plan helped us a little bit. It was hard work and we all tried to rebuild our lives.

❧ Jean Kulmala

I was born Jean Kennerley in Nottingham, England, on September 15, 1939, so my memories of the war are a child's memories. In fact, the war even affected my birth date. As she tells it, my mother went into labour a week earlier in the night and her labour was stopped. Two days later, again after dark, her labour started and was again stopped. When my mother went into labour again, she told no one until the birth was so far along that it couldn't be stopped. I arrived on the 15th of September during the afternoon. It was only after my birth that a nurse explained to Mother that the reason my birth had been stopped before was because it was nighttime. The hospital had no blackout curtains in the labour and delivery rooms and they were not allowed to use the lights. They had blankets hung over the windows in the ward.

My father was a farmer, an occupation designated essential, so he could not go into the army. Instead, he became a foreman in what was called the Land Army. His responsibility was to take over a farm, put it into food production, then go on to the next farm and do the same. The Armed Forces had to be fed and food production was a priority. As the war went on, and the Armed Forces of the Allies gathered to prepare for the invasion of Europe, food production became even more critical. Due to Dad's job, we moved around a lot, staying about half a year at each place.

Through stringent rationing most people had less, but everyone had enough. Meat was especially scarce. Usually, the general population could only get mutton, not lamb, two or three times a week. However, Dad's work was in the country and he was a good shot with his twenty-two, so we often enjoyed rabbit or pigeon pie.

When I was about a year old and my sister Olga was 4, we had an experience that affects me to this day. We were living in a row house on the outskirts of Sheffield. Because we were so far from an air raid shelter, Olga and I were put to bed every night under the dining room table, which was pushed into the corner of the room with the chesterfield along one side and the two chesterfield chairs blocking off the fourth side to shield us from flying glass in case of a close bomb. Dad, like all able-bodied men, had to do fire control duty in the evenings.

On one particular evening, Mother was also helping rescue people trapped in a bombed home not far from ours, when another bomb struck a house further down our row. Our home sustained considerable damage. A wall fell in on top of the table Olga and I were sleeping under. We were terrified. It was dark and dusty, but Olga had been well coached as to what to do.

Our parents had, of course, foreseen this eventuality. Mom had drummed into Olga's 4-year-old brain, over and over, that this might happen, but that someone would surely rescue us. Olga gave me a drink and talked soothingly to me; occasionally, we would scream and cry a little. Eventually, just as Mom had assured, the fire control and rescue team came and pulled us out. We were dusty, tired and frightened, but we were unhurt. However, we have always attributed our claustrophobia to this traumatic incident.

Once, when I was just about three, Olga and I were sent by our mother to take Daddy his afternoon tea. We were living near Luton at that time. Olga was carrying the tea in a silver-coloured pail and I had scones wrapped in a napkin. We looked forward to taking Daddy his tea because time spent with him was so special, and he always shared with us.

But this time, as we made our way down a grassy path toward a paved road, I felt some tension in Olga. She wasn't just holding my hand; she was clutching it. We could see Daddy driving a tractor on the other side of the pavement. It was the widest road I had ever seen. We carefully looked both ways several times. Olga seemed hesitant to start over it, and even as we crossed her head was on the swivel. I thought we'd never get to the other side, as we scampered the last few feet. Daddy was happy to see us and his tea and cautioned us to be careful on the way back, to go straight home and not dawdle. It was years later, when I asked Olga about my memory of that incident that I learned we had been crossing a taxiway at the Luton Airport. The need for extra land was so great that the Land Army was even cultivating the land between runways to raise potatoes. The traffic Olga was so wary of was not motorcars, but airplanes!

By 1944, Mother was also working full-time in the Land Army. German prisoners augmented the numbers in the Land Army on the understanding that they would not attempt to escape; the prisoners were happy to be occupied in this way. Not having anyone to care for Olga and myself, Mother took us with her when we were not in school. So, of course, we worked too.

I can clearly remember cutting the tops off turnips in the early summer. Those greens were sold as a vegetable to a population that found it harder and harder to feed itself. The turnips easily grew a second top to feed the tubers. What amazes me now is that Olga and I, at 7-years-old and 4-and-a-half, were given sharp knives to cut the greens and place them into a jute sack. We were expected to keep up as we all moved row-by-row across the field. And we did!

The Land Army was amazing. As a crop was ready to be harvested, several khaki-coloured trucks would roll up, the canvas-covered backs would be flipped aside and a flock of women would jump down and go to work. The food was gathered promptly, with nothing being allowed to spoil. As a child, I had no understanding of how this happened. But now I realize that it was as well-organized as a military campaign, which, in a way, it was.

There is one other memory I would like to share. Towards the end of the war, when the bombing in England had tapered off and people felt that the end of the war was possible, the Germans developed the V-1 rocket. This was a self-propelled bomb, which fell randomly whenever its motor cut out. They were sent over in swarms and were a terrible scourge on the war-weary population because there was no way to defend against them.

I remember one evening Mom and Dad had taken Olga and I to the neighbours for a visit. We were playing on the floor with their children while the adults were playing a game of whist at the table. Suddenly, they stopped their game and looked up, listening. Then I heard it - the distinctive whine of a V-1 rocket or doodlebug. Everyone held their breath while the adults' eyes tracked the bomb as it passed over, and the sound faded in the distance. Then, the tension relaxing, they went back to their game and we went back to ours. It was only if you heard the engine noise stop that you had to take cover in the few moments it took for the bomb to fall and explode.

I will always remember my parents with admiration for their efforts during the war. Under intolerable pressures, they worked long and hard. On occasion they were forced to leave Olga and I unattended and their anxiety must have been unbearable. And yet, that was the way people had to live their lives at that time, so they managed. My parents - Annie and Frank - gave Olga and I a wonderful childhood, in spite of the war. It wasn't only the troops who were valiant!

Many years later, when my daughters were having children, my mother said that she wouldn't want to be raising children nowadays. "It's so dangerous, with all the drugs and traffic and perverts all over the place." "Mom," I said, "at least nobody's dropping BOMBS on them!" She looked at me, puzzled for a moment. Then, recollecting, she smiled sheepishly. "Oh well," she said, "it didn't seem so bad at the time. And it came out alright, in the end."

🍁 Freda Leenders

Freda, 1942.

I was 4-years-old when the war started. I was born on a rented farm and grew up in a small, new village in the south of Holland. The beginning of Mariahout, or Marywood in English, came about when a church was built in 1933. My parents bought ten hectares of sandy land, which they cleared, mainly of heather; they built a house and a barn and planted an orchard. I was one of six children, two brothers were older and two brothers and a sister were younger.

We were barely settled in Mariahout when World War II began. The next five years were difficult. I have the clearest memories of the last year, when the long and painstaking campaign began in August 1944. Among others, the Canadians were ordered to advance from France through Belgium and into Holland to liberate us from the Germans. The long and difficult struggle to free us from the Germans ended in May of 1945. Many died, including Canadian soldiers who fell in those nine months of conflict.

I didn't understand war and our parents shielded us as much as possible. But we sensed the fear towards the enemy and the stress that our parents had to endure. The Germans stole all they could from us, our horse, bikes, radios, etc. At night, we were terrified when we heard the air raid sirens and the bombs falling. Our parents would comfort us by saying they are the good guys. But if there was mention of the Germans, Mum hauled us out of bed, grabbed her purse and rosary and herded us into the underground shelter, which Dad lined with bales of straw. I remember a bomb hitting the house that went through the kitchen ceiling and into the cement floor below; it left a hole, but never exploded.

We were fortunate to live on a farm; we were never hungry. But in the northern regions, with its large cities, the people had almost reached the end of their endurance from misery and starvation. They suffered what became known as the "Hunger Winter." Food supplies were exhausted. Fuel had run out and transportation came to a standstill. Thousands of men, women and children perished.

On our farm, we had a few cows, pigs, chickens, grains and vegetables. Dad and our neighbour grew rapeseed and together made a contraption that extracted the oil. Food became so scarce that people were given coupons, but even the stores ran out of food. Hungry city folks would come and trade their household possessions for some food. Some would eat cats and tulip bulbs to survive!

Dad baked bread and lots of it. I remember seeing him standing in a big trough in the stable kneading the dough with his feet. Mum made butter. They killed pigs and nothing was wasted. Our parents were always on the watch for inspectors who would stop them from such illegal acts. We did not know whom to trust. Some Dutchmen were lured or forced to work for the Germans. One time, when Mum was pregnant, she was buttering the milk when an inspector came. She quickly sat on the milk can in the corner of the hallway and pretended she was in labour. The inspector left.

Our family risked their lives by hiding Jews. They helped on the farm for their nourishment. The Jews that were found by the Germans had their gold jewellery confiscated, even their gold fillings were retrieved after they were gassed in the concentration camps! I remember a young Jewish girl, in particular, by the name of Hettie. I always wondered what became of her.

The people in the south of Holland were liberated first, as the Armed Forces came in through Belgium. I'll always remember seeing the Canadians with their big trucks, tanks, jeeps and cannons. The falling of many parachutes was a sight to behold. They occupied our barn and fields and parked their equipment against the bush with one canon facing close to our house. But they were Canadians and we were free!

The young soldiers gave us crackers, chocolate bars and cigarettes. We would trade eggs from the henhouse for more goodies. I was only a child, but can you imagine how easy it was for older girls to fall in love with the handsome young soldiers. Many did and became war brides. My husband had two older sisters. At that time their orchards were full of tents with soldiers. His mother kept a close watch and made sure the girls were inside in the evening.

The war left Holland devastated and poor. Farmers had to start over again. It was a disgrace to send young farm boys to factories to work and the idea of immigrating started. "Go to the land of our liberators" was written on posters and preached in churches. English lessons were offered. The war brides became the first immigrants. From our small village alone, one third of its population, mostly large families, went to Canada. The Dutch and Canadian Government worked together. Holland paid Canada with immigrants. "Go to the Promised Land," we were told.

Then came the rumours of the Russians coming and people became more anxious to leave to avoid yet another war. Dad would have gone to Brazil, Australia or New Zealand to speed up the process, but really wanted to follow his brother and sister who had already left for Canada with their families. We sold our farm and had an auction sale. All the money was needed to pay for the boat journey to Canada. After nine days on the boat we arrived in New York, and then went by train to Oakville. People had courage, which was what they needed to begin their new life in a strange country.

Our sponsor picked us up at the train station. He knew us all by name. Mum and Dad were in the front of his pickup and we were in the back. After working for him on the dairy farm for one year, we bought a house. We stayed there for two years and Dad and his brothers went to work in a factory until there was enough money to buy a new farm. A hundred acres!

We will always remember and thank our liberators. Sometimes I wonder who those soldiers were who gave me the chocolate bars almost 60 years ago. The Germans stole our food, but the Canadians stole our hearts!

🍁 Shirley Lefler

The war started a month after my fifth birthday. My little brother was just a month old. I can remember my mother's concern when she heard the news on the radio. We were a long way from the war zone; we lived in the country near Paris, Ontario, but I remember having some fears.

In our rural schoolhouse, Grade 1 and 2 were dismissed at 2:30 p.m., while the older pupils stayed until 4:00 p.m. So my big sister and brothers could not accompany me home. I walked home with a neighbour boy. Sometimes he thought I was too slow and he ran ahead, leaving me alone. The big airplanes flew overhead from time to time and I was afraid the war might come here. I told him about my fears and after that he was kind and didn't run ahead of me.

Another time I remember being afraid was at the Canadian National Exhibition (CNE), probably the last year it was held until after the war. My sister and I went to watch the Grandstand Show. My eldest brother was at the CNE showing his calf and he came to sit with us. During the show, the airplanes kept flying back and forth along the lakefront. When the fireworks started, they made such a noise that I thought we were being bombed. Thank goodness my brother was there to tell me differently.

My teacher was great at the piano and she taught us many patriotic songs. One was "Hats Off to Mr. Churchill." We sometimes sang as a school group at the Home and School Meetings. I remember The Happy Gang singing a song about spitting in Hitler's face. We didn't like to see pictures of Hitler.

During the war years, the older pupils at school knit squares, probably for the Red Cross to make quilts. The younger pupils sewed cotton squares together into quilt blocks. I think a ladies group in the community made the quilts. We also knit scarves for the soldiers. I was a terrible knitter. I dropped stitches and picked up extras from the splitting wool. If there wasn't enough wool, mine was usually ripped out and the wool given to a better knitter to complete.

I remember VE Day well, when the Penman's Whistle blew long and hard. Our teacher sent us home. Later in the day, my sister and I went with a neighbour lady to Paris to celebrate on the main street.

Marlene with her parents and brothers, June, 1944.

🍁 Marlene Lehman

My father, Charles Searle, was working at the Ingot Iron factory in Guelph during the first few years of the war. The men were being called into the army according to their age. My dad was over 30 by this time. He didn't wait to be called up to join the army; he left before his call came. I remember the day the War Department called to tell him his time had come and my mother proudly said, "He's already gone!" He joined the Essex Scottish unit in London, Ontario, and was sent to British Columbia to train in the mountains.

On February 22, 1944, my birthday, I was playing down on Perth Street and along came my dad in his army uniform. He was home for a short visit before being shipped overseas. My family was complete for a while – Mother and Dad, Don aged 7, myself aged 5 and Bill aged 2. We went to a studio in the square in downtown Guelph and had a family photo taken.

Then, off we went to the train station at Eramosa Road and Cardigan Street. What a crowd! Everyone was there to say goodbye to the Guelph soldiers who were being shipped overseas. My grandparents and many of my aunts, uncles and cousins came to wish my dad the best. I can still hear the whistle of the train as it pulled away from the station. All the soldiers were leaning out the windows and waving. Everyone was crying and waving and trying to be brave. My 7-year-old brother Don told Mother, Bill and I not to worry, he would look after us while Dad was away protecting our country.

I was in Miss Piggott's class at St. Agnes School in Guelph. We prayed every day for the soldiers; I especially prayed for my dad and for peace! I was so proud to have a Daddy fighting for us across the ocean. All the children donated 50 cents each week for War Savings Stamps. That was a lot of money in those days and Miss Piggott printed our names on the chalkboard as we purchased these stamps.

For Easter in 1944, my brothers and I sent my dad a Soldiers Catholic Prayer Book. In the front we wrote "To our daddy with love, Don, Marlene and Bill." My dad wrote letters home to my mother and individual letters to each of us. The Knights of Columbus and the Salvation Army supplied Dad with his writing paper. Dad was always telling us to be good! When Dad was on leave in Belgium, he bought us wooden shoes. He had our names printed on the side and sent them home to us.

My dad met up with my mother's brother, Bill McCluskey, overseas. They spent some time together. Uncle Bill had lied about his age and joined the army before his eighteenth birthday. He was with the Red Cross and was on the front lines most of the time. He carried his guitar with him for six years. When he came home, Grandma asked him where his guitar case was and he said he traded it for some food. Uncle Bill had many stories to tell when he came home. He said that the worst thing he had to do was to take the bodies of children out of a school that had been bombed. He told of being with a dying soldier, trying to make his last moments comfortable. The soldier gave my Uncle Bill his pink, glass rosary in a brown leather case to carry with him. Uncle Bill gave me this rosary for my First Holy Communion.

Early in 1945, my mother received a telegram stating that my father was missing. I remember her face, but she never lost hope. She was a strong woman. Then, on February 19, 1945, Dad was killed by a sniper's bullet during the liberation of Holland, just three days before my birthday. We have the telegrams from the War Department saying he was killed and buried in Germany. Later his body was reverently exhumed and moved to Holland. He is buried in Groesbeek Cemetery in Nynegen, Holland. I remember my father's funeral at the Church of Our Lady in Guelph. Father O'Reilly said the Mass. Dad's coffin was draped with the Union Jack and his name is on a plaque in the Church of Our Lady. Father O'Reilly and my dad used to go fishing together.

🍁 Berta Lindenstruth

I was born in Germany. I was the sixth child; I had six brothers and four sisters. We lived on a farm. Every time the Allied bombers flew over to bomb the cities, the air raid sirens would go off; they were terribly loud and frightening. We all rushed to the basement in the dark and sat on the pails full of black coal. All the windows in the neighbourhood were broken as a result of bombs dropping, and there were cracks in the house walls that were wide enough to stick your hand through.

We frequently watched paratroopers jump out of planes. And at every bombing raid, day or night, advance planes dropped silvery metal strips. People said they were to confuse the German anti-aircraft radar. All of the children used to collect them since they looked like Christmas tree limetta.

When I started to school in 1945, there were classes with up to 80 boys and girls. The teachers were all retired teachers that had been brought back since all the others had been drafted into the army. Schools were often unheated and had no window glass. If students wanted heat, the parents had to come up with a stove and firewood. Classes were also held in the basements of hospitals, since many schoolhouses were bombed out. On our way to school, we would sometimes meet army trucks with soldiers sitting in the back under a canvas cover. Sometimes they threw us chewing gum and Hershey chocolate bars, which made us very happy.

As a child I collected cigarette butts to retrieve the remaining tobacco. The tobacco could be exchanged on the black market for shoes, clothes, coffee or blankets. For my First Communion I wore a coat that was made from a dyed army blanket and coat. There was a shortage of shoes for us children, so we walked a lot in our bare feet. A chronic shortage of food was our daily worry. But there was an appreciation for one another and lots of family love and togetherness. I have a tremendous amount of respect for my parents who worked around the clock to feed us.

🍁 Annette Lindop

I grew up in wartime Germany. My hometown in the Ruhr Valley was flooded by the waters of the Moehne Dam, which was hit by bombs on the night of May 17, 1943. Eighty million cubic metres of water rushed down the valley, submerging everything in its path. To this day I remember my dad shaking me awake after a loud knock and a shout at the door warned us. Dad told me the dam was broken and it was too late to risk running to the hills. There was not much time, so we went up to the attic of our two-story stone house.

As my parents rushed up and down the stairs trying to save what they could, I looked out the attic window. At first I saw only the dark, deserted town. A small trickle of water came down the street. Then all hell broke loose! The trickle turned into a torrent, then I saw a raging wall of water carrying screaming people, struggling animals, huge trees and household furniture. It soon covered the treetops, but still the water rose, almost to our attic.

Afraid for our lives, we climbed onto the roof and clung to the shingles until early morning, when the water slowly began to recede. It was a night of terror! The deluge left the first and second floors of our home ruined, and everything soaked and caked with dirt. The basement was so filled with mud that we couldn't go down there. Many of our friends and neighbours were drowned. They had hidden in their basements thinking the warning was for an air raid. We were thankful to escape with our lives.

❀ Joan Lowcock

I was 5-years-old when the Second World War broke out. I lived with my parents in the industrial town of Darlington in the County of Durham, England, where my father worked as a plumber in the railway repair yard. We were spending a weekend with my grandparents when the announcement was made. On returning home we found our short street lined with army vehicles and soldiers milling about outside our house. I was only allowed out of doors to play in the back garden behind a locked trellis gate.

My father was ordered to work on the repair of ships which limped into the River Tyne. For many months, Mother and I lived on in Darlington, until we could move into the bungalow we had leased to other people when we had moved out four years earlier. Father could live at home again and travel the ten miles daily to the dockyards. Some nights he had to stay on firewatch, as the Germans flew over nightly dropping incendiary bombs along the river.

During this time, my mother had a serious operation and I was sent to her parents. They lived in the tiny village of Allendale, which was in a valley of moors with the River Allen running alongside. I spent seven months there, in safety from bombs and war, until my mother came for me in December.

When living with my grandparents in Allendale I was not free to roam the moors and river alone, as I had been able to do when visiting the occasional weekend prior to the war. Many German airplanes were so damaged by the anti-aircraft gunfire that they crashed into the sea or onto the moors. Pilots may have escaped by parachute. Everyone was warned to always be on the lookout for strangers near the village and report sightings to the police. Most of the pilots were eventually caught, lived in prisoner of war camps and worked for farmers in the area.

A prisoner of war camp was built about a mile up the road from my grandparents' home. Sometimes I cycled by and spoke with one or two of the young men. They showed me photos of their families, parents, wives and small children, and I realized they were people with homes and families like me.

We no longer had butter or margarine on our bread, only homemade jams from the fruit we found in the woods or grew in the garden. We had a small ration of candies per month, so we bought the smallest ones we could find. There was little sugar, so we substituted saccharin or golden syrup. Extra sugar was available for jam making in the summer. There were no bananas, oranges and lemons, only at Christmas. We gathered nuts from the woods, mostly hazelnuts. A halfpenny bottle of milk was supplied at school, a gill bottle each morning and afternoon at recess. For poor children, it was free.

There were coupons for everything, food, furniture, clothing, etc. We were measured every few months at school and if we were tall for our age, as I was, we were given an extra allocation of shoe coupons. My toes were misshapen from wearing shoes that were too small for me. Clothes were altered to fit or they were remade. Young children contributed to the war work by collecting hips and haws from bushes in the garden and woods. We were paid sixpence for a one pound jam jar full. This was made into rose hip syrup and used in place of concentrated orange juice for babies and children.

We had moved in with my mother's sister in 1941, as Mother had become an invalid. At 7-years-old, I was at home looking after her. My aunt and uncle took us in or we would have been split up, Mother to a home and me to an orphanage. They had a bomb shelter dug deep into their garden and many a night we spent in it. Mother was unable to be moved, so Father or Uncle stayed in the house with her. In August 1942, my mother died.

One night after Mother's death, Father and Uncle were outside the shelter watching dogfights overhead, deciding if enemy planes were hit by the tracer bullets from our town guns. Something loud whined nearby. They jumped into the shelter, one after the other, the last one holding the loose heavy wooden door behind them, like a shield. After the all-clear sounded they looked at the door and found a large piece of jagged shrapnel stuck in it. There were other pieces in the garden. The bomb had exploded over a field at the end of our street, but the shrapnel could have killed any one of us.

One day, when I was 7, a friend and I were walking to school. Halfway there, we passed a fire hall with a siren on the roof and the alarm went off. We stood stock still, deafened, not knowing whether to run on to school or back home. We ran down back lanes to school, banging on the door of our shelter to be allowed in. Every class was allotted a shelter and we were counted so nobody was left outside. The shelters were built of brick on the schoolyard against the fence. We often spent hours in them, seated on wooden benches built around the walls. Our teachers led oral lessons and games and we sang songs and rounds. Candles, oil lamps or flashlights were our only source of light. The effect was quite eerie!

At school, it was instilled in us to watch for strangers, or people acting suspiciously, as they could be spies or escaped prisoners. Later on, I attended a school on a street behind the seafront. We were asked to watch for any ships we might see approaching our coast. Our town was five miles north of the mouth of the River Tyne, and often there were warnings of a possible German invasion. Norway was only a few hours sail across the North Sea.

Apart from occasional hair-raising happenings, life had to go on as normal. People went to school, to work and to shop; they cleaned house and cooked meals as best they could. Train travel was minimalized as they were used for troop movement. There was little gas for buses or cars. My grandfather's car was in his garage, unused the six years of the war. We got around by walking on "shank's pony," as we called it, or cycling.

After the war, many of the women, who had been employed in munitions factories, learned a trade, drove tractors as farmworkers and did many other jobs usually done by men, decided to keep on working. Many needed to continue to work because their menfolk returned from the war injured and were unable to work in their previous jobs, if they were able to work at all. Other women preferred to have extra money for themselves or holidays.

During those years, our animosity was bent on Hitler and Mussolini and their cohorts. We felt sorry for the people of Europe who were suffering from bombings. Anyone who fought alongside us was a friend. Our political leader was Winston Churchill and we lived and died by his words. King George VI and Queen Elizabeth were also part of our strength.

Katherine with family friends.

🍁 Katherine Lynch

I was 11-years-old when our Canadian Government declared our country's involvement in World War II. My memory of life during these years is from a home front perspective. I grew up in a small town on the Prairies and World War II touched us mainly through newspapers and the nightly news on the radio. Everyone talked of the newsman, Lorne Greene. They feared the nightly news with its list of casualties. The happy part for our family was the safe return of all its members.

Mail was a long time coming, was censored and often pieces were cut out. No addresses could be given, so it was just from "somewhere in Europe." The Red Cross was a big help to Europeans in getting word to them from their families.

D-Day was a great day of celebration, but I have more vivid memories of the VJ Day parade in town because my brother was in it, along with many other returned veterans. They marched with pride at having done their part to bring freedom and peace to the world. I was proud of them.

Sheila and her dog Colonel, summer, 1944.

🍁 Sheila H. Lyttle

My father built airports and factories during the Second World War, so he was away most of the time. We lived in Chaput Hughes, just outside Kirkland Lake in Northern Ontario, right across the road from a gold mine with armed sentries.

Life was difficult for my mother who had sent parcels to her brother at Vimy; now she sent parcels to his son, my cousin. She wrapped everything in thick brown paper and sewed the whole thing into cloth sugar bags and wrote the address on every layer with indelible purple ink. One parcel reached him overseas, still sewn securely, with nothing left in it but one pair of socks.

Ration books were a trial to Mother, though it sounds so trivial when compared to what we knew of the lives of friends in England and Europe at the time. Mother didn't drink tea and I was too young to qualify for coffee rations, which I seem to remember were a quarter pound a week - just one pot, really. Our neighbours with three grown children were tea drinkers, so they'd exchange coffee coupons for Mother's tea rations.

When I had my appendix out early one spring, Mother had a battle with the hospital over my ration book. They had taken all my coupons for the weeks I was in the hospital and had even taken my sugar coupons for canning, which didn't come due until summer. She conceded the hospital the month's meat, butter and sugar rations, even though I ate nothing but cream of wheat most of the time.

There could scarcely have been a more patriotic group than school children of that period. Every week we brought our quarters to buy War Savings Stamps. We peered into cupboards at home and said things like, "Do you really need all these pots and frying pans?" We wanted them for the metal collecting drives. The minute a package of coffee was empty, we snagged the heavy foil.

One Halloween, because of the absolute lack of candy, our school had an evening costume party with National Film Board movies. They showed one of flowers unfolding in time-lapse photography, which was a step up from the monthly lantern slides we saw at Sunday school. Instead of collecting candy, we went around the neighbourhood selling sheets of milk tickets and went back to collect them just before the party. The child who collected the most was given a prize. We were all indignant about one man who wouldn't distribute them, but gave all of his to his own son. The proceeds from the tickets went to England to buy milk for children whose homes had been bombed.

On VE Day all the pupils marched around the school grounds singing. I couldn't stop crying and one of the teachers came over to talk to me and was quite cross. "Lots of people here lost someone close and you don't see them making a scene," she said. That didn't keep me from grieving that the war hadn't ended sooner. My cousin who got the one pair of socks died in Holland two months earlier to the day.

❧ Grace A. Macaulay

My life before World War II had been like most middle class girls in England – school, sports, trips to the coast once a year for a couple of weeks holiday – pleasant, but uneventful. My mother died when I was 14, and as my family then consisted of my dad and two brothers, who were already out working, I guess I had more responsibilities than the average teenager.

When war broke out, I was 17. I had just finished two years at a commercial college and had started working for the National Amalgamated Assurance Company in London. I lived in the suburbs of London and travelled an hour by underground to get there. I remember the day at the office before war was declared, we heard newspaper boys shouting out the headlines. Anyone in the office near a window, opened it, listened and passed on the news that Hitler had invaded Poland.

The following Sunday I was walking to church and as I passed by a house, I could hear Neville Chamberlain on the radio saying in a solemn voice that we were at war. Almost before I could think about it, the air raid warning went, an eerie, frightening sound that was to be heard hundreds of times in the next five years. I ran to the church, meeting the vicar on the way. Most of the congregation was already at the church. Nobody knew what to do, but to everyone's relief the all-clear sounded within a few minutes. Later, we learned that it was a false alarm set off by a lone plane crossing the coast. There were several similar incidents in the first month of the war and they became like a rehearsal for the real thing.

People started preparing for the worst. I became a volunteer at the local Air Raid Precaution (ARP) Depot and received training on what to do in the event of a raid. I remember the evenings spent on duty there as stressful. But before there were any raids, my life took another turn. The company I worked for held employment records and dealt with unemployment insurance and work-related compensation. As the records were considered to be of national importance, the entire office and its staff of about 2,000 personnel was evacuated to Eastbourne, a resort town on the English Channel where it was thought such records would be safer than in London.

The offices were located in what had previously been a private boys school, complete with underground passages. The staff was housed in guesthouses or small hotels, which had been requisitioned by the government. For the first few years, I lived in a small guesthouse, sharing a room with one other person. The elderly lady who owned the house still lived there and managed it. We had two meals a day there, breakfast and dinner. There was no choice of meals. What you were served is what you ate. At lunchtime, we bought whatever was available near our office.

As war progressed and rationing came into effect, our landlady took the food coupons from our ration books. We were given a ration of butter each week, which was kept in the dining room with our name on it. The rest of the coupons were used for whatever she chose to serve us. We were never hungry, but there was little variety. As there were few food items that were not rationed, lunchtime became a bit of a problem. After a while, the government set up home kitchens and for a minimal cost you could eat there at midday, usually rabbit cooked different ways and, of course, potatoes. Not as bad as it sounds!

We also had ration coupons for clothing. If you planned carefully, they were adequate. But you did not buy frivolously. The only exceptions were hats and shoes. Needless to say, many of us used our hats to satisfy our fashion sense.

Movies were a form of escape for everyone, usually romantic, glamorous and dramatic love scenes, which never progressed beyond long, lingering kisses. The themes were sometimes war-based, but I do not remember any graphic war movies. Between shows, newsreels showed war news that had passed the censors.

Eastbourne, thought to be a safe place at the beginning of the war, underwent a dramatic change in June 1940. At that time, the war was going badly in France and our troops had to be evacuated from Dunkirk and with only the English Channel separating us from the German troops, we were put on an invasion alert. Travel out of the area was not permitted for a couple of weeks. Most of the peacetime population of Eastbourne had already moved out, but it was simply not feasible to move us again. The whole south coast was put under tight security. Only authorized personnel were allowed in and many different regiments were stationed on the coast and in the surrounding countryside.

By September 1940, the war on the home front began in earnest. The bombing of London – the Blitz – had started and the bombers came over nightly. People in the hardest hit areas of London took to sleeping on the platforms in the underground. They would routinely go down there with makeshift bedding when the air raid warning sounded. I felt sad and angry that people had to spend their nights that way, but at least they were relatively safe and I believe their moral was boosted by shared hardships. When nighttime bombing didn't bring the country to its knees, daytime bombing began and other places besides London were targeted.

By 1941 in Eastbourne, life became routine on the surface. We went to work and no longer took shelter when the air raid warning sounded, as often planes were en route to London. Consequently, a different warning sound was designed for the coastal areas, which got nicknamed "the coo koo." When this warning sounded, we knew it meant immediate danger. Often this warning came a little too late, as it was a plane that had come in low under the radar or it was a lone plane returning from a raid and wanted a last shot with its bombs. We knew that certain areas, such as railway stations, were prime targets and hoped not to be in that area when "the coo koo" sounded.

Women also received their call up papers. If you had no children and were not working in an essential job, you had to do war work of some kind. Although our jobs were considered essential, some of the girls felt they could do more and left to go into the services, nursing, the Land Army or a munitions factory.

Sometimes a notice would circulate in our office asking for volunteers to help out local farmers. We would be picked up after work or on a weekend and taken to where we were needed. I vividly remember helping to pull flax, which was needed to make parachutes. For a short period of time, a team of three was asked to patrol the area where we lived. We took a stirrup pump with us to put out any incendiary bombs that were dropped. Later in the war, another request came to knit string socks to go over the boots of Russian sailors to prevent them from slipping on icy decks. The string was provided and several lunch hours were given over to this miserable task.

It is difficult to condense five eventful years of life into a few pages of writing. We learned to take for granted the blackouts, food shortages, V-1 and V-2 bombs and the rules that had to be obeyed. On reflection, considering the focus of war is death and destruction, in daily life people were kind and considerate of each other. In spite of the blackouts, there was little crime. In lineups or queues, which occurred for many reasons, nobody pushed or tried to get ahead. For the duration of the war, we became a moral, hard working and friendly society. The radio was our link to the world. Everyone knew the voice of Winston Churchill. But they also knew the voice of William Joyce, who broadcast propaganda from Germany in the hope of demoralizing us.

At the beginning of the war, I was a young girl. Six years later, I was married and leaving home and country to travel to a strange land 3,000 miles away, fully confident that I could handle whatever the future had to offer.

❦ Liane Maitland

S ix years old, precocious, just one darned sweet kid - that was me in
1944! My mom, brother Stu and I travelled with my dad, a Royal
Canadian Air Force (RCAF) mechanic, to many air force bases in Canada
during the Second World War. At that time, we were stationed in Vulcan,
Alberta, a small agricultural village, turned air base. It was exploding at the
seams. Days were full of excess activities for what used to be a sleepy rural
town.

Sharp looking young men in those "special blues" and their "saucy caps"
were everywhere. Schools, churches and commerce were at the extreme.
The skies were dotted with the sight and noises of the Avro Anson twin
engine training aircraft, the most widely used trainer aircraft of World War
II. Housing was at a premium. Any building that had four walls and a roof
that wasn't collapsing was remodelled into living quarters.

We occupied the dilapidated old Snodgrass Funeral Home. "Oh my
heavens," my mom exclaimed, as she perused the sight before her. "I can't
live in a place like this!" But in her heart she knew that there was no
alternative. This derelict building had been left to rot for a number of years.
Due to the housing shortage, it was renovated into two living quarters and
we were to reside in the back. It really wasn't big at all and the ramp to the
back door was rather ominous. But new linoleum, a paint job here and there,
brought about a little rosier view of the place we were to call home for the
next couple of years.

A friendly couple occupied the front apartment. He played the guitar and
sang. As days went by, I would find myself drawn to his music and songs –
mostly the war hits of those years. Soon, I was singing along with "gusto!" I
had started Grade 1, attended Sunday school and enjoyed each and every
day to the fullest. My mind did not comprehend the seriousness of what was
going on in the world at that time. I was just a happy-go-lucky little girl,
who took everything for granted.

Soon, our Sunday school teacher was preparing our classes for the
Christmas concert. Because I had such a good singing voice, I was chosen
to sing a solo. "Boy, am I ever lucky," I reasoned one night after practice, "I
could even sing something else, if my teacher wanted me to." But my mom
quickly replied, "You just need to do what you've been asked to do Liane,
and that's all!"

The concert night arrived and a warm glow encompassed the audience of
proud parents. I wowed the crowd with my solo. The gathering clapped
loudly and the rest of the play went off without too many hitches. Santa
would be arriving soon and we would all get to sit on his knee and tell him
which toy we wanted and that we had really been good little kids – all year
round! Then we would get that wonderful little brown bag with the orange
and the candy stick in it.

141

But first, our teacher got up on stage and made a request, "Is there any little boy or girl that would like to perform anything else for our audience tonight?" My eyes lit up and excitement overtook my mind. "I think she's asking me," I thought. "I can sing good – and I know all the songs that Brian taught me." And with that, I threw up my hand and yelled, "Me! Me! I will!" I literally skidded onto the stage in anticipation.

People were smiling and gave a little round of applause, as I was preparing my offering. I spied my mother. She looked a little perplexed! With no accompaniment and in perfect key, I belted out the first verse and chorus of "Pistol Packin' Mama" before my astounded Mother could wiggle through the congregation, onto the stage and drag me off in the midst of the second verse. I spied my dad with a huge grin on his face, and I wondered why my mom was so upset. The audience was on their feet and their applause was deafening. My debut was complete!

As adulthood shaped me into a much less precocious person, I reflect upon my little misdemeanour and consider the fact that it would have been a heck of a lot more embarrassing for my mother had I sung the verses to the "North Atlantic Squadron!"

🍁 Winnifred Mann

I was almost 9 when war was declared. We had a battery-operated radio. My father would hook up the car battery to the radio, and when the volume was getting faint, he would exchange the batteries so as to charge up the battery in the car. My parents were horrified to hear that war had been declared and they tried to keep up with the newscasts.

One of my cousins joined the navy and was sent to Esquimalt, British Columbia, for training; another cousin joined the army. They both survived. We were encouraged to correspond with them to help keep their moral high.

My public school teacher was a great influence on our war work. She encouraged my school friends and I to do as much as possible for our servicemen and women. We enlisted the help of neighbours, friends and relatives to give us soap, washcloths, combs, candy, gum, decks of playing cards, shaving cream, etc., to put into ditty bags, which we had sewn, to give to those in the service. It was at this time that my grandmother taught me to knit with four steel needles, turn a "double" heel and knit, knit, knit! I knit at recess, lunchtime and again at home at night. The woollen socks were either given to individuals or sent in a shipment overseas.

My father taught me to drive an English Fordson tractor with steel wheels and studs for traction. Then I could help with some of the outside work. Money was scarce and so were strong, young men to hire for farmwork.

Near the end of the war, I had begun Continuation School. Even the girls were divided into platoons and taught how to march, to stand at attention and to be dismissed.

🍁 Bernice Marsland

My memories of the Second World War are rather sparse, as my brothers and I were babies or toddlers during that time. My parents had quite an intense interest in the war, however, as they had several first cousins fighting overseas, stationed in Britain, Europe and even in Rawalpindi (Punjab), India. Also, my mom's brother was in Britain working as a mechanic. Consequently, every noon hour the radio was on to catch the latest news.

My mom also enjoyed music coming over the radio and often would singalong as she bustled about doing her daily household tasks. I thought that one song, "A Little Girl Dressed in Blue," was about a little girl like me, but years later learned that it really was about a soldier admiring a pretty, young lady.

Some of the sounds, however, coming across with the radio static were quite ominous to a small child, and especially as they were punctuated with Dad's colourful, expressive and ongoing spot editorials. Other radio sounds I was taken with included the gongs from Big Ben and the powerful doom and gloom dramatic voice of Lowell Thomas, who always started his broadcast with, "This is Lowell Thomas and the news."

Being bombarded with so much talk, we developed an early sense of geography and a distorted view of what or who Germans really were. I recall sitting at the kitchen table, pointing to the east and saying that the Germans came from over there. Another impression was that Germans were worse than boogiemen, more like giant, hairy monsters that killed innocent people.

My brother Fred and I had a chance to get a close look at one, a German that is, when the threshing gang came to our farm about 1944 or '45. Through neighbourhood talk, we heard that a German prisoner of war was staying on a nearby farm and would be brought along to help with the grain harvest. Fred and I were both excited and frightened at the prospect of seeing a real German. Nonetheless, after the threshing gang arrived and began working, we mustered enough courage and headed for the barn to get a peak at the "monster." Once in the barn, we quietly snuck up on the granary where the "creature" was working. What a revelation! A German was really human after all! My curiosity was satisfied so I left, but Fred stayed and became better acquainted with Fritz.

Wars, even for children on the fringe of them, can warp a child's sense of reality and truth. It took me many years to destroy the hate I felt for one group of people and to separate in my mind the ordinary peace-loving citizen from the destructive war machine.

❦ Catharine McKenna

I was in public school when World War II broke out. I lived in Ilderton, about 12 miles northwest of London, Ontario. Students were encouraged to purchase War Savings Stamps, which cost 25 cents each and were affixed to a certificate. We were awarded pins based on our sales. We also gathered bags and bags of milkweed pods, which were used to stuff life jackets and parachutes. I was too young to be interested in politics, but I do remember listening to the radio war news. Every day at school we covered current events regarding the war.

We were a tightly knit community and each person who enlisted was given an engraved wristwatch at a "going to war party." Every month, our Women's Institute (WI) packed each person a box, whether they were serving in Canada or overseas, and it was considered really cool to help them. Of course, when bad news arrived about the wounded, or those missing or killed in action, we all grieved because we were truly a family.

How well I remember the weekly knitting classes for the Red Cross, where scarves, vests, socks, etc., were produced. Although I was young, I was a good knitter and so I was assigned the task of teaching the art to beginners. How crass I was when they came the next week with holes from dropped stitches. I just told them, "Rip it out and start over again, and for goodness sake, count every stitch of every row!"

Our close proximity to the London Military Base meant that we often had servicemen and women for dinner on a Sunday. My grandmother was a terrific cook and made scrumptious desserts. I remember company giving her some of their ration tokens, so they could return for more "home cooking."

It is strange what will evoke memories of long past, but every time I slice a Spanish onion, I remember a young man who wrote home saying the thing that he missed the most was Spanish onions. His mother was a WI member and the Ilderton Branch went to work on how to accomplish this mission. The children went door-to-door collecting tobacco tins, which were washed and dried. A Spanish onion was encased in cooled, but still pourable, paraffin wax within the tin, which was then sealed with wax. With baited breath, we waited for word, and when it came, it said, "Thanks a million, the WI did it again!"

❦ Iris McManus

I was 6-years-old when World War II broke out. My first memory was of my mother gathering my sister, my brother and I and taking us to the closet under the stairs after a warning siren had gone off. It was dark inside the closet and she told us to be quiet. I cannot say how long we were in there, but it was a frightening experience at the time. When the siren went off again, indicating it was all-clear, we emerged from the closet.

School carried on and we were all issued with a gas mask, which we had to carry everywhere we went. Concrete shelters were erected on the school grounds and we had practice drills evacuating the school. As a child, I never realized the danger; I just thought it was a great adventure!

Now and again at school we received parcels from America and Canada. Everyone in the classroom was given a number that went into a box. The teacher would pull a number out of the box and if you were lucky you got an item from one of the parcels, like tinned fruit, soap or oranges, and many other things that were in short supply at that time in England.

While there were clothing coupons, you had to use them sparingly. My mother unpicked old sweaters and wound the wool on a tea tray, making skeins, which were washed and hung to dry. Then she knit up new sweaters, hats and mittens for the winter. This wool was unpicked and knit over many times into various items. My aunt gave my mother two blankets, one was a khaki colour and the other was the air force blue. She made two winter coats from these blankets - one for me and the other for my sister. I had the khaki one; I hated it, but it was warm.

People erected Anderson bomb shelters in their gardens, where they went if the bombing got bad. Many people made them into really comfortable dwellings. Because we had a cellar in our house, my father decided to turn this into our shelter. So he whitewashed the walls, built bunk beds and placed a table and chairs down there. My mother had stocked a cupboard, so there was always something to eat. As well, there was tea and sugar, and she would always bring milk to the cellar whenever we had to go. Mother had a little primus stove to heat water to make tea. My sister and I thought our cellar dwelling was great and we took turns sleeping in the top bunk. While we were down there, my father taught us all kinds of card games and we played Ludo and Snakes and Ladders. We also had jigsaw puzzles.

The most frightening thing I remember while in the cellar shelter was hearing the bombs falling and dropping to the earth and shaking the ground as they hit, especially when they started sending over what were known as doodlebugs to bomb London. You could hear them going over, and if the engine noise stopped it was the most frightening because you knew they were going to drop. My father also built an escape hatch from the cellar shelter in case the house was bombed. Fortunately, none of my family was injured despite the many close calls due to the bombing.

🍁 Ruth Metcalf

In 1939 I began my training at the Winnipeg General Hospital to become a nurse and I graduated in the fall of 1942 as a Registered Nurse. World War II in Europe was in full swing. I signed up for overseas duty with the

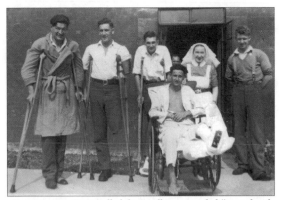

Patients, sometimes called the "walking wounded," posed with a nurse from No. 23 Canadian General Hospital.

Royal Canadian Army Medical Corp and was commissioned as a Lieutenant Nursing Sister. Initial training at Sussex, New Brunswick, included armaments and gas warfare. In early 1944, our hospital unit left Canada from Halifax on the huge troopship, the *Empress of Scotland*, formerly the *Empress of Japan*. The name had been painted over and the ship was stripped of all its glamour and luxuries. My journey overseas was a frightening experience at that time.

Our unit was No. 23 Canadian General Hospital. We landed at Greenock, Scotland, near Perth, and from then on it was troops, trains and convoys. Eventually, we were stationed at Leavesden, outside London. In July 1944, we began receiving severely wounded troops from the D-Day assault in Normandy. There was no time to worry about the buzz bombs, the V-1s and V-2s dropping around us. We worked 12-hour shifts from 7:00 a.m. to 7:00 p.m., boiling up our needles and administering morphine and penicillin around the clock. We received many cases directly from the front lines, some with maggots in their wounds. Actually, the maggots were important as they cleaned up the infected flesh and there was a limited supply of penicillin.

I was doing my duty for my country and it was indeed a privilege to nurse those young servicemen who fought so bravely. These lads were from all across Canada. We found ourselves being real sisters to them, writing their letters home and consoling them in their troubled times.

🍁 Mary F.S. Miller

My home was in a small village in east Scarborough in Ontario. Early in 1939 it became clear that war was inevitable; then it was declared. I was engaged with a wedding date set. My wedding dress was purchased and many preparations were made. However, my fiancé decided he must join the Armed Forces. He persuaded me that we should postpone our wedding until after the war, as he did not want me to be left a widow in case he did not survive. At the beginning of the war the casualties were high, so I finally agreed and stored my wedding dress away.

I was a Junior Women's Institute (WI) member. Our Branch had a membership of 20 and was deeply affiliated with the Highland Creek Women's Institute where the membership numbered 45. All members immediately became involved in war work and secured a charter under the War Charities Act, Department of National War Services. Each year, the Branch had to report to Ottawa to renew the charter and provide details of the war work that we had done, including the amount of money expended. To raise funds for this war work, our WI sponsored euchre parties, bingos, dances, potluck lunches and progressive dinners.

Our Branch participated in the provincial and national war efforts, providing jams, jellies and honey to send overseas. My parents' home was like a small factory four or five days a week. Each day, five to ten members would show up for work. Some 600 quilts of varying sizes were made for use in homes in Canada and for families overseas whose homes had been bombed.

Several days of the week, my mother cooked lunch for these members. She established a connection with a local butcher and it was amazing what interesting and nutritious meals she served using meat such as liver, kidney, tongue, tripe, bones and cuttings. Meat was rationed, so better cuts were not readily accessible and were costly. Members paid 15 cents each for lunch. We had our own chickens and ducks, so some days an egg or chicken dish was served. Other days, members brought their own lunch. Sugar was rationed, so no one used sugar in tea.

Materials had become scarce. Mother established another connection with the manager of Dry Goods and Fabrics at the Robert Simpson Company. He would phone me at my office downtown and I would walk over from Victoria and Queen to Yonge Street and pick up any fabrics he had. Cottons were 20 to 50 cents a yard and flannelette was 10 cents a yard. By this time the members had donated any surplus fabrics that might have been on hand. Every evening, it was my chore to cut and sort quilt patches and strips for use the following day. It became a joke in my home when someone came to visit. They were warned to hang onto their pants and skirts, or they might find them in a quilt!

In addition to baby layettes, diapers and knitted items were made for overseas and home use. We had a new Williams treadle sewing machine, but Mother purchased her first electric machine. Some of the quilts were tied, some quilted by sewing machine and some by hand. Many quilt tops were made and taken home by the members to finish. There were some 200 men and women from our small community involved in the war at home and overseas.

Our members knitted scarves by the yard and dozens of balaclavas, gloves, socks and mitts. Sailors' jerkin vests were made from old fur coats. Parcels were regularly sent overseas containing cheese, honey, candy, cookies, fruitcakes and cigarettes, along with the knitted goods. At the outset, each parcel contained a "Housewife's Kit," which contained thread, needles, buttons and wool for darning socks. It was most heartwarming to hear the letters of gratitude.

In the meantime, my fiancé had become a training officer stationed at various camps across Canada. As years passed, it seemed the war would never end, so we decided to get married. He was granted a three-day pass over Easter weekend, 1944. My wedding dress was brought out of storage, and we were finally married. Lo and behold! Two months later he was sent overseas as a replacement officer to see duty in France, Belgium and Holland. He returned home in January 1946.

Some of our local men married British, French or Dutch girls overseas. They began to arrive in our community, some with babies or small children. They were welcomed into our midst at a large garden tea party sponsored by our Women's Institute. Each bride and child was given a gift.

❧ Nellie Montgomery

When World War II broke out I was 18-years-old, fresh out of Peterborough Normal School and ready to begin teaching at a little country school in Victoria, Prince Edward County. My sister and I had gone to the Canadian National Exhibition (CNE) in Toronto for the Labour Day weekend. We awoke the morning of September 3, 1939, to the sound of a newsboy on the street below shouting, "England Declares War!"

Canada declared war on Germany on September 10. Our local regiment, fondly called "The Hasty Pees" (Hastings and Prince Edward), was one of the first to be mobilized. They left for overseas in December of '39. With Canadian Forces Base Trenton just across the Bay of Quinte, we began to see much more activity in the skies overhead. In 1940, Royal Canadian Air Force (RCAF) Mountain View was rapidly constructed in Prince Edward County. This base had two school wings – the No. 6 Bombing and Gunnery School and the RCAF Air Armament School. Soon, they were churning out navigators, air gunners and bomb and gun armourers, etc. There were Canadians, Britons, Poles, New Zealanders and Czechs in training. There was living accommodation for more than 3,000 military people. But that was not sufficient. My parents had a large farmhouse near Mountain View, so they, like many others, rented out a few rooms to married couples that lived off the base.

While I was teaching, one of the mothers helped me organize a Junior Red Cross Society at Victoria School. The children collected tinfoil from cigarette and tea packages. They scoured the fields collecting milkweed pods. We opened the pods and bagged up the silk to be used in down jackets. Several times a year we had paper drives; the children came to school pulling their wagons laden with newspapers. We took a collection at each meeting and sent it to the Red Cross. So, in many small ways, we were helping the war effort.

In 1942 I married a farmer from the community. We operated a dairy and apple orchard farm, so supplying food was our war work. Eating well was no problem as we grew a large vegetable garden and all kinds of fruit. Sugar rationing presented a challenge, however, with so much fruit to be canned. I remember canning raspberries with no sugar at all. We used saccharin on fresh fruit and in applesauce, but used it sparingly as too much made a bitter taste. At threshing and silo-filling times, we were allowed extra ration coupons to feed the men. We would have to go to City Hall in Belleville to apply for and obtain the extra coupons.

I joined the Rednersville Women's Institute in 1942. Our President at that time was Miss Audra Brickman. Audra and her parents operated a small canning factory. After having received a letter from the Canadian Red Cross Society asking the Women's Institutes to make jam for children in Great Britain, the Brickmans offered their factory one day a week to make jam for the Red Cross. A faithful bank of Institute members and other volunteers gathered during the fruit season to make jam. We all helped when we could.

The jam was cooked in large enamel dish pans on coal oil stoves. The Red Cross supplied the directions. No Certo was to be used, just fruit and sugar weighed out carefully. The jam was made from strawberries, raspberries, red currants, gooseberries, plums and peaches. A lot of the fruit was donated, but some peaches were purchased. Permits were obtained through the Red Cross to buy the sugar required. Other WI Branches in Prince Edward District gave financial assistance for the purchase of sugar and fruit.

The jam was packed in four-pound pails and shipped in crates. The Canadian Red Cross Society supplied the pails and crates. Mr. Brickman would load the crates of jam on a trailer behind his car and deliver them to Burford's Transport in Belleville who trucked the jam to Toronto without charge. He sometimes brought back several bags of sugar. On one occasion, someone reported Mr. Brickman to the police after seeing him drive through Belleville with several bags of sugar on his trailer. Two policemen showed up at the Brickman factory to check out the use of the sugar. They were told that all of the jam went overseas for evacuated children living in hostels and wartime nurseries. The policemen left satisfied that it was a legitimate operation.

A Canadian Red Cross Society label was put on each pail of jam; the label included Mrs. Brickman's name and address, as she was chair of the War Emergency Committee. She received many letters of thanks and appreciation from evacuee hostels and nurseries in England and Scotland. The Brickman's processed and shipped a total of 8,800 pounds of jam during the war. Honey was also purchased and shipped overseas.

During the Second World War, Rednersville WI held many quilting and sewing bees and the knitters were busy with their needles. The Rednersville WI contributed 151 quilts, 475 pairs of socks, 30 sweaters, 105 pairs of gloves, 52 hospital gowns and 20 suits of pajamas to the Red Cross. At Christmastime, they packed boxes to send to our local boys overseas. As Institute members, we all did our part to help the war effort.

Many cousins and friends were in the services and most of them returned home safely. My young brother joined the army in 1944 and was in training at Camp Borden when the war ended. My husband lost a first cousin; he was in the RCAF and was shot down over the North Sea.

🍁 Shirley Moore

At the time Canada entered the Second World War, I was 6-years-old and living on a farm near Florence in Southern Ontario. My three brothers were serving in the army - Robert (Bud) joined in 1939, Gordon in 1941 and Lloyd in 1943. I often think of the constant apprehension my parents must have felt having their boys facing death every day.

I attended the rural public school and on my way home collected the daily mail from the box at the end of the lane. My father had told me to bring any letter I didn't recognize to him, whether he was working with the horses in the field or wherever. I guess he didn't want my mother to open bad news. Once there was a picture of an injured soldier on a stretcher, somewhere in Italy. This soldier looked just like my brother Bud. In fact, some people called our house thinking it was Bud. I can't recall how my mother found out it wasn't him, but I do remember anxious times.

Bud returned in 1945, Gordon and Lloyd in 1946. I remember going to the armouries in downtown London to meet Lloyd from the train. But he didn't arrive at the expected time, so Mother, Dad and I went to wait at my future sister-in-law's home in London. At one point, I walked out in front of the house and coming down the street, walking arm in arm, were my three brothers. A sight to behold!

🍁 Ruth Morrison

I was 13-years-old when the war broke out in 1939. My brother Jack joined the Royal Canadian Air Force (RCAF) in April 1942. He trained in Galt, Ontario, and in Ucluelet on Vancouver Island. Jack was a mechanic with rank of leading aircraftsman. He worked on warplanes in England. My brother Ross joined the RCAF in August 1942. He trained as an air gunner in Lachine, Quebec, in Macdonald, Manitoba, and in Monkton, New Brunswick. Ross was promoted to Sergeant before leaving for England. He said he wasn't actually seasick on the boat, like hundreds of others, instead he said he was "damn sick of the sea." He started with No. 427 Squadron and later transferred to No. 405 Squadron.

Ross's first crew seemed to have bad luck. On their third mission over Germany – December 3, 1943 – they had engine trouble and lost two engines. They had to jettison their bombs and head for home base. They were losing altitude and the pilot ordered the crew to bail out. Ross wrote that it was quite the experience coming down from 8,000 feet in eight minutes. The next day, he went around to the parachute section and personally thanked them for the good job they had done packing the parachutes. The pilot managed to crash-land the plane two miles from base. The pilot and the crew survived, but the plane was demolished.

On January 20, 1944, after eight hours in the air, Ross and his crew were returning from Berlin. They were short of petrol and crash-landed short of their home base. They hit overhead wires, as well as a tree. Three members of the crew were killed and others were seriously injured. Ross was badly shaken up. He was promoted to Pilot Officer. In a letter home after that incident, he told us about the worst week of his life. He told of visiting the families of his crew who had been killed and attending the funerals.

A German fighter plane attacked Ross and his crew while on their way to Russelsheim, Germany, on their fiftieth bombing mission on August 25, 1944. Their plane was hit by gunfire and it seemed doomed as it spun out of control. Ross and two others bailed out over enemy territory. The other two were taken as prisoners of war, but Ross was never heard from again and his body was never found. It was a sad occasion at home to hear that he was missing. The family hoped and prayed he had been taken as a prisoner of war, but it wasn't to be. Ross is commemorated on the Runneymede Memorial near Windsor, England.

My brother Leo joined the air force in September 1943. He trained in Lachine, Quebec, and in Macdonald, Manitoba, as an air gunner. Leo served with No. 408 Squadron in England. By the time he and his crew had completed their training, things were coming to an end. They had three missions over enemy territory. Leo was promoted to Pilot Officer.

My brother Barry, the baby of the family at 9 years of age, was in need of a new suit for church. The Red Front Store in Stratford had suits for boys similar to air force uniforms that came complete with brass buttons and a little cap. Barry was proud to wear that suit.

My mother kept all the letters from the boys and when Jack and Leo returned safely, she may have burnt them. Ross's letters and his logbook and medals were all kept together in a box.

❈ Hilda Muir

I was born in Eastbourne, Sussex, England, an only child. My father worked on the double-decker buses. We lived on the outskirts of the city. I was in the last grade of an all girls public school when the war started.

Most of the girls were evacuated to Gloucestershire, but my parents wouldn't allow me to go. They thought we should stay together. I did get some more schooling by going in the mornings to a new high school on the outskirts of town. I remember our classes were often taken to the South Downs where we would gather rose hips. Apparently it was impossible to get cod liver oil for babies and the rose hip oil was a substitute.

When I was 14, I applied for a job as a Ledger Clerk in a large department store and got it. It was right downtown in the city. My mother used to say that she never knew if I was going to return home at night, as Eastbourne was densely bombed. We were opposite France on the English Channel and the German bombers would sneak in real low under the radar, drop their bombs and be on their way home again, sometimes even before the air raid siren was sounded. We got to know the sound of their engines, compared to our air force planes and we knew to head for cover when we heard them.

One day we had a real bad raid and a thousand pound bomb was dropped on the chapel next door to my workplace; it did not explode. Everyone was sent home while the engineers dismantled it. The next day, all the girls from the office went over to see it. It came through the roof, making a large hole and was resting in the aisle. We all sat on it and scratched our names on it. It looked like a large beached whale.

One weekend, my aunt who was a cook in the Navy, Army and Air Force Institute (NAAFI) canteen, stayed with us and we walked over to the cemetery to tend my grandmother's grave. I heard a plane and I knew it was German. I said, "We must hurry home." We didn't quite get there, but ran into a neighbour's house. After the raid was over we went back to the cemetery and found that both it and the church were badly damaged. Churches were usually targeted because in Germany they kept their munitions in them.

Lewis and Hilda, June 12, 1944.

In 1942, Britain started its offence. Two Canadian soldiers who spent their weekends with my neighbour survived the Dieppe raid, but there were thousands who were killed. They met a German convoy in the English Channel on the way over. Dieppe was a mistake. That's when it was discovered that our tanks were obsolete. They couldn't move in the shale on the beach.

About that time my husband and I started going together. He was one of the Canadians who spent the weekends next door. Many people opened their homes on weekends to enlisted men. He was in the Royal Canadian Engineers. He volunteered in September 1939 and was overseas for five and a half years. We planned to get married in August 1944, but my husband found out in June that he was going to France again. We had no telephone, so he sent a telegram which said, "Get married Sunday or Monday, or not at all!" I knew what that meant. My mother booked the Presbyterian Church for Monday morning, but couldn't get the organist. I borrowed a wedding dress from a friend at work. We were married at 11:00 a.m. then had a few friends in for tea. That evening, they sent an army truck to take him back to camp. Shortly after, I applied to come to Canada.

I left home with 900 other war brides on a troopship in convoy on April 29, 1945, and arrived in Ontario on May 15. The girls who had children had staterooms. The rest of us slept in a four-tier bunk and were told never to get undressed. A German U-boat attacked us as we approached Canada. We were seated for dinner, when the boat suddenly went sideways. All of the food landed on the floor. We never knew if it was depth charge or not. The stewards would not tell us. We never did get our dinner. Then, Winston Churchill's voice came over the radio saying that the war with Germany was over.

As we landed at the dock in Halifax, we saw the German submarine, which had surrendered. I was glad I didn't have any children on the trip. Army personnel put us on trains to our destination. I arrived in Elora, where I was met by my sister-in-law and taken to live with my mother-in-law. My husband came home in August on the hospital ship *Letitia*. The benefits that the veterans received after returning home were a great help. We were able to purchase a house in Preston through the Veterans Land Act.

🍁 Marjorie Nesbitt-Thom

One day our tall and handsome teacher was standing in front of the classroom tossing the chalk in his fingers trying to keep our attention. Everything in our two-room public school in Dundas County was ordinary and familiar to those of us in Grades 1 to 4. The next day we arrived at school, a small smiling stranger was standing primly at the door, waiting for us as we filed to our seats. What was this lady doing in our classroom? Where was Mr. McIntosh?

Everyone was quiet as the principal came in from the Grade 5 to 8 room, and explained to us that this lady would be our teacher until the end of the school year. Stunned expressions were on all of our faces, but the silence remained. Continuing the explanation, we were told that Mr. McIntosh had left to join the air force. Wow! Our teacher was going to be in the war.

Maybe he would learn to fly one of those double-engine bombers that flew over our farm. We were not far from the Ottawa airport. When we heard those planes, my brother and I would run outside and watch until they disappeared out of sight.

We were all aware that World War II was being fought across the ocean, so far away, and Canada was helping by sending the army, the air force and the navy "over there." Soon, many other young men also left our community to become soldiers, even our neighbour Charlie.

We were kids in Grade 4. How could we help? For some reason tinfoil was needed. We were asked to collect tinfoil from gum and cigarette wrappers and anywhere we could find it. It was rolled into a ball and it became a contest to see who could save the largest ball. These were handed in to our teacher and they disappeared. I later learned that the tinfoil was shredded and dropped from the airplane to interfere with enemy radar signals.

In the fall, some of my friends gathered ripened milkweed pods by the bagful. There were contests to encourage children to gather more. It was discovered that milkweed fluff had natural buoyancy making it useful as stuffing in flotation devices and flight jackets.

My dad continued to work our small rural farm. He was past the age that was expected to enlist. He was too young for World War I and too old for World War II. I was secretly glad about that. It was such a worry for the families who had boys in the war. There would be news of terrible battles with hundreds killed. I always wondered if Charlie was among them? It was usually quite a while before we knew.

Rationing was imposed on our country, things like sugar, meat, butter and gasoline, but we learned to live with it. Perhaps the farmers were better off than the village or city folks. Mom had a big garden. We always had lots of veggies and fruit. The preserving cupboard in the cellar was gradually filled every fall. We were given coupons to buy sugar. I'm sure our share was used wisely where it was most needed. As a substitute, Mom bought pails of liquid honey from a neighbour who kept beehives. It was so delicious on breakfast cereal and this 8-year-old didn't feel deprived while the war raged on.

Coupons were also used for gasoline. If you used your coupons too quickly you were out of luck until the next ones were issued. Green tea was in short supply. If you were lucky enough to find some, it became a treasure and was used sparingly. Meat was no problem. We slaughtered our own beef, pork and chicken. We made our own butter by putting the milk through a separator to get pure cream. The cream was placed in the churn. To a little girl it was a privilege to make the churn tumble and shake the milk until it began to thump, which meant the cream had turned into smooth and delicious butter. No one suffered from hunger on our farm during this awful war way "over there."

Daily the adults gathered around the radio to listen to the BBC news. Children knew to keep as quiet as mice when the broadcast was on. The grown-ups were very serious and didn't want to miss a word. We all lived with fear and anxiety, more so as the war escalated year after year. I remember large posters and billboards advertising that the "Walls Have

Ears."

On our road, we tried to keep track of Charlie, our teacher and Lyle from the village. If Charlie's family received mail from him, they shared it with us. I was a child and I was safe, but there was worry all through our neighbourhood.

In 1945 VE Day was memorable and momentous. Some friends and I were staying at a cottage when an announcement came over the radio that the war was over in Europe. Neighbours came out of their houses and gathered together hardly able to believe it was true. Horns blew and everyone cheered and the streets filled with exuberant, jubilant people wanting to share the good news. What a relief! The war was over.

Our local soldiers started to return. When we knew they were arriving the school allowed us to go and line the streets of the village to cheer and welcome them home. Charlie and Mr. McIntosh came home, but Lyle didn't.

🍁 Muriel Nichols

At the age of 18, I joined the Women's Division of the Royal Canadian Air Force (RCAF) and requested, so-called, "secret work" in the hopes of an overseas posting. My only regret in three years of RCAF service was that I never got overseas. However, I did work as a filterer in the operations room of the Western Air Command Radar Unit in the basement of the Belmont Building, across from the Empress Hotel, in Victoria,

Muriel, 1943.

British Columbia.

We scanned for Japanese attacks, a real threat to the country at that time, and tracked both Canadian and American pilots with the aid of "bush" radar stations strung along the remote coast of BC. During quiet times these men were more than happy to chat with us, the ladies of the airwaves. For a while, war imposes and enforces camaraderie amongst its fighters; it also relies upon the loneliness and isolation of those who stand and watch for the safety of all. That is, in effect, what I did for the war effort. Of all the events that transpired, I wish to recall one short, but typical, moment.

One night an American pilot crashed into the Pacific Ocean. Lost pilots, especially those in training, were an unfortunate but all too common reality. On this particular evening, however, I imagined his family, his friends, his lover, etc. That he be saved was of prime importance for some reason. Fortunately, we were able to give the rescuers his exact position and he was saved. I never met him, but I imagined his life and was both proud and happy to have had a part in returning him to the people in his life. That is what we did; we saved some and lost others – all from the basement radar operations room of the Belmont Building in Victoria, BC.

🍁 Adrienne Noble

In 1939, I was 20 years old and full of enthusiasm having just completed two years at Gipsy Hill Training College for teachers of children aged two to eight. I had spent two wonderful years living in London, England, and was then appointed to the newest, most up-to-date school with outstanding facilities. I was most eager to start. War was officially declared a few days prior to my appointment, so previously arranged plans to evacuate children from high-risk areas were set in motion.

While my school was not high-risk, all teachers were needed for evacuation. I had to report to a school in a squalid part of the city. So with the 10 children in my charge, I boarded a bus. Everyone had a gas mask. Understandably, mothers were hesitant to let their children go to an unknown destination for an unknown length of time. It was an emotional departure to say the least! After boarding a train, we travelled from station to station, whose names were hidden for security reasons. The journey was not far into the next county.

Months earlier, residents had volunteered to take in evacuees, but some of them were now unwilling. Consequently, we walked the streets to try to get the last children placed. What a nightmare! After a night at my own billet, I was told to return home. My relief was tremendous because my widowed mother was in the hospital about to be discharged.

Back at school there were many changes. Five long air raid shelters, one for each class, had been dug into the beautiful grounds. Fortunately, there was still the sandbox, the paddling pool, the little garden, the outdoor play equipment and the hardtop for outdoor gym. The school kitchen had become headquarters for the local volunteer Air Raid Wardens. I think they had their own phone for receiving warnings, at which time the siren on the roof would be activated. The roof post was manned every night, all night.

The school itself was equipped to be a Rest Centre in case of emergency. That meant all available storage was used for blankets, non-perishable food and first aid material, etc. Another staff member and I volunteered to attend a Saturday afternoon course to prepare us for the eventuality of a possible confinement. Mercifully, this never occurred. But there were a few days when we did receive evacuees from the inner city and we had to share our school with other children and their teachers.

Another change at the school included the enrolment of 3-year-olds, provided they were toilet-trained. This change came about because most of the young fathers were in the Armed Forces and many mothers worked in munitions factories. The teaching staff also helped distribute milk and cod liver oil every day. In spite of severe rationing of most food items, children were a priority and were taken care of as well as possible.

✤ Shirley E. Orr

It was September 1939. I was 16. We were having Sunday dinner at my aunt and uncle's farm at Singhampton when the radio announcer let us know that Canada was answering the call to go to war in Europe. Also at that table was my uncle's nephew, a fine strapping young fellow of eighteen or nineteen. His immediate reaction, "I guess a lot of us will be going there." Most people from rural areas were not well travelled. This war certainly changed that.

Letter writing became important to sons, brothers or cousins who were stationed far from home and all things familiar. As the fellows moved overseas, airmail became the "in" thing. A sheet of pale blue, onion-skin-like paper could be written on and then folded to form its own envelope. Everyone learned to write a "finer" hand so more news would go on each page. Many letter writing friendships continued after the war ended; some blossomed into romance, including my own.

In 1939, there were few tractors in rural Ontario. The bulk of farmwork was done manually or with horses. As the able-bodied men enlisted, those left at home worked until the jobs were done. Women, girls, the elderly and children helped in harvesting, gardening and fruit picking.

We lived about 15 "crow" miles from Camp Borden and, believe it or not, when we would hear the hum of an airplane we would run outdoors to see it. Those adventurous pilots doing dives and rolls were a source of amazement and entertainment to their scattered audience.

Some homes had battery-operated radios; we relied on the daily newspaper, the *Mail and Empire*. Headlines often appeared stark and frightening. The casualty lists were carefully perused.

Some rural girls worked in munitions factories in the city. I worked in the meat department of an A&P Food Store. At that time working in a butcher shop was considered male territory. I was not required to lift carcasses or heavy boxes, but I could tend counter, weigh and parcel and, of course, clean.

Every person in a household was issued a ration book to allow for the purchase of meat, butter and sugar, with additional pages in case rationing of tea, coffee or other goods became necessary. Each automobile owner had a ration book for gasoline purchases. In the country, sugar was the commodity most sought after, as most farms had their own supply of butter and meat.

Every housewife tried to save some sugar for canning and some experimented with canning with no or little sugar. At our house, my mother doled out our sugar carefully. My grandfather had a sweet tooth and could have used up the family ration by himself. Rather than skimp on his cereal, he would eat his porridge without sugar for several days, so he could have it

157

to his liking on occasion.

Our community honoured those bound for overseas with wristwatches. Many care packages were packed by individuals and by service clubs. In our area, the local Red Cross Society was an active group of nearly 50 women and girls. It was actually a community enhancer, as women from different church groups worked side-by-side in the Red Cross Society and became more familiar with each other. Neighbourhood parameters were extended and when the war ended those friendships continued and our Women's Institute Branch was born.

🍁 Veronika Osske

My childhood years were carefree and happy. My father was a high school principal and when war broke out in 1939, we lived in the town of Kolberg, a beautiful summer resort on the Baltic Sea. We lived in a lovely spacious apartment in a big house. The location could not have been any closer to the dunes, the beach and the sea. We spent our whole childhood summers playing and exploring. It was an idyllic life. But when the sirens became a part of our daily lives, life became uneasy.

My father was an officer in World War I and World War II. He went with his troops to France and later to Russia. When Father developed diabetes, he was then sent home, since he was not well enough for the front line. My older brother was conscripted into the army and my two older sisters were already studying and living in West Germany.

We had to leave our beautiful home on March 4, 1945, never to see it again. The Russians were quickly advancing toward our town. Really, it was almost too late to leave, but families with younger children had been allowed to pack up and go first. My brother was 9 and I was 14-years-old, when my mother told us to choose a few precious things to take along in our backpack which we would carry. That was a hard thing to do. We managed to get a ride in an army truck, but not far. The truck was needed elsewhere, and we were left stranded. At nightfall, we could see our beautiful town burning behind us and we knew that there was no turning back. From that point on, we had to walk.

Along the way, we stopped at a farm, where we were given a meal. For the first time, we felt like refugees. At night you could see the houses and barns burning in the area. Before leaving this farm my parents decided that one of the stables would be a safe place to bury the family jewellery. There was not a doubt in their mind that we would return to recover what we had left behind.

We were warned not to continue our journey, but my parents wanted to get us out of danger. Retreating civilians encouraged us to seek shelter because the Russians were quite close. There was a small abandoned house nearby that became our refuge. We heard the "Hurrah!" in the distance when the Russians first started to attack. All night long, we heard grenades and bullets fly over our shelter. It was a sound that I will never forget. My father told us that if the Russians got too close, or won the skirmish, he would use his revolver because he would never let them take us. He knew that women, in particular, were in danger.

At dawn, after many frightening hours, there was a sudden silence and we did not know who would appear or what to expect next. We heard the rattling of tanks and saw that they were our soldiers. We were so thankful to still be free and the journey went on. It was an unforgettable sight to see the many dead soldiers and other innocent victims of crossfire. One such victim was the mailman, with his delivery bag and bike nearby.

Our next destination was a little harbour called Dievenow, where we would find a boat to take us to Swinemunde. We were cold and hungry when we finally got on the boat that would help us continue our journey. There were soldiers on the boat with civilians, but they were forced to make more room for families. An hour and a half after our departure, the town was bombed by a huge air raid. Many people died. Later, we heard that the Baltic Sea crossing had many mines planted in it, but somehow we manoeuvred through them safely. We stayed overnight with relatives and the next morning we found a small motorboat, which took us to the next town. From there, we boarded a train and took it to a town where we stayed with some friends before starting the last leg of our journey to Demmin.

A few days later, my parents decided to go on to Rotenburg, where one of my sisters lived. Once again it proved to be in our good fortune. The Russians took over Demmin, and it too was given to soldiers to plunder and do other dreadful things. Finally, we arrived at my sisters, exhausted and shell-shocked. We had no idea what the future held for us.

My father had to convalesce in a hospital for a few weeks and my mother found a place for us to stay on a farm. We hardly recognized Dad. He was so skinny; he must have been starving for some time. We were thankful that he was alive. Once Father got his strength back, he started to work as a farmhand, as did I. This was the way that we earned our food. My family stayed on this farm for eight years.

🍁 Zina Ottokar

World War II started in 1939. Germany had declared war on Poland around the first of September. I was a young teenager then in Estonia, living in our capital city of Tallinn. Knowing the impending danger, the citizens began to move away to other countries. The first ones to leave were the so-called "Baltic Germans," who left for Germany. It turned out to be the best decision for them because when the Russians came to occupy the country, they would have been deported to Russia.

From 1939 to 1941, I attended a business college. The first semester was uneventful, but after the Russian occupation everything went downhill for many people. My mother foresaw many things ahead. She bought large bags of sugar and flour and also many good fabrics for dressmaking purposes.

The first thing that happened to the Estonian people was the confiscation of their radios, so that they would not be able to listen to the news. Then everyone had to give up their cars to the Communists, without any remuneration. Later, storeowners had to give up their stores. Some were lucky and could work at their former stores as store managers. At the same time, homeowners had their homes confiscated.

I got a job in a Russian office. Those were dangerous and difficult times for everyone living in Estonia. The Russians hired people who would spy on the workers, and if anyone did not measure up, they could be easily arrested and sent to prison. I had to report to one of the Russian office directors who wanted to know if I believed in God. I said, "Yes, I do." He looked at me and said that his god was Joseph Stalin. I was lucky after that incident that I was left alone. I was fired when the German Army started closing in to take the country from the Russian Communists. I was sent, along with many other young girls, to dig ditches around the city to keep the German Army out, which of course was a ridiculous idea.

Citizens were forbidden to be on the city streets after 10:00 p.m. One day, I went to a summer resort with my girlfriend. Upon returning home, we realized that it was too late to walk over the bridge to go home; it was already after 10:00 p.m. The only place where we could be safe and spend the night was an old cemetery, and so we spent the night sleeping among the graves. I will never forget that fearful night.

On another occasion we wanted to take the bus home from the same summer place. There were two buses packed with people. The bus did not stop to let people get off; instead the bus driver took us out of the city to dig more ditches. It was dark outside and when the bus finally stopped, I just ran away. I was lucky. I left everything, my family and my beloved homeland hoping to return some day when the war was over. I was 19-years-old.

War propaganda was heard everywhere in Estonia, as well as in Germany. The Communists forced the working people to go to designated places in the City Square where there were propaganda speakers. It was a must to take part in these hated meetings and to listen to all kinds of speeches that you knew were propaganda. And there was someone who was watching to be sure that every worker was at those meetings. In 1941, when the German Army took over our country from the Communists, I did not hear any more propaganda speeches.

I fled to Germany and got a job. I just hated entering a government office where you had to lift your hand and say, "Heil Hitler!" During those years, I was forced to move from one place to another, depending upon where the Communist Russians were moving and what part of Germany was being given to them.

At the end of the war I was living in West Germany. There came the golden opportunity to emigrate to one of many places. Estonians could find a new home in Australia, Canada, the USA or Argentina, or stay and work in West Germany. I am so thankful that I chose to have my new home in Canada, the best of all countries in the world.

❧ Lois M. Parker

At the time World War II started, my family and I were living at the corner of Hess and Hunter Streets in Hamilton, Ontario. I was getting ready to start Grade 6 at Ryerson Public School on Queen Street South. My new friend Irene Thorburn was starting her first day in a new country. Irene had been sent to Canada to live with her aunt for the duration of the war. She was one of a boatload of British children sent out from Glasgow, Scotland, to a safe haven in Canada to escape the war that was looming on the horizon. Irene was my closest friend and she lived kitty-corner across the street.

A block away, at the end of Hunter Street, where the T.H.& B. (Town of Hamilton & Buffalo) Tunnel comes out into the open, there was a corner grocery store. Almost every day, I would go buy a penny's worth of candy from the grocer who would fill a paper cone with candy that lasted all day. He was popular with all the neighbourhood kids. A few months went by and we heard that the owner of the store had been arrested for being a Nazi spy. He had been sending radio messages over to Germany about the steel and munitions factories in Hamilton.

One lovely summer day, I heard that a famous person was attending a Garden Party at one of the large homes on Jackson Street West. Of course, I went to see what I could from the sidewalk. There was a crowd around and lots of noise, but soon a speaker announced a special request and a singer began to sing. It was the voice of Gracie Fields singing "Say a Prayer for the Boys Over There." This party was given to help the war effort and to sell Victory Bonds.

In the early autumn of 1940, Dad announced that he had bought a farm on Chippewa Road near Mount Hope. It was 10 miles away from downtown Hamilton where he worked. Dad had been born and raised on a farm and he was always interested in farming. My two brothers, Aunt Margaret, mother and myself would help do the farmwork. Now we could raise meat, make butter, boil maple sap down for sugar and enjoy the fruits of our labour.

Our farm was only two miles away from the airport at Mount Hope. On a clear night we could see the training planes taking off and landing. The searchlight kept going around as long as any plane was in the sky. The airport was built for a training base, mostly for English airmen. The officers brought their wives over to Canada to be with them and every few months some squadrons and officers went home to England. We had a large 10-room, brick house, so my parents rented rooms to a couple of officers and their wives. I went to the United Church in Mount Hope and we put on a special evening of entertainment once a month for the airmen.

The spring and fall were particularly bad for foggy weather. One foggy day, a training plane came down in a field nearby. The pilot was not hurt, but the plane was damaged, so it was taken apart and trucked away. In other accidents, however, there were airmen killed.

While I was in Grade 8, I had the chance to be a Farmerette in the spring of 1942. Starting in May, I was allowed to skip school to work on the farm to help the war effort. It meant I did not need to write any exams to pass into Grade 9. We were also able to get a student from Westdale Secondary School to work on the farm for his board and a small wage. His name was Rodger Allen and the next year the student was Kenneth Bates. We had to milk cows, feed the chickens, mix the mash for the pigs, gather the eggs, kill and dress the chickens and geese and churn the butter. Fieldwork was the hardest – hoeing the crops of turnips and beans and driving the team of horses. The worst part of farming was having to give up summer holidays in Muskoka.

My Aunt Margaret Alton enlisted in the air force in 1943 as a photographer. She did her basic training at Rockcliffe and then she was sent to Aylmer, Ontario, for her studies. She was commissioned to go to McDonald Gunnery School in Manitoba for the duration of the war. She continued to study aerial photography using a type of gun camera. A picture she had taken in the air turned out to be a surprise because the airplane was actually an American Stearman, similar to a Canadian Harvard, and not immediately identified.

Aunt Margaret, 1944.

Volunteering for the Red Cross was one of the more pleasurable things I liked to do. My future mother-in-law, Mrs. Parker, was the quilt convener at Welcome School on Saturday afternoons. Every week we went there to make quilts. We set up two at a time and eight or ten ladies from the community came to work. We made six or eight quilts every week. The Red Cross supplied the yard goods and we put them together as fast as we could. Mrs. Parker would take them home to finish the edges, then take them back to the Red Cross office in Caledonia the next week and pick up more supplies for the Saturday quilters. At the end of the war, we all were awarded a Red Cross pin for our efforts.

Our farm neighbours had two sons in the Royal Hamilton Light Infantry;

both boys were killed in the Dieppe Raid in France. Their parents were overwhelmed with grief when they received word of their death, having just buried a wee son killed in an accident at home. There were others lost in the war from the community, as well as one of my cousins. We thought the war would never end, but by the grace of God the Americans jumped into the battle, which gave us all a tremendous lift.

🍁 Bertha Pattenden

When World War II was declared, I lived in Northern Ontario near a little town called Matheson, with a population of 400 people, 40 miles south of Timmins. When war was declared I was 9-years-old and I didn't really understand what it meant. But all of the young boys around started enlisting in the army. Before they were sent overseas, I would see them in their uniforms on weekends. It was the time of the big bands and my stepfather played a base fiddle every Saturday night in our community hall. We would have dances as entertainment for the soldiers.

My stepfather, Tom Longstreet (bottom right), with his base fiddle.

A lot of the teachers, men and women, were joining the Forces in our area. Consequently, an older woman was asked to replace the teacher in a small school not too far from our home. She needed someone to help her with her housework, and so she asked me if I would help. This was in 1943. I was 13-years-old at the time. I accepted and worked there for two years for $20 a month.

A lot of women had to go out to work to take over jobs that the men and boys had always done. It was a positive thing though because it got women out of the house and taught them to manage things on their own.

Every Saturday afternoon, at the Matheson Community Centre, the

National Film Board of Canada would show a cartoon followed by a main feature all about the war. After that they would show another cartoon so everyone would stay until the end. We all enjoyed the cartoon, but not the war feature.

🍁 Jean Phoenix

W ho can forget those days in the summer of '39 when war was declared? The excitement of preparing for a new adventure, a year at Mac Institute in Guelph, was overshadowed by newspaper reports. They stated that war was imminent. The war clouds were real and frightening. Finally, the day came in September when there was no doubt. Hitler, after declaring war in Europe, turned on the United Kingdom and as their Allies Canada was in for over five years.

The first year, war was no closer than school chums and acquaintances leaving for training. Then, gradually, a number left for the front and reports would follow of some that were killed in action. But the war was still far away. We were on a farm and my brothers were kept busy there.

Just one year after war was declared, I dated Stuart who became a Flying Instructor and was posted to Dauphin, Manitoba. It was apparent he would be in Canada for some time and so we became engaged.

In February 1942, we were married and for one and a half years I followed Stuart wherever he was posted. I was a real war bride. It was an exciting time. We adjusted to travel by train and bus and cramped living quarters with used furniture. We met many young men from the United States, the United Kingdom, Australia and New Zealand came to Canada to train. Stuart instructed mostly on Harvards and Yales.

Three months after my arrival in Dauphin, a new posting came through and we moved to St. Eugene on the border of Quebec and Ontario. Our 48-hour leaves were spent in Ottawa or Montreal. The French Canadians' treatment of Anglos was cool. Many young French men were able to avoid conscription, which caused a rift between the two nationalities. In the French Canadian home where we had an apartment with others, we were treated well. Our landlady saw a chance to make money and she turned every available space into living quarters. Her daughter and niece slept in the hall.

Jean and Stuart, February, 1942.

By September 1943 fewer students

were being trained to fly and Stuart received a posting overseas. It was rather a shock! After one month of training as a fighter pilot in St. Hubert, Quebec, Stuart was on his way. I boarded with friends in St. Lambert in Montreal for the next month. By then, Stuart was a Flight Lieutenant and had left on a convoy for England. I stayed with relatives in Halifax during Stuart's two weeks of preparation for leaving. Due to engine trouble his ship had to return to Newfoundland. Later, he was sent to New York, where he boarded the *Queen Mary* along with several thousand others. During Stuart's two years overseas, I entered the Toronto Baptist Seminary for a three-year course. I seem to remember some disapproving remarks for not joining a war effort somewhere.

During those two years, letters flew back and forth. We promised to write a letter every day and almost did, with as many as six or seven in the mailbox at one time. There was a constant fear of the dreaded telegram. I was in a friend's home in Toronto when one came regarding her brother. It was devastating for the family. When the war was over, I burned my letters, something I have regretted since.

In the summer of 1945, when the war in Europe was over, Stuart came home on leave with orders to return to the Japanese front. In the mid-Atlantic the news reached him that the atomic bomb had been dropped on two places in Japan. The Japanese had surrendered and Stuart would be home for good. It was an exhilarating thought!

Stuart joined me at the Toronto Baptist Seminary. He was thinking of entering the ministry, but was soon convinced it was not for him. That summer, he taught veterans who were catching up on Grade 13 Chemistry and other subjects in order that they might enter university or the business world. They were eager students from Kitchener and London, Ontario, and were satisfying to teach. They used gratuities for their war service and Stuart earned a good salary for these extra classes.

In September 1945 an offer came to teach in Ethiopia, which we accepted. I saw this move as restlessness left over from the war. I did not complete my three years at the Seminary as our son Leigh was born in June 1946. Leigh was 8-months-old when he travelled with us to our new home in Jimma, Ethiopia.

❧ Inta Purvs

From Viking times, the Daugava River has played a large part in the geographic and political history of the Baltic States. It starts far away in Russia, crosses Latvia to the Baltic Sea. It was a main trade route and valuable real estate, opening doors for the Vikings going to Russia and for the Russians going to Europe. It was a crossroads country between East and West interests. The Russians had demanded an army base in the Baltic State of Latvia in 1939, although they didn't formally occupy us until the following year. Nothing was as inhuman as the Russian occupation.

My mother and father were divorced. Mother remarried a widower. My stepfather was a chaplain and was drafted into the Latvian Legion when I was 12-years-old; my brother Ivar was 7 and my stepsister Barbara was 4. The Germans were occupying Poland and advancing into Leningrad. They drafted Estonians, Latvians and Lithuanians. People were shot if they didn't comply. Then the Germans retreated, while the Russians advanced and the two Latvian Legions were faced against the Russians in Kurland. Even though Father was in a Latvian Legion, he had two strikes against him. He wore a German uniform and he was a clergyman. The Russians were determined to destroy any evidence of religion.

When we left Riga in 1944, Father was not with us. Mother was alone with the children. The army was going west to escape the advancing Russians. Bombs were falling and we could hear machine guns. The only trains running were loaded with wounded soldiers trying to get to a seaport and on a boat to Germany. A train was stopped in the station, but not taking civilians. Mother gave a bottle of cognac to the conductor and three families piled into the last car loaded with blankets. The train stopped every hour to unload the dead. There was no medical help. I can still hear their screams of agony. That 15-hour journey was the first time I'd come face to face with death.

We were reunited with Stepfather for one week at the Baltic Sea where the German ships were stationed. He stayed at Danzig and we were shipped further west, as we did not know who was coming first - the Allies or the Russians. Mother bribed a bus driver, again with a bottle of cognac, to allow us to get on the bus going towards the Allied Forces at Lubeck. The bombs were falling and we got off to hide in the bushes. Brother got trampled and his arm was broken. When we reached a friendly zone, his arm was immobilized. We spent a year in a Displaced Persons (DP) Camp run by the United Nations (UN). The American camps were the best, Canadian camps were okay, but the French camps were by far the worst economically. Trade schools were started under army supervision. Some people lived for 10 years in these camps. Thousands refused to leave and be sent back to the occupation of the Russians.

During our year there, lights would go off at 10:00 p.m. Then Mother would tell us stories. I could sense her intense fear. When the Russians came to her office in Riga, where she was working in municipal government, they tried to force her to spy on her co-workers. She constantly refused and even considered suicide. They even threatened to remove her fingernails and harm her children.

Another woman in the barracks told us that because her son had appendicitis, they had to stay behind. She tried to look old, stooped and repulsive, and even painted her teeth black to avoid bad treatment by the soldiers who demoralized the population. Men had their hands tied behind their backs and toothpicks stuck in their eyes; they were forced to watch the repeated raping of their wives and daughters. Mother knew women and girls who drowned themselves in a pond after being repeatedly raped. The Russians were brutal!

Mother spoke of the Russian atrocities. She related how inhuman the Russians were during the occupation of the 1940s. They came at night to collect families. The men were separated out and shipped to Siberia to work in the uranium mines. Most lasted only six months. The women and children were loaded on cattle-cars and the doors were locked. They were deprived of food and water, and heat in the winter and ventilation in the summer. They tore holes in the car floors to excrete. Many went mad with the deprivations and killed themselves. When they were let out in the wilderness in Siberia, they dug holes in the ground for shelter and even resorted to eating tree bark for nourishment.

The Russians came back again in the spring of 1944. Grandfather was a horseman and there were many young foals. He had many barns for the cows, pigs and chickens and owned a large acreage. He lingered to look after the livestock. The Russians came in fast and he did not escape. He also employed people, which the Communists considered a crime. He lost all his land, buildings and inventory. He was shipped to Siberia for five years. When he came back home, he was old and sick with bone cancer. There were hospitals and medications only for the Russians. I used to send him a birthday card every week with pain tablets taped inside to help relieve some of his misery. It took him three years to die.

Grandmother was too old to be of much use in Siberia. She had been allowed to take only one of everything - a spoon, one pair of shoes, one pair of panties, etc. Her only means of survival was to act as a servant to a Russian family. Many children were put in orphanages, so that the women could work harder. The children were given Russian names so they never knew their identity.

Mother received a small pension, so I was working to support my brother and sister's schooling. I sold candy in a cinema during show intermissions. While the show was on, I would pull out my books and study hard. I became fluent in English and Swedish. Mother asked the Swedish Consulate to help us enter Sweden - a neutral country - where we hoped to find Father. We could not find him. When Mother realized he had not escaped, she had a nervous breakdown. Two years later she learned that he had been taken prisoner and shipped to Siberia. He had been able to get only one note to Grandmother. That was the last we knew of him.

When Mother's health improved, she started working in a lab, analyzing margarine, and I was able to go to high school. One was required to choose a career first. I was looking to a medical degree, so I took extra courses in chemistry, biology and physics to shorten my time at university. I learned of an essay competition, which I entered and won second prize, a one-way trip to Stockholm for a weekend to take part in a youth festival.

While in Stolkholm, I decided to go to the opera. I asked a nearby youth to direct me to the opera house, instead he led me there; it seemed like miles. My new shoes were hurting, but he assured me the opera house was just around the corner. I told him I'd call the police if it weren't. It was, and I thanked him and bought my ticket. Then he bought one too, for the next seat. I eventually married him. His family had been lucky enough to escape to Sweden via a fishing boat carrying escapees. Later, I came with his family to Canada in 1951.

A friend of ours who immigrated to Hamilton the year before sponsored our family. My mother found employment in a lab at McMaster University. The rest of my relatives were either killed or died in Siberia.

🍁 Cynthia Rabstein

I was 4-years-old when war was declared between Germany and Great Britain. I lived in Devonshire in a village called Lympstone, about 80 miles south of the town of Exeter. My father was an Anglican Rector of the Church of the Nativity and Chaplain to the Marine Camp based in Nutwell Court, the estate of the late Sir Francis Drake.

The Germans were always trying to find this Marine Camp. Their bombers would fly across the English Channel and follow the River Exe. They managed to bomb the whole of Plymouth on the other side of the Exe, and Exeter was badly bombed. However, they never did find the Camp; it was so well camouflaged that even the locals could not find it.

My father and mother were firewatchers. They wore a uniform and a helmet and took turns with other villagers standing on the roof of the church tower at night, looking for enemy aircraft or fires from dropped bombs. I remember my mother getting me up at night and putting me in what I called a Puffersuit (snow suit). Once the air raid sirens were sounded we had to go to a shelter, which was underground at the bottom of the garden with a hedge hiding the opening. Sometimes we did not make it to the shelter and we had to hide under the stairs or the dining room table.

Our tennis court was turned into allotments or gardens for the villagers to grow fruit and vegetables. We also had a large garden and chickens and ducks for meat and eggs. I overheard my mother telling my father that she had heard something whistle over her head as she was walking up the driveway coming back from firewatching. She thought it was a flying bomb. Even after asking around the village, no one else had heard it, until she met an old parishioner who had been in the First World War. He confirmed what she had heard and together they got the Bomb Squad and there it was, ticking merrily away, just over the wall of Nutwell Court.

Everyone had to carry a gas mask and there would be mock gas attacks, which were unpleasant if you were caught in one without your mask. My parents bought me a gas mask with a face like Mickey Mouse. It had a floppy nose and blue cheeks. I refused to wear it, even when ordered to at school. I had to stand in the corner, but even that did not work. My parents had to get a miniature adult one for me.

My mother worked one evening a week at a canteen for the soldiers in Exeter. An army lorry picked her up and brought her back. Quite often it was an American lorry, and those soldiers gave me my first taste of candy. It did not take me long to learn to wait at the gate for them!

One day I was out on my swing when a German plane flew overhead, 50 feet from the ground. It was being chased by two of our Spitfires. I could see the pilot and the gunner clearly. My mother was leaning out the bedroom window yelling at me to lie down on the ground. Luckily the pilot was too busy trying to avoid our aircraft and the trees to shoot at me.

I remember the day victory was declared. My parents took me for a walk down to the village at night to see all the windows and street lamps that were lit up and the villagers dancing in the streets.

After I immigrated to Canada, I married a German, who had far worse experiences than I. We vowed that peace had to begin with us and that history should always be remembered.

🍁 Delight Rath

I was a teenager going to school when the war started. I was born and raised on a farm in Colchester Township in the County of Essex, Ontario. I helped my dad farm, as I had no brothers. At this time, the Ford Motor Company of Windsor hired my dad. Ford produced war materials for overseas.

When I was about seventeen, I went to work at a small factory in Harrow. We built wooden boxes or containers for Ford to use to ship parts overseas. We worked long hours, six days a week. My girlfriend and I made all the wood ends for the boxes. We had to make ends for boxes of varying sizes. Our job was to put four lengths of lumber cut-to-size together with 2½ and 3-inch nails, which we could sink with two strikes of the hammer. These ends were made on steel tables. The women on the lines put heavy black waxed paper on the sides and bottom. Then lids were put on. The boxes were taken to the Ford Company by truck.

Many items were purchased with stamps from our ration books - coffee, tea, butter, sugar and meat. We had white margarine with colouring in a bag, which you had to mix to make it yellow. Restaurants had meatless days on Tuesday and Friday each week. Once the soles or heels on your shoes wore out, you took them to a shoemaker to have them fixed. Gas was rationed, but it was a little easier to secure than tires. You had to be doing a wartime job in most cases to purchase tires. We were lucky; we had our own fruit and vegetables, pork, beef and chicken. We made our own butter in a churn. Our meat was stored at the cold storage in Harrow. Many people in town had a Victory Garden and grew their vegetables.

During my school years, I was President of the Junior Red Cross. We were taught to knit scarves, socks and mitts. I often wondered what poor soul had to wear them. There were many dropped stitches and uneven sides on our scarves. We made up boxes, which included things like chocolate bars, cookies, cigarettes, shaving supplies and writing paper, to send overseas to the servicemen. We packed the boxes with loose peanuts in shells to hold the articles in place. We collected all the foil we could get out of cigarette packages. We asked people we knew to save the foil and we made large balls out of it for the war effort. We had fundraisers to buy War Savings Stamps, which were put in a book. When I worked, I saved my money and bought Canada Savings Bonds.

Every family knew each other in a small town like Harrow. We were like a family. The residents of Harrow had many sad times and many happy times together as servicemen came home. We had many young men who were wounded, killed or missing in action or were prisoners of war. My first cousin joined the Essex Scottish Regiment and was killed in action. His brother joined the Royal Canadian Air Force (RCAF) and became an air force officer and navigator. He flew 43 tours and returned home.

There was one family in town that had four boys in the service. I believe three joined the Essex Scottish Regiment; the oldest joined the air force. The two youngest were taken prisoners in different camps. The older of these two engineered four different escapes but was caught and returned to camp. The Germans were impressed with his attempts to find his young brother. The youngest was hit with shrapnel, and after returning home had several pieces come out of his body. All four boys from this family came home. The whole town was thrilled!

I also had a young friend who joined the Army Tank Core. His tank took a direct hit by mortar shell. There was a bad fire and he suffered a great deal. He was able to return home and he brought me a silver three-pence bracelet.

As a result of the war, I grew up quickly and had a far different outlook on life. It made me a more independent adult. The war made a great change in the way women were treated. Every woman who was able held some type of wartime position. Many joined the army, navy and air force. They also worked in factories on assembly lines. Women did all the jobs men had done. They were well respected and did a great job.

I ended up marrying a returned air force veteran who had served in Ceylon, Holland, Belgium, Germany and France. He saw the Belsen Concentration Camp where he witnessed bodies being put into large pits. He said it was something he would never forget.

🍁 Myrtle Reid

My first recollection of the effects of the war was that mail was not coming from our relatives in England to my grandparents who lived in Ontario. I also remember Mom packing boxes of baking, jam, butter and chocolate for my Uncle Vic Plant who was serving somewhere in England. He was not allowed to give his address so the enemy could not trace their campsites. The letters were censored, as stated on the envelope, but I do not remember any of his written words ever being blotted out.

Gasoline was rationed. But we were allowed enough for one seven mile trip to Brampton and one twelve mile trip to west Toronto to deliver eggs, dressed fowl, fruit and garden produce once a week. One elderly customer even gave me 10 cents for a handful of freshly cut garden flowers every week. There were some hills on the egg route and Mom would shut off the car engine and coast to save gas. New rubber tires were almost non-existent. Every driver carried a repair kit to patch the inner tubes and a hand pump to inflate slow leaks. Farmers were sold gas with a colour additive to use in their machinery. Car owners were fined if caught using the coloured gas.

We did not have enough gas to also attend our regular church, a six-mile trip. So we walked two miles to a community church. During the service, some of the women would knit socks, scarves and mitts for soldiers serving overseas. This caused some controversy, but they argued they were only being patriotic. Individuals would set a goal for themselves of so many units per week, with the wool being supplied by the Red Cross.

Dad canvassed a certain local area selling Victory Bonds; there were two campaigns a year. Some nights he would come home with as much as $200. He entrusted me to carry this to school and at noontime I would walk into the village to deposit it in the bank. What a responsibility on my shoulders. I had to do this secretly without anyone else knowing. Dad was a private man, but years later he told me that a displaced Japanese family who lived in our community were the best supporters of these Bonds. He also told of how he had been sworn to secrecy, but the canvassers had been informed during their "pep rallies" that German U-boats had already entered the St. Lawrence River from the Atlantic Ocean. This encouraged the canvassers to get as many dollars for the war effort as could be persuaded.

I had two cousins who were a few years older than I. They quit school and went to work in factories, building airplanes and making ammunition. In my young eyes, these girls were so sophisticated in their combination coveralls. They wore bandanas to cover their hair. They developed a style of starched front knot for the bandana, which would stand up quite high behind their bangs. There were no silk or nylon stockings, so the gals would paint a brown lotion on their legs, complete with a dark line up the back to imitate a stocking seam.

All the young men in training for the army, navy or air force wore their spiffy uniforms. I was not ready for the sociability of dances and leaves from training and weekend passes. Seeing my cousins swooning and wooing seemed like a fairy tale. They did marry servicemen, but then the reality of overseas duties and the anxiety of relatives missing in action shattered their young dreams.

My parents hosted Farmerettes, city girls and businesswomen who contributed to the war effort by spending their holidays on a farm helping with the manual work. Dad was never too hard on them, but encouraged them to feel good about their efforts.

We got some news of the outside world on the tube radio. When peace was declared in 1945, we drove one and a half miles to visit Grandma Dennis. She had her Union Jack flag waving from the veranda and red, white and blue bunting hung over the doors. She was a staunch Brit. The economy of the country started to improve and everyone's mood turned to rejoicing.

After the war, Europe was coping with displaced persons. Many of their youth immigrated. The Canadian Government located them in rural areas, even though they might have had a carpentry trade and came with their box of tools. These young people were happy to have food and accommodation while learning the English language, finding a place in a community, settling into a new way of life and adjusting to long distance family relationships and homesickness. We hosted two such lads on our farm. They had sailed by boat and I met them at the Toronto train station. They both eventually moved on to other occupations.

Many of our returned soldiers did not talk of their horrendous overseas experiences. My Uncle Vic arrived home safely. He told me that he drove supply trucks in Belgium and Holland, but could not drive at night because headlamps were forbidden. He was supposed to sleep in a ditch. One night when he decided to sleep on his load of sugar sacks flares hit his vehicle. The enemy dropped flares to illuminate the ground so they could see the convoys and villages. Then the next wave of planes could see where to drop their bombs. When he woke up, one of these flares was burning the sole of one of his boots. A bomb dropped on his truck and blew off the radiator.

🍁 Doreen Riggin

I was a Grade 8 student in London, Ontario, at the start of World War II. I was 12-years-old, the oldest of five children. My Grade 8 teacher returned from retirement to replace someone who had enlisted. In geography class, we had a large map and everyone listened to the news for the names of places in Europe. We would then find these places on the map and learn as much as we could about the area. History lessons became more personal and relative to our lives. I think all of the students actually looked forward to these lessons each day.

The news was a large part of our daily lives. Each morning and night the family would gather to listen to the events of the war. Many people were late for work or school on the morning of the Dieppe raid, subsequent evacuations and the D-Day invasion.

During my high school years, we were given classes in first aid, aircraft recognition and uniform designation; as well, air raid drills were conducted. We had periods set aside to knit socks and scarves for the Red Cross. Several of my classmates were children who had been sent to Canada to stay with relatives. Their families wanted to remove them from the dangers caused by the air raids in Britain. Many of their friends had been sent to stay with families in northern Scotland. The British Government instigated this program for the children's safety. Our job was to try to make them feel at home and include them in all our social activities and sports. None of them had ever played basketball or baseball. They all adapted to Canadian life and several immigrated to Canada as adults after their schooling was completed in England.

As the war dragged on, all teens were encouraged to work during the summer months. Students from farms, and others willing to go to a farm, were excused from classes during the latter part of May and the months of June and September to assist with planting and harvesting. Many farmers had enlisted and farm help was badly needed. Women helped out by taking jobs in factories. My dad's unmarried sister took just such a position and remained with the company after the war. She derived great satisfaction from her war work experience and felt she was helping her brothers overseas.

VE Day was announced during school and everyone cheered and threw papers in the air. Schools and businesses closed for the day, but celebrations were tempered with the realization that our military was still abroad and many would still be fighting the Japanese. When VJ Day arrived in the summer of 1945, the factory I was working in closed early and everyone got together and headed for Victoria Park in downtown London. There was a spontaneous street party. The music store piped music outside and conga lines danced along Dundas Street. The buses and streetcars stopped running.

They were not able to navigate through the crowds anyway. My friends and I had to walk about six miles to get home. At work the next morning there were many tired but happy people.

The war years had an impact on our high school years, which in retrospect wasn't all bad. We shared good news and consoled each other during bad times. We were forced to make our own entertainment. With the help of the Kiwanis Club in London, we ran Friday night dances or games (ping pong, checkers, chess, etc.) at our high school so that the kids would have a place to get together. We learned how to be responsible and how to organize supplies and our time. Mostly, it brought home the need for cooperation and how to make the best of each day with the resources at hand.

As a teenager, I felt that the war made us grow up and accept responsibility. I learned to take nothing for granted and that each new day was one to be lived to the best of my ability. Little things that could be done to make the day better for someone also made the day better for you as well.

🍁 Ada Roeper-Boulogne

Although I was born in the city of Haarlem, North Holland, I don't remember much about my birthplace because in 1934 my parents departed for the Dutch East Indies (now known as Indonesia), where my father was installed as a teacher-missionary. The mission was called Safe Haven and was set up to help poor native people find meaningful work. In my memory I see our bamboo house surrounded by coconut palms and banana trees, among which my older sister and I frolicked. Soon a younger sister was born, and later, in a more central part of Java, my brother arrived. On Java, we lived in what was known as The Boys' House, part of a complex of buildings that housed mentally challenged persons. My mother and father had been asked to be the boys' parents. We children lived a rather carefree life, surrounded by mountains and beautiful tropical flowers, but soon rumours of war threatened our peaceful existence.

We found ourselves sitting in front of the radio listening to the announcer reporting the bombing of Rotterdam. Hitler's Nazis had attacked Holland, and since both of my parents were born in Rotterdam, it was an anxious time. The Dutch colony was now cut off from the motherland, but we had our own government, which kept going much as before. However, another threat was looming - the advancement of the Japanese Army. On December 7, 1941, Japan made the mistake of attacking Pearl Harbour in Hawaii. That's when the Americans became involved along with their allies, which included the Dutch Indies.

I had just turned 10 and remember feeling uncertain. Schools were closed. Most of the men were drafted into the defending army. My father was exempt because of his position at the Boys' House. Trenches were being dug everywhere. We wore rope necklaces with a piece of rubber on it to bite on if there was an air attack. In our dining room a makeshift bomb shelter was set up - the table surrounded by iron bedsteads. Refugees from Borneo, a lady and her son, came to live with us. We also had a visit from a survivor of the Safe Haven mission, who told the horrible tale of how it was destroyed by rioters.

In March 1942, the Japanese Army overran the island of Java and occupation began. We watched while part of the conquering army drove into our town, going slowly to save gas. The survivors of the Dutch Army were already interned in prisoner of war camps. Everyone else had to be registered and the Japanese Government began a process of imprisoning all civilian white men.

For a while, life seemed to go on as usual. Over the radio we heard a different language. I was intrigued by a certain song, which seemed to be played over and over again. One day I was happily humming that tune when right out of the blue the lady from Borneo snapped at me, "Your father has just been picked up and you're singing that song?" It turned out to be the Japanese national anthem. I felt so guilty about that! I also had not known that my father was taken prisoner.

My mother went to the authorities to explain my father's position, while my three sisters and I strolled around outside in the town square. When Mother returned, she was horrified to see that two Japanese soldiers had approached us and were taking pictures. They were polite and let us go. Much later we understood what had happened. My mother liked to dress us identically and we wore white frocks with red polka dots on it, which the soldiers probably took to be in honour of their flag. My mother's efforts were successful because my father came back home. However, our joy and excitement did not last long because two months later he was taken to a camp in East Java.

For several months the women struggled on their own without the men, and it was almost a relief in December 1942 when we were transported to our own camp in Central Java. At our destination we walked from the train station to our new abode, each laden down with our most prized and needed possessions. A vivid memory still stays with me of my mother telling us, "Children, watch where you are walking. These are the last steps you are taking on free ground." Although this was not to be true, I have never forgotten it.

We were the first people to occupy that old army camp and we filled three barracks. There were bunk beds inside on which we put mattresses we had been given. For a few days, everyone was busy settling in and then the women got together for a simple Christmas celebration. My mother said that it was the most memorable Christmas she had ever experienced. All I remember is that three neighbour boys, together with us three girls, sang the song "Jesus bids us shine, with a pure, clear light." We were holding candles in the three colours of the Dutch flag - red, white and blue.

I felt lost and forlorn during those first few days in camp, because I could not find my mother anywhere. I finally located her in the camp kitchen where she was helping to prepare the meals in big cauldrons. At first, the food was still adequate, but deficient in protein and certain vitamins.

In the beginning, our camp wasn't totally closed off. We were still able to walk across the shaded town square to another camp, where many of our friends stayed. A big surprise for the children of Barrack III came when some Chinese friends sent a big box of toys. From the oldest child on down, we were asked to choose a toy. I had my eye on a doll with braids, but someone else had the same idea ahead of me, so I picked a celluloid doll. We survived the camp together.

Two of the women started a children's choir and we sang at Easter and on Mother's Day. On Christmas Day, 1943, we went around the camp and sang a different carol at each of the nine barracks. Soon after that, all these kinds of activities were forbidden. Slowly, the camp became more of a prison, especially after the Japanese Army took over the management. Everything became stricter and stricter.

At first we had one schoolroom where the different grades took turns for one hour a day. No Dutch was to be spoken and only Malay taught. This rule was ignored, of course. Then schooling was forbidden. Books too were taboo, so learning had to be hidden. Mothers usually tried to teach the younger children to read, write and count. It was the older children who lost out on their education. We had sporadic lessons from teachers in the camp, but it did not amount to much. We did not have materials either. When we had filled a page in pencil writing, we rubbed it out and started all over again.

We weren't allowed any money, but cigarettes and sugar were hot commodities for trading. My mother washed clothes for other people and received sugar in payment, which she then traded for other things. For my thirteenth birthday she gave me a New Testament with a handmade embroidered cloth cover. I used to read it, lying on my top bunk, praying fervently for the war to end.

Religious services were allowed outside, but no word was to be spoken. So the leader would write out the order of service on the blackboard and would point to each item, so that we could all read the same passage in our Bible together and "sing" the hymns in our head. Sometimes a Japanese VIP would come and inspect the proceedings and sit through the whole service. In our second camp, we even celebrated Holy Communion, or the Lord's Supper, with cornballs and water, because there was no bread and wine.

We heard almost nothing at all from the men. Once in a while we were allowed to send a postcard with prescribed sentences, which were censored, and sometimes we even got a postcard back. People would be happy and think, "At least my husband is still alive," until they looked at the postmark, which might be a year earlier. Radios were forbidden, so we heard no news.

Many rumours did the rounds and once in a while they proved to be true. We had heard that the big civilian men's camp in East Java was to be closed and the men divided between the other camps. A train was supposed to arrive in Ambarawa Station filled with men. Since the tracks were right beside our camp, most of the women went at the appointed time and sure enough, there came the train. But the windows were closed with the blinds down, and after the event was over, the women went back to their bunks, totally deflated.

After the war was over and before we were reunited with our father, we wrote back and forth from our camp to his. In one of his letters he mentioned the train ride. It so happened that he was in one of the toilets at that moment of passing our camp, and there was a little hole through which he could see all the women. He wrote: "Were you also standing there with all those women? Oh, how I wished with all my heart that for one moment I could see you, but the train went by too fast."

Another blow for the women was when their sons turned 10-years-old, they were taken away and placed in the men's camp and it was not necessarily at their father's camp. My father wrote later that he took a lot of those boys under his wing and taught them what he could. But the uncertainty of not knowing what happened to their boys must have weighed heavy on the hearts and minds of those mothers. Luckily, my brother was just under 10 when the war ended.

In general, the women in the camps had a higher rate of survival than the men, mostly because they had the children to take care of and could not allow themselves to sink too deeply into despair. It was interesting to note that many of the Japanese soldiers really liked small children. The commandants of the camp were usually brutal men, but many of the regular soldiers had been forced into the war and probably missed their own children. You often saw them walking around with a string of children hanging onto their hands.

Every morning we had to assemble for roll call and had to count in Japanese. We all had a camp number we had to wear. Mine was 5934. Every time we saw a Japanese, we were supposed to bow and woe to those who did not bow deeply enough; they were often severely beaten. I think we gave most of the Japanese commanders nicknames, such as "John the Hitter." There were days when the whole camp was punished, by withholding food for one day.

On the other hand, sometimes more encouraging things happened. One day, the camp got parcels from the Red Cross. There was supposed to be one for each person, but many had been lost or pilfered. What was left was divided equally between all of us. Yet, we were overjoyed with our one-eighth can of tuna and our one-sixteenth can of beans, and we savoured every bite.

By this time rations were pretty slim - some rice with vegetables, some watery starch and sticky bread. Once in a while we got an egg. My mother had remembered some tricks from the First World War and fed us crushed eggshells as medicine, which we hated of course, but I think it helped save our lives. We moved to our second camp in January 1945. Here we got a lot of indigestible corn for supper and Mother added yeast and made it a palatable dish for breakfast. Soon all the other women stood in line and exchanged a cup of regular for fermented corn to start their own batch. My mother tried this with soya beans too, but the lid of the bottle blew off and everything sprayed onto the ceiling. What I remember most about the second camp is that we were close to the gate and could hear the beatings that some women received, mostly those who dared to speak up like the doctor, for instance.

In June 1945, we were transported to yet another camp, this one close to the coast. From the station we had to walk three hours in the hot tropical sun. When we arrived, again there were beatings because some of the women had hidden money in their underwear. In this camp we felt lucky to be put in a little house, even though our room was only as big as a bathroom. At least we had privacy for a change. While our family enjoyed a certain amount of freedom, the state of things in this camp of 8,000 did not look encouraging. The constant lack of nutrition finally took its toll. People were dying left and right and most of the women looked like scarecrows.

My mother and older sister put their name in for a crew that would work outside the camp, which would earn them a little extra food. One day this crew was sent back without explanation and rumours started flying. That same evening one of my mother's friends came in and started whispering to her. It was then we learned that America had dropped two atomic bombs and that Japan had surrendered. We weren't told this officially until the end of August and we hardly dared believe it.

We didn't know that the war in Europe had been over for three months already. Then one day we heard low flying airplanes and we could clearly see the American flags on them. They dropped food parcels down to us. We finally let go and danced in the streets until we were dizzy. Right away the bamboo fence came down and a brisk trade began with the Javanese people, who wanted our clothes, while we were desperate for the food they offered. There seemed to have been enough food outside the gates, while we were starving inside.

Soon lists of the survivors at the men's camps were posted and happily our father's name was among them. Other people were not so fortunate and the end of the war only brought them more grief. My father was in a camp in West Java and we started corresponding on any little scrap of paper we could lay our hands on. There was no regular mail service, but the Red Cross took care of it. We couldn't be reunited right away because everything was so chaotic, so we had to wait for a transport. Finally in November 1945, after a separation of almost three and a half years, we were brought over to our father's camp. Six months later we were on a boat to Holland, and another five years later we took the big step and immigrated to Canada – the "Land of the Future."

❦ Blaikie Rowsell

Blaikie, Halifax, 1944.

On September 3, 1939, war was declared. That was also the day I arrived in Montreal by train from rural New Brunswick. It was the day my three years of training to become a nurse began. The nurses' residence at the Royal Victoria Hospital (RVH) was a sheltered environment for a country girl in the big city. We were spared any privations the war might bring. Rules and curfews were a part of our life. Classes and long hours on duty occupied most of our time and energy. Upon graduating in September 1942, I decided to remain at the hospital to work in the Operating Room.

My application to join the Royal Canadian Navy (RCN) was accepted in February 1944. Soon I was on the train en route to Halifax; I arrived at 2:00 a.m. At McAdam House, the residence I was to make my home, a friend and classmate from RVH welcomed me. She had joined the navy earlier and was able to direct us to a vacant room. The residence, one of three in the area, was a two-story home taken over by the navy. All rooms were used as shared bedrooms, except the living room, and there was one bathroom shared by 10 or 12 nurses.

The hospital was nearby. Conditions for work were pleasant. Our patients were mostly young sailors from ships coming into Halifax. Few of the patients were seriously ill. There were lacerations, fractures and burns. Respiratory infections were common. We worked with top physicians and surgeons. Life in residence and work at the hospital protected us from the shortages felt by the general public. After a few weeks working on the general wards, I was assigned to the Operating Room (OR).

Nurses did not traditionally "go to sea." However, groups of four or five nurses would be assigned to a ship for one day. In the pre-dawn light of a chilly March morning, we boarded the minesweeper HMCS *Fundy* for our experience. The *Fundy* swept the area outside Halifax Harbour daily to ensure the safety of the convoy of ships arriving or leaving each day. Beyond the gate ships, which marked the harbour entrance, waves of the Atlantic made themselves known. I am not a sea traveller. So after a few hours and an attempt at lunch, I surrendered to "mal de mer," or seasickness. A young officer kindly allowed the use of his bunk for my comfort. We were thankful to return to harbour after a full day ensuring the safety of the shipping lanes. Our understanding of the challenges faced each day by those who served on minesweepers, and other ships of the Royal Canadian Navy, was somewhat heightened.

A second "sea time" experience came with an invitation to spend a day aboard the Dutch aircraft carrier *Gadilla*. The ship would leave port and once it was a safe distance away, the planes would be flown aboard from the Naval Air Base HMCS *Shearwater*. These planes would search areas where the convoy would travel looking for enemy submarines or warships. It was an amazing sight to observe the planes landing one after another, arrested by a cable strung across the deck to prevent them from going into the ocean. Each plane was then lowered into the hangar space below deck before the next one landed. Back in port, *Gadilla* would be ready to accompany the next convoy departing, probably within hours.

In May 1945 when victory was assured there was great rejoicing. At noon the next day I was called to the OR. Sailors in Halifax were out of control, looting and damaging downtown stores. In so doing, lacerations and fractures were sustained. It was 2:00 a.m. before we had treated all injured in need of sutures and such. It was a black day for the Navy. Halifax had been overwhelmed during the war and was not deserving of this mistreatment.

With the end of the war, my OR experience made me a candidate to be transferred to the RCN Hospital at HMCS *Naden* stationed in Esquimalt, British Columbia. In 1948, I returned to Halifax. That summer a group of medical students from Toronto, who had served at sea during wartime, came to work at RCNH Stadacona. One of them, Roy Rowsell had been assigned to HMCS *Warrior*, an aircraft carrier. He would on occasion visit his friends at the hospital where we met. In December 1952 we were married in the Naval Chapel on HMCS *Naden*. It had been a long-distance romance!

🍁 Sheila Sciarra

I was 14-years-old when war was declared and was living on the Isle of Wight in England. I remember listening to the radio and hearing Prime Minister Neville Chamberlain saying that we were now in a state of war with Germany. I was young enough at the time that it didn't seem to upset me that much, but we soon learned that every man, woman and child in England would be affected in some way during the next six years.

I was still a schoolgirl in 1939, but decided that I was going to leave to find a wartime job, which I did much to my parents' dismay. I got myself a job in a factory making barrage balloons. My mother was quite upset. But since I didn't want to go back to school, she quickly enrolled me in a night school to learn shorthand and typing, which I hated. I was now working day and night. So much for my freedom!

My first glimpse of the enemy came early in the war. My family was awakened one night by the sound of the air raid siren. My dad got us all out of bed and we watched from the bedroom windows. We saw an enemy aircraft caught in the searchlights and then heard the sound of anti-aircraft guns. At that point, Dad hurried us all downstairs into a cubbyhole under the stairs, which seemed to be the safest place at the time.

Those of us who lived on the Isle of Wight were usually the first to hear the German bombers going over to Portsmouth and Southampton. These were the two largest ports on the south coast and the cities were in direct line with the island. On their way back across the Channel, they dumped any remaining bombs on the island.

The Isle of Wight was primarily a seaside resort, but we did have a shipyard that built destroyers and an aircraft factory in Cowes, which was where we lived. We were considered quite a target and suffered many air raids as a result. Moonlit nights were the worst. But we also had many raids from dive-bombers that would come in under cloud cover and machine gun and bomb anyone or anything in their path.

We were a happy family – Dad, Mom, my brother David and myself. We all had our jobs to do. After my job at the barrage balloon factory, I got a job in the aircraft factory office. My mother was more pleased about that, but I really enjoyed my barrage balloon workmates. I wasn't in my new office job long when the whole place was bombed one night during an air raid. They soon opened up again and we were all relocated.

Somehow though, I felt that I was not cut out for office work and I wanted to contribute more to the war effort. I applied to the Southampton Borough General Hospital to train as a student nurse. Again, my mother was not too happy, as I would be leaving home to live in Southampton, which was not the safest place to be.

I often thought that mothers were the ones to bear the brunt of the war, as their husband and children were all working in different places or at school. My dad worked in the shipyards, I was away from home and my brother was still at school. He was a Boy Scout and after school he delivered many telegrams that often brought sad news.

My mother was a Northwood Women's Institute (WI) member and the ladies had all sorts of things going on for the war effort. They ran a canteen for the Armed Forces on the island. They had first aid centres and knitting circles organized among neighbours and friends. The government supplied the wool to make socks, scarves, sweaters and balaclavas. At one point, the women canned vegetables and fruit for weeks, anything that could be harvested to help out with food rationing.

During the war, there were many small classes of nurses, which started every three months. There was such a shortage of nurses that they needed to

Sheila (front left) and fellow nurses, Southampton, England, 1943.

get them in hospital wards as soon as possible. There were six of us in my three-month period and we were no sooner fitted out with cap and uniform, than we were put to work. I was assigned to a surgical ward and in my first two weeks of training was already in the operating room. That was an experience I will never forget.

The surgeon asked me if I was a new recruit and when he found out that I had only been a nurse for two weeks, he had me stand beside him while he explained everything he was doing during an appendectomy. We were all assigned to ambulance duty, as well as our regular 10-hour shift. We had to go with the ambulance during air raids, often with only a nurse and a driver. We were learning our nursing skills on the job! In addition, we had to fit in our nursing lectures, which is where my shorthand came in handy.

The most memorable time for me at the Borough General was the D-Day invasion and the weeks following. Southampton was a coastal city and the first casualties of the assault on France were brought to our hospitals as soon as possible. I will never forget seeing all the poor, wounded boys being brought in, stretcher after stretcher. Some were without arms or legs, covered in blood and sand and all with seawater. Some had been blinded. We had been preparing our special wards to receive them, but nothing could have prepared us for what we saw.

There was one young soldier I will remember all of my life. I often wonder what became of him or if he survived. He was a Canadian boy. We knew that because of the blue patch on what was left of his uniform. He was a handsome boy, his face never suffered a scratch, but he had both legs and arms blown away and he was blind. He would not eat and he never spoke. We never knew his name as his dog tags were missing and it was almost as if he was willing himself to die. Needless to say, we were all upset. What a waste of a young life.

There were countless similar cases. The four operating rooms were occupied day and night. Surgeons and nurses came down to Southampton from other parts of England. The wounded were operated on, patched up and sent inland by ambulance to make room for new casualties. We also had German prisoners of war to look after. They were kept separate for obvious reasons, but were treated the same as our own boys. Most were grateful for the care they received, but some were not.

My husband was wounded in the battle of Caen in Normandy. He was not a patient in the hospital where I worked, but I met him while he was on convalescent leave in Southampton. We were married in England in 1945, just after the war ended, and I came to Canada in March 1946. I travelled on a hospital ship with hundreds of other pregnant war brides. I was not long in Thorold, when my husband and I became the parents of triplets – two boys and one girl.

🍁 Lydia Scott

On April 18, 1940, in Lwow, Ukraine, then under German control, my mother, knowing her time was near, attempted to get to the hospital on the streetcar. Someone noticed that my mother was alone and in advanced labour and they brought it to the attention of the conductor. The driver drove straight to the hospital without stops. I didn't wait and was born on the way. Our stay wasn't long. Mothers and babies weren't always safe in hospitals.

Mother told of a nurse who ran through the ward, warning mothers that the next morning someone was coming to take the babies to be raised by "good German parents for the glory of the Fatherland." The mothers quickly gathered their newborns and fled into the night. I too was bundled and whisked out into the chilly night. At the same time, my four-and-a-half-year-old brother was being passed off as girl. He had long hair and wore dresses so the German authorities wouldn't take him away to be trained as a Hitler Jugend or Hitler Youth.

During this time, Jewish people were being hunted down and deported. The decision was made to move us out of the city because life was becoming more and more uncertain. We moved to the small town of Belz. Then one summer evening, when I was about three, disaster struck. I was whisked out of bed, taken to the glassed-in porch and shown the red glow on the horizon. The Russian Army was advancing and the German Army was evacuating villages, then setting them on fire so that nothing useful would be left behind that could help the enemy. The next day, German soldiers came and recruited all able-bodied men into their army; my father was among them. Those who resisted, or were caught hiding, were shot on the spot. The rest of us gathered all we could carry and were herded out of town before it was set ablaze.

The full brunt of the war caught up with us. Without a home, alone with her two small children, my mother wandered over much of Germany, following the German Army to which my father was now attached. Throughout this time, Mother always made sure we had some means of transporting our belongings. A wagon was used until snow made that impossible, then she traded it for a sled. We were on the road during the winter of 1943 to 1944.

How cold and tired we'd become, trudging up and down hills amidst the throngs of humanity, escaping the main fighting and trying to find a safer haven. One day, bundled warmly against the bitter cold, I had been placed on our belongings on top of the sled. Mother pulled and my brother pushed. On a straight stretch, I was taken down and told to walk to restore my circulation and to give my perch to my tired brother. I walked along for a while and then just sat down in the middle of the road. Someone behind us shouted at my mother, who turned to see a tank bearing down the road with me sitting in its path. Mother ran back in time to snatch me out of harm's way. After a warning of how dangerous it was to stop, I again plodded along behind the sled.

With each step I grew more tired and hungry. The last meal had been hours before. I pushed the sled with my eyes focused on the snow-covered road, when I saw a parcel lying before me. This time, I shouted for Mother, who picked it up and tucked it among our belongings. Wrapped inside were two pairs of warm felt slippers and some butter. At the next stop, my mother and brother put the slippers on their cold feet and the butter was spread over hard rye bread. As long as I live, I will never forget that wonderful taste.

As we travelled, many sights became etched in my mind - a lone movie camera, still set up on a tripod, standing beside the fallen photographer; a baby carriage off to the side of the road from which we heard a faint cry, the baby having been abandoned by its mother and no one stopping to help; tiny planes, high in the sky, dropping their load of bombs on a distant city; everyone shepherding their own, moving away from areas where the main bombings were occurring; thick, yellow crayons that I found on the road, left behind by some army unit, and being so happy that I had something with which to colour; my brother's pants made out of canvas were so stiff they stood by themselves when washed; kind people who helped us along the way, with great risk to themselves.

Although we spoke German, our papers listed us as Ukrainian, and that wasn't a safe thing to be just then. One farm we stopped at put us up in a nice warm room, only to be roused and asked to leave during the night before any soldiers arrived. That kind lady gave me a warm pink blanket.

During this time, we hitched rides on trains, hopping on as they moved out of the station. One time, a row of flat cars, known as gondolas, were slowly pulling away, so Mother helped brother up, threw up our belongings and was ready to hand me over to him when someone shouted a warning that this train was on its way to Siberia. My poor brother had to throw our bags off and then jump off himself as the train gathered speed.

Occasionally, we managed to find Father's unit and arranged to stay near him. One day some other children and I were playing in an abandoned searchlight, using it as a merry-go-round, when I was grabbed and hoisted up by a strange man. I screamed and fought against him in terror, until I noticed a gold tooth in his grinning face. It was my father! We spent a few days together before he moved on.

Shortly after, we were in Berlin, trying to board a train. Because of the bombing, we had to hide in the underground tunnels. My brother got separated from us during a raid, so Mother sat me on our suitcases and told me not to move while she went to look for him. Finally, Mother found him under some bombed debris, but came back only to find our belongings. They grabbed the cases and ran farther into the tunnel calling for me. The noise was loud from all of the people crammed in there; Mother was frantic! A Red Cross worker who found me all alone on the suitcases carried me off thinking I had been abandoned. From my vantage point in this person's arms, I saw Mother pushing toward me calling my name. I was crying and trying to get to her as I struggled in my rescuer's arms. Mother finally got to me. My brother told me that I was so filthy from the soot and tears that he didn't even recognize me.

Up in the train station, we had to wait for an empty train. A woman approached us, begging Mother to mind her two boys and baby while she went to get her ticket. She never came back. Hours later, Mother turned the little group over to an attendant. I always wondered what became of those three children.

The summer of 1944 was one of the best times since leaving Belz. Father was stationed in Weimar and Mother found us a place on a farm, just out of the city. The war seemed far away on that farm and days passed in play and adventure. The farmer had a small son about my age who became my constant companion. Father visited us often and during one stay, we all went for a walk, stopping at a creek to rest and eat lunch.

The fighting was again closing in on us. One day we were all ordered out of the house into the barn, while the house was used as a headquarters for a troop of soldiers. Everyone was scared to disturb the soldiers, so we stayed in the loft, only going down for chores and necessities. Because we had to leave the house in a hurry, I forgot my only toy, a little pitcher, hidden in the oven. Wanting it badly, I crept away and boldly marched into the kitchen demanding to get it. All those stories of soldiers harming us fled from me, as these men and young boys let me retrieve my pitcher and loaded me down with sweets and food. Upon returning to the barn, I was severely scolded and warned about what could have happened to me.

Once again, we were in the midst of fighting. While at the train station, looking for passage to safety, Mother was approached by a large woman officer asking why a big boy like my brother wasn't in the uniform of the Hitler Jugend. The officer started to lead my brother away when my mother's fury exploded. She threw herself at that officer and they began to fight on the train platform. Mother was a small woman and got the worst of it, losing some teeth and receiving many bruises. We three remained together, but we were arrested and sent to Buchenwald, a concentration camp just outside of Weimar. We stayed there until we were liberated in May 1945. Father never knew what became of us, until long after the war was over.

🍁 Leona Serbey

World War II started on September 3, 1939, but for Belgium, my homeland, war began on May 10, 1940, when the German Army invaded my country. I was living in Ghent and I was 14-years-old. Listening to the radio, we knew that the German troops were advancing fast. So, as many Belgians did, my family took refuge in France. We travelled through Dunkirk, Calais and Boulogne, but everywhere we went, the German Air Force would bomb us. It was terrifying to spend the night in basements and to hear the bombs falling during the day wasn't much better. The planes would attack the endless lines of refugees. After two weeks Belgium surrendered and part of France was occupied. We were allowed to go back to Ghent. Luckily our house was intact.

After a few weeks, school resumed and life seemed to be normal again, but it didn't last long. The supplies in the stores were going fast and soon every shop was nearly empty. Everything was rationed and although we had stamps to buy food, there was hardly anything to buy. Winter was coming and there was practically no fuel to heat the houses. The only way to get supplies was the black market, and we were lucky that we knew a farmer who would occasionally sell us butter, eggs and milk.

Many Jewish people lived in Ghent; they had moved from Germany after Hitler came to power. They were well educated; many were doctors and engineers. They all had to report to the Gestapo (German Secret Police) regularly and were obliged to wear the Star of David on their cloth. It was terrible to see people tagged. Quite a few Jewish girls attended my school. One day, one of my classmates came to school in tears. The Germans had taken her father during the night. A few weeks later, she didn't come to school and we learned that she had been taken away with her mother. Soon, all the Jewish girls disappeared with their families.

The Belgian Resistance was active, but every time they sabotaged the Germans would take some hostages. Even listening to the BBC was a crime, punishable by prison. In August 1942, the Canadians landed in Dieppe, and we were so sure that the war would be over soon, but unfortunately it wasn't so. But now, we had hope! The highlight of our evenings was listening to news on the BBC with neighbours; the news that was more and more encouraging.

D-Day, June 6, 1944! What a day! The British liberated Ghent on September 6. How happy we were! I remember people kissing and dancing and welcoming their liberators! But that joy was short-lived, when during the night the German Artillery bombed Ghent. Our house was badly damaged, all the windows were shattered and the furniture destroyed. We found pieces of shrapnel in our beds. Luckily we were in the cellar when it happened. The bombing lasted 10 long days and finally the Germans retreated. Ghent was a favourite town for soldiers on leave from the front. Many people, and we were amongst them, opened their houses and their hearts to these brave men.

Around Christmas 1944, the German offensive in the Ardennes Forest of Belgium began and it was feared that we would be occupied all over again. One morning my sister and I were walking, when suddenly the sky was filled with German and British fighter planes. Bullets were flying all over the place and we could see the sparks on the pavement. If it weren't for the people who pulled us into their house, we certainly would have been hit. Finally, the Germans were stopped and the Allies crossed the Rhine on their way to Berlin. The war ended on May 8, 1945.

What a joy! There was music and dancing in the streets for days and nights. And somehow the hardship of the last five years seemed far away. War is so senseless. We thought we hated our enemies, but with time, our enemies became our friends.

🍁 Corrie Slangen

It was 15 days before my tenth birthday. We were living in Sittard, in the middle of the province of Limburg in the Netherlands. The day started as a beautiful spring day, when around six o'clock a.m. we awoke to a huge bang - an explosion. People ran into the streets asking each other, "What was it? What happened?" The explanation came not long after we saw the Dutch Army running and crawling through the fields. They had blown up the bridge by the border crossing. We lived only a few kilometres away from the German border, and before we realized what it all meant, we saw the first German tanks rolling toward the town. War had started.

People ran to the stores to buy what food and supplies they could. Our parents had long talks with us children; there were five at that time aged three to 10-years-old. As the oldest, I was told what and how to do things in case something should happen to my parents. That was the day I became a grown-up at the age of 10.

The war progressed and our daily life returned to a somewhat regular routine, except that we saw the German troops everywhere. We had to blackout our windows, so that at night not a speck of light could be seen. During the night, English airplanes loaded with bombs flew over on their way to Germany. Curfews, identification cards and rationing coupons were initiated. We all had a plastic-covered card on a cord around our neck, which included our photo and personal information. Bit by bit, our lives became more controlled by the Germans. Our nights were spent sitting for a few hours in our basement waiting until the sirens gave the all-clear that the English airplanes had returned home. We heard the shooting of the artillery trying to shoot the planes down.

In 1942, my father, who worked for the Dutch Railways, was transferred to Susteren, a small town not far away. This was the largest railway-shunting yard in the country. My father was placed in charge here, and we lived right next to the rail lines. The war began to get worse. At first we went to school, but eventual had to stay close to home because daytime bombings started and you never knew when the sirens would go off. Our food and clothing was rationed. We grew our own vegetables and potatoes. Our parents had a hard time feeding and clothing seven people.

Being the oldest, I was 12 by then, I had to get up early, as soon as the curfew was lifted. Each morning I had to go to the baker, butcher or grocery store and stand in line to get some of the things that were to be delivered that day. With money and rationing coupons in hand, I waited and waited until it was my turn. We did not always get what we wanted. Many times we were told everything was sold and that we had to wait days until the next delivery. Some days as we stood waiting for food, German trucks would drive up and load all the food in the trucks and we received nothing.

My sister, who was one year younger, and I walked and walked for hours from farm to farm for a few handfuls of grain, bread, a few eggs or some milk. I knew that farmers had lots of things we couldn't get, especially knitting wool. Even at that young age, I was an excellent knitter, so I let them know that I would knit socks, sweaters, hats and gloves for them in exchange for food. The orders came in and I used to knit every minute I could, walking to school, at recess time, on the way home - knit, knit, knit! I had to help my parents. There was no more time for a normal, young life. Our generation went from being young children to being grown-ups.

Then the time came when the few Jewish families living in town were rounded up, put in army trucks and transported to the concentration camps. We also saw long freight trains passing our home, full of people pressed into cattle cars. We found out later they were Jews on their way to concentration camps. I will never forget their hands sticking out of the rail cars as it rained, trying to catch some raindrops.

German soldiers came to our schools to pick out girls to work in the fields to help the farmers. I was selected and I worked for many days in the spring planting and later harvesting. We did this for two years. They were long hard days. When we were not needed in the fields, we went to school. And then the razzias started the roundups. The Germans would go house-to-house and get men, boys and sometimes girls and load them in trucks and take them away to work.

From secretly hidden radios we received news that invasions were being planned; that gave us hope that the war would soon be over. However, that was not the case until June 1944, when the Allied Forces landed in Normandy and started the long fight to overtake the Germans. We were so happy. We felt the end was in sight. But our happiness was short-lived. We had to endure a lot more. The front line stopped about five kilometres from our home.

On November 6, 1944, the Germans posted orders all over town. By noon the next day, the town had to be evacuated. We had to walk to a town 35 kilometres north of us. We left everything behind, except what we could put on or carry. We put clothes over clothes. We loaded the baby carriage with as much as we could, but so that the 2-year-old could still sit on top. My father had a wheelbarrow full and my mother had the bicycle loaded with bags. We waited until the last possible minute, in case the orders were changed. We walked on a snow and ice-covered road. It was one long and silent parade of people; nobody said much and the people cried.

The Germans drove motorbikes and trucks up and down the road keeping us moving. Airplanes flew overhead. The next small town was already empty. The people had left ahead of us. My father's friends gave us the name and address of a family who were willing to take the seven of us and feed and help us. We arrived there late in the evening, hungry and half-frozen. We were taken to a room with a pot-bellied stove, a table and a few chairs. In the corner of the room, they had placed wooden beams to make a box type frame that was filled with straw. That was the bed for all of us for the next three months.

Mom and Dad were happy with the small room. It was better than the cold school basement or some other cold hall with hundreds together. We had enough to eat and drink and we were warm. The German SS (Schutzstaffel) troops occupied another room in the house as an office. When they were there, my father and I had to go into hiding. Otherwise, we would have been taken into Germany to work in the factories. The people who took care of us were in their pension years and made sure we were hidden from sight. How we made it through those three months, I still cannot understand. The Lord was surely watching over us.

On January 26, 1945, we heard shooting. There were small clusters of Germans left in the woods behind the house. The English troops were coming; the last Germans were taken prisoner. We were free at last. Everyone cried and cried. We were so happy. My father had received secret messages on the situation in our town and he knew that our house was gone. So we had to find another place to live. The next day, he spoke with an interpreter to an English soldier. He agreed to drive us all the way to my grandmother's house. My parents had to start from scratch to make a new home for us.

I had really grown up during those years and experiences. Six years later, when my boyfriend and I decided to get married, there was only one choice - leave the country and start somewhere else. Everything was still in turmoil. There was not even a room to be had. You had to put your name on a waiting list for an apartment. It could take years. So we chose to move to Canada, where we have been living for more than 50 years.

🍁 Jane C. Smith

I want to relate my memories of May 8, 1945. I was 12 and in Grade 7 at Aurora Public School. All of a sudden the church bells and the fire bells started ringing. Our teacher Mr. Babcock told us the war was over in Europe!

The staff at the school arranged for all the students to attend church services. When I got to my church, the minister's wife, Mrs. Canon, was ringing the church bells with much vigour. The tears were streaming down her face as she continued her joyous task. It was a bitter sweet moment for her because she knew her only son would not be coming home. He had been killed in action the year before.

I remember seeing my mom sitting in our family pew. My mom was in her father's old pants and shirt because she was doing the family's wash. Our neighbour was also there. She was getting ready to go to the Liberal Women's Convention in Niagara Falls, so she was all dressed up. They were quite a striking contrast to each other, but they both dropped everything and went together to church to be a part of the Victory Celebration.

The best memory of all was when my dad came home after being away from us for four long years. What a great day that was!

🍁 Juanita Snelgrove

When World War II broke out in 1939, I had just finished my education, suffered the death of my mother and became the "homemaker" for my stepfather and baby sister. To a young woman in her twenties, I confess to much personal impatience at my inactivity in the area of "the glamour and dedication of war service."

While the boys I knew so well went off to war and a number of the girls entered the women's branches of the services, I joined the war effort on the home front, unglamorous as it appeared to me. I dealt with ration coupon books and stood in line at grocery checkouts for items in short supply - "Only one to a customer, please." Often, I carried the bag of groceries because gas for the car had run out.

In general, I lent a hand, where and when I was able. I joined The-Hostess-To-The Boys-on-Leave-Brigade. In Montreal, the YMCA held frequent Open House hours for servicemen on leave, as well as at a number of large restaurants popular with young people at that time. The Mount Royal Hotel set up a registry where officers from the various forces could receive invitations to dinner or other social evenings.

I once invited two air force officers to dinner, one from Australia and one from New Zealand. The air around the dinner table got rather hot and heavy when I intimated at the lovely climate they must all enjoy. I knew nothing of their geographic separation! One hotel where I was closely involved provided constant snacks and overnight accommodation for servicemen on leave. While making sandwiches, there were constant battles with "the help" to keep them from using an entire sandwich ration of butter on one slice of bread.

I spent a day a week with the Red Cross unit in the beautiful, ornate ballroom of the McGill University Faculty Club sewing hospital supplies and rolling bandages. What a gracious setting we enjoyed in this magnificent Victorian Montreal mansion, filled over the war years with a battery of all manner of sewing machines and cutting tables.

I packed and sent care parcels to friends in England and boys in the Forces. A lifelong friend in the Women's Royal Naval Service (WRENS) drove navy personnel up and down the coast of Scotland. She was so cold all the time in the damp, foggy weather that I sent her "a bottle of cheer" wrapped in a hollowed out loaf of bread. I continually knit her bed socks and bed jackets, which she said "kept her in one piece!"

As my grandmother was still in her house in the country, I spent as much time as possible with her, especially at holiday times. My younger sister loved these outings, and twice I was able to include a young "guest from England." There were several of these little girls in my sister's class at school. While visiting my grandmother, I joined the Red Cross working unit in the village, sewing and ferrying wool and string back and forth. Grandmother turned out an amazing number of mitts for sailors. The string covering on the mitts kept them from freezing to ropes and gears on the icy seas.

Column after column of war casualties appeared daily in the press. Tears of sorrow and tears of joy were constantly intermingled. Keeping a stiff upper lip was the order of the day. Looking back on those harrowing years, I marvel at how much women on the home front accomplished. I think that I am a stronger person for the experience.

🍁 Doreen Stewart

The scene opened with Ronald Coleman, the dashing, young soldier with amnesia, wandering away from the asylum on Armistice Day, 1918. He becomes disoriented amid cheering throngs of British subjects, only to be rescued by the beautiful and vivacious Greer Garson, who restores him to health and gives him back his life. As an impressionable young woman watching this opening scene from the 1942 movie *Random Harvest*, I vowed, with tears in my eyes, that I would be in England when the

Doreen in uniform.

Armistice was signed for World War II.

The Second World War began on the day I entered nurse's training in Ontario. When I graduated three years later, Canada was sending troops and medical personnel overseas. Nothing could stop this determined young woman from enlisting in the Canadian Army Medical Corps as a Nursing Sister.

When the telegram finally came, I reported for duty at Kingston Military Hospital and was inducted into the army at Fort Henry. Transferring to Camp Borden, I learned how to protect myself in the event of enemy attack or gas warfare. I then went to Debert, Nova Scotia, for vigorous training. There I awaited my commission. All military personnel were sworn to secrecy. I couldn't even tell my mother that I was leaving for overseas. Ironically, my mom worked in Ottawa at a government building registering postings overseas. What a shock it was to see her own daughter's name on the list!

On board the *Empress of Scotland*, it took eight days to cross the Atlantic Ocean because the ship had to steer clear of German submarines. When I finally sailed up the Firth of Forth to Glasglow, I saw the most beautiful sunset I had ever seen - the majestic hills in the foreground and off in the distance, farmers' fields laid out like a checkerboard. Along with five other nursing sisters, I was posted to #18 Canadian General Hospital in Colchester, Essex, in England. We lived in the gardener's cottage at Blenheim House, since there wasn't room for us in the barracks.

The hospital in England was shaped like a spider, so the wards were called Spider A, Spider B, etc. The body contained the nurses' offices and the pharmacy, kitchen, stores and lavatories. On night duty, two orderlies and one nurse were responsible for the care of 120 wounded men. Twenty patients were in each ward, which were the legs of the spider. It made my heart ache when convoys of suffering soldiers arrived at the hospital. Many of them had been wounded long before and were barely breathing. Some of them were in such excruciating pain that they just wanted to die. I not only had to tend to their bodies, but also to their spirits.

As they recovered, the boys were taught to do embroidery, needlepoint pictures, leatherwork and even sewing stuffed animals as part of their occupational therapy. Of course as a nurse, I had set routines to follow and I wasn't about to change the rules. One night, as I was doing rounds, I delivered five large tablets to a young lad who was making a cute stuffed rabbit holding a carrot. Now these tablets were hard to swallow and I knew it would take him some time to get them all down. Since the beds were quite close together, I turned to the patient in the next cot to administer his pills. The giggling from the others guys gave the lad away. As I turned back to him, he was diligently sewing the last little stitches on his bunny. I undid the stitches, and lo and behold, as I reached down with fingers, there were the five tablets still intact. That was one very sheepish soldier!

Although we tried to keep life as normal as possible for the patients, they always feared being blown up in their beds. Invariably, whenever on night duty, my charges and I would hear the roar of a German buzz bomb. We held our collective breath until it stopped and exploded somewhere nearby. Whenever any of the staff received parcels from home, they would have a ward party, sharing their goodies with the guys under their care. When they were not on active duty, the staff played cribbage with the patients to help take their mind off their troubles.

Some soldiers returned to their units when they recovered from their injuries. The more seriously wounded were sent home to Canada. As if the fear and terror on the battlefield were not enough, some soldiers had to endure the physical trauma of lost limbs or eyesight, as well as the anxiety of returning home not quite whole. Many of these soldiers were to spend the rest of their lives in Veterans Hospitals, never again knowing the pleasures of the freedom for which they so diligently fought.

When the war with Germany ended in 1945, I was on leave in Belfast, Ireland. Imagine my excitement as my friend Kitty Brady and I led the parade up the main street of Belfast as the whole town turned out with flags waving and voices soaring! I had the option of going to the Army of Occupation in Europe or the Far East. I opted for the Far East and nursed psychiatric patients on the hospital ship The *Lady Nelson* returning to Canada. Upon reaching Ottawa, I was proud to be asked, along with my Lieutenant Nursing Sister and friend Kitty Brady, to lead the parade on Parliament Hill on Remembrance Day, 1945.

🍁 Gerry Sweezey

I was born and raised in the Netherlands. We lived in a resort area about 20 kilometres northeast of Rotterdam, one of the most densely populated parts of the Netherlands. The Germans attacked our country in the early morning on May 10, 1940. I was not quite seven. I remember waking up early that morning and looking out of our bedroom window and seeing my parents and all of our neighbours standing on the road, watching airplanes fighting over the lake. Most of the people were half-dressed and nobody seemed to worry about the bullets flying around.

We did not go to school that day or for weeks afterward. Everybody was glued to the radio to hear what was going on. I remember being outside later in the day and running into the house as German planes flew over. My mother had a hair appointment the next day and she went to the city on her bike. On her way home, the sirens went off, but Mother just peddled along until she got home. Later on, we realized how foolish she had been. That same day, I saw the first bombs being dropped from an airplane. It was a chain of bombs, which missed the bridge.

The Dutch fought back and there was some fierce fighting around Rotterdam. The Germans had not expected this and told the Dutch that if they did not surrender, they would flatten Rotterdam. While the surrender terms were being worked out, they bombed the heart out of the city. I remember the city burning; there was a downfall of ashes and burnt paper. The Dutch surrendered that same day.

I don't remember too much about the first few years. I know that all our radios were confiscated. I remember my aunt pulled hers apart and hid the pieces all over the house. She had not been married long before her husband got shipped out to Germany. Our men were sent to work in their factories as forced labour to replace the Germans who were in the Armed Forces. My aunt did not see her husband again until the war was over. The thing I remember most about those years is being told to keep my mouth shut. You could not trust anybody. We had several traitors among us. I remember a neighbour down the road who wore a uniform and carried a rifle over his shoulder. He was responsible for several men being sent to work camps in Germany.

Gradually, things got worse. Food became scarce. We got ration stamps for food and textiles. My dad was a green grocer and he was told to deliver vegetables to the Wehrmacht. He told them he could not handle that and sent them to a German sympathizer. As it happened, the local commander was not a hard head, so my dad got away with it. As a rule, the army was easier to deal with than the SS or the Gestapo.

The bombings got worse after the Normandy invasion. We lived about 10 minutes by bicycle from the expressway that ran between Rotterdam and Utrecht. The Allies shot at everything that moved on this road. The planes would fly low over our house and the shell cases would rattle down the roof. The Germans put anti-aircraft guns in imitation houses set among the regular houses in a neighbourhood. At night, they would use powerful searchlights. When a plane got caught in the light, it would get rid of its bomb load, which fell among the neighbourhood. This killed a lot of civilians. I remember waking up in the middle of the night and diving under the bed.

In the summer of 1944, the Germans were all over the place. People disappeared. More and more men were sent to Germany. My father had what was called an "Ausweis." People in essential services got this permit. However, in the latter part of 1944, this did not mean anything anymore and most of the men went into hiding. The bombing by the Allies got much worse. They dropped bombs on every train station, railroad track and bridge and shot at everything that moved. Our local hospital was built in the shape of an "H." The one wing had German soldiers in it. The other side was still used as a hospital. They bombed it but took the wrong wing, so most of the patients died.

The winter of 1944-45 was cold, colder than it had been for many years. We had hardly any fuel. We heated one little room. My mom would not start a fire until shortly before noon. We stayed in bed as long as we could. I would have my young brother in bed with me to keep him warm. My mom had a friend who would bring us some peat blocks. She would bring us 10 or 12 at a time, hidden in bags on her bike.

At that time, the razzias, or German Secret Police, swooped in and searched the houses looking for men. They picked up anybody from 15 to 19 years of age. I remember one morning the soldiers came for my dad. They had bayonets on their rifles and this soldier stuck his under my bed looking for my dad. All the men had hiding places. They did not bother children too much, so people would send them out to warn each other that the soldiers were around. The men they found were marched along the expressway to Germany. This was one way the Germans could move some of their supplies.

This is one of the saddest things I remember about the war, all the people walking along the expressway with soldiers pointing their rifles at them and their wives and children walking alongside. They were afraid they would never see them again. All the men had rucksacks ready just in case they did get captured. The Germans did not give you time to pack a bag.

We did not go to school at all that winter. We had little food. A lot of people died of starvation. My brother, who was about two years younger, and I used to leave the house at 6:00 a.m. and walk for about an hour to get to this farm. We would line up with a lot of other children and most of the time we did get a cup of milk. We would be so proud to take it home to my mom. Sometimes we would be gone for hours, going from farm to farm, begging for milk. One day my brother got a full bottle of milk and I got a watered-down bottle of buttermilk.

We were lucky that my dad had bought beans, peas and chickpeas the summer before. We had dried them in the sun, so we had them in the winter. My grandfather gave us some potatoes. My mother would mix them with sugar beets and make pancakes. Dad also made sauerkraut, which he would sometimes trade for cooking oil, but we had no meat, dairy products, bread or eggs for a long time. People would stand in front of the windows and beg for food. Sometimes, my mother would make up a plate and feed someone, but we had little ourselves.

We all had "water bellies," so we had to go to the washroom many times. My mother would take a large galvanized pail upstairs at night and we would use this like a chamber pot. In the morning, the pail would be full to the brim. One morning, my mother dropped it and everything went down the stairs.

Our village had what was known as a soup kitchen. You would turn in your food stamps and then once a day, you would go and get whatever soup or stew they had that day. A lot of the time, it was awful looking and smelling stuff. People would fight over who was going to get the last bit out of the pot.

Some women would go behind the German lines to get food for their families. They would travel at night and hide during the day. Some came home with bags of grain, but others had it taken away from them. Many a family ruined a good coffee grinder grinding wheat into flour.

I saw the last German plane on New Year's Day, 1945. There were three, flying low over the lake. The Allied planes never stopped; they made a steady drone day and night going over to Germany. They also dropped a lot of leaflets with pictures of Churchill, Roosevelt and Stalin.

Not too long before the war ended, food started to come through from the Swiss Red Cross. We got a loaf of bread, a pound of butter and a pound of sugar. When my mom got home, she made us all a sugar sandwich. That was the best sandwich I ever had. A few days before the war ended, the Allies dropped food from airplanes. We also got army rations from the Canadians. They were large biscuits, which you softened with water, and they tasted terrific.

We all lined up to welcome the Canadians. They threw chocolate bars and cigarettes and everybody was in a mad rush to catch them. We celebrated for days. All the traitors got picked up and jailed. The women that went out with the Germans got their heads shaved and a swastika painted on their baldheads. The Canadians could do no wrong. All the girls and some married women went to entertain them and if a husband or boyfriend objected, nobody paid any attention. If they went to the dance halls to get their women, they would not be let in. Those were wild days!

🍁 Elizabeth Ten Hove

I was a child of 7 at the outset of World War II. The political aspects of the war were beyond my grasp, but the terror was not. At first the only noticeable change was that the German soldiers were heavily patrolling the area. Fortunately, I lived in a rural area at Ofslider Dike, with my parents, two younger brothers and two boarders who worked on the same farm as my father. This farm had five or six cows, but growing seed potatoes was the main crop. Naturally potatoes were our main food source.

Our family was rationed a litre of milk per day and one pig per year. It was a real treat to have butter on Sunday. We had our own produce garden and I helped my mother do a lot of canning. Sugar was scarce, so Mother made her own by grating sugar beets and boiling them down on the back of the old woodstove. Hard, dark brown bread could be bought, but Mother preferred to make her own. She'd make a meal out of ground barley flour boiled with milk. Things got so bad that some people ate tulip bulbs, which were pretty tasteless.

As the war progressed, people came from the cities on bicycles that had rubber strips on the wheels because inflatable tires were no longer available. If you did have good tires, they were stolen. These people went from one place to another begging for food until they had enough to head back to the city. My mother would always give them a big potato.

In 1943, the war was taking its toll. We were without electricity. For light, we put a cork with a wick in a glass of water with a thin layer of oil floating on top. Our only source of heat was the cookstove that was fuelled by wood that I had to scavenge.

It was fairly safe to play outside, but I stayed inside most of the time. I cherished my doll and my toy sewing machine that I got before the war started. I spent hours sewing my mother's cleaning rags together. It only made a chain stitch that could quickly be pulled out. Clothes were scarce; you basically had the clothes on your back. Nothing was thrown out. I remember Mom making me a dress from the curtains. If it could be altered it was; if it could be patched it was - again and again and again!

School carried on as normal until 1942 when the Germans took the benches out. When they took over the school, we held our lessons in a tulip farmer's barn. Later, as things got worse, a group of five or six kids my age would meet in our kitchen on Tuesday mornings. A teacher would give out our assignments for the next week. Church also became too dangerous to attend, so we prayed in our homes.

The Germans were constantly patrolling the roads on their bikes. Occasionally you would see army trucks rumble through, but parts to keep them operating were scarce. The older soldiers were tolerant of us, but near the end of the war young lads around sixteen who liked to throw their weight around replaced them. Thinking back, these youngsters had no place in the war. They should have been sitting around their own kitchen table, doing their lessons and praying with their own family.

I found that the Dutch collaborators, people who sympathized with the Germans, were the worst. They were one of us, but they couldn't be trusted. You had to watch everything that you said or did around them. Everything had to be kept secret. I found out after the war was over that our two boarders were part of the underground. They would sneak out at night and help downed pilots and others get out of the Netherlands via France, through the Pyrenee Mountains and into Spain, which was a safe country.

There wasn't much bombing in our area. The cities were the main targets. Occasionally V-1s or V-2s aimed for England would go off course and land nearby. I'll never forget the day the German soldiers came and told us the Canadians were coming. My mother ran out and put up the Dutch flag, only to have the German patrol take it down again when they made their rounds. It was several long days before the Canadian military arrived. What a moment! What a sight! Seeing the khaki green uniformed soldiers with their white arm bands. There is absolutely no way the joy of seeing these men could be put into words. They were our heroes!

The Canadian soldiers searched the Germans before they were allowed to cross the dike back to Germany. If they had anything like a blanket or scarf, it was taken from them and thrown into the crowd of onlookers. One German had a sleeve of bullets sewn into his scarf. Another had a gun hidden in the bandage on his horse's leg. The Canadians weren't happy with this man and gave him a trouncing and threw him over the dike.

In my heart the Canadian soldiers were so special. I would have loved to carry them on my shoulders. I fell in love with Canada before I knew what it was like. I am now a Canadian citizen and proud of it.

🍁 Bernice Thompson

In September 1939, two things happened in my life. As a young rural 12-year-old girl, I started high school and World War II was declared. There were no school buses, so if you wanted to attend high school you had to stay in town from Sunday night until Friday afternoon. For a few dollars you rented a room and prepared your own meals. The war all seemed many, many miles away. We only heard of the bombings in England on the radio. The lady that I stayed with was English and had survived the bombing during World War I. She impressed me with the horror of it all.

After two years, I went to a larger school a little further away, but the living arrangements were still the same. The war, however, seemed closer as a number of my friends went into the Armed Forces. Each week more of the older students left, along with many of the teachers. The principal was a Major in the local battery, so everyone in the school became cadets. The boys dressed in typical uniform and the girls in navy skirts and white blouses. We trained and trained. We were also expected to join the Red Cross, where we learned first aid and how to knit for the armed services.

When the list of casualties began to arrive, the war took on a whole new meaning for all of us. An air force base was opened nearby, so dances were organized. I was only 14-years-old, so I couldn't attend them. But I did attend the local parties with my friends, which was one of the bright spots in our young wartime lives.

My mother, a middle-aged farm wife, left the farm during the winter months and went to the city to work in ammunitions. This made a big change in my life because after a week away at school, I came home on the weekends and had to do the laundry, baking and cleaning, as my mom only had Sunday off after an exhausting week in a factory. As well, there were a lot of other farm chores that I had to help out with that my mom normally would have done.

My boyfriend joined the army and went to Europe. Now there were letters to write and care packages to send and long waits for mail. Those who were left at home tried to fill our time with knitting and making things for our hope chest. By this time I was working in a bank, a field where only men worked until the war. Also, women and girls wore skirts and dresses until the war, but this changed when women entered factory life and there was a need for the more practical long pants and slacks.

After the war and while I was still working in the bank, one of the local fashion stores received a shipment of silk stockings. Up until then, we had worn those horrible lisle stockings. As there was only one pair of silk stockings per customer, the bank manager let us each go to purchase a pair. While on the subject of feet and legs, wartime shoes were something else! I had a pair that had soles made out of recycled tires. We only had a couple of pairs. We also wore galoshes over these in the winter. Our legs were not the most attractive part of our wardrobe.

In May 1945, the war in Europe was over. I remember the church bells ringing and everyone was so happy. Then the veterans started to return home. My boyfriend returned, but had signed up to go to Japan. His homecoming was bittersweet. Although I was delighted to see him and we became engaged, we knew he would be going away again in one month. Then the atomic bomb was dropped in Japan and the war was over. He still had to return to Camp Borden. There were lots of tearful goodbyes and long lonely walks back to my boarding house, but he would soon be home for good. We were married one year later.

🍁 Fay Timbers

I lived in the village of Westboro, outside of Ottawa, with my family; there were 13 children, 6 boys and 7 girls. I was 6-years-old and going to Broadview Avenue Public School when war broke out. The first we heard of the war was on the radio. I remember coming home from school to find my mother crying because she was from the industrial city of Birmingham, England, and her family still lived there. I didn't know much then about England at that time, but the radio was always on for the war news. All of the children had to sit down and be quiet so that everyone could hear the news.

We were a large, poor family. I had two half-brothers who were old enough for service, and both Jack and Norm left home to join the army. Jack was sent overseas and Norm was stationed at Camp Borden. My mother would always have us sit down in the parlour to read their letters, and then we would all sing the old songs, like "It's a long way to Tipperary" and other war songs of the day. I can remember a letter from my brother

Norm telling us that he had killed a pig with his tank and had to pay for it, but he didn't even get a pork chop!

Rationing didn't affect us too much since we were a large family and had sufficient ration coupons. My mother used to trade coupons with other families in the area. We had chickens and a pig in our shed for meat, but my mother needed sugar for preserving. I remember going to the grocery store early, about seven o'clock a.m. before it opened, to line up for those items that were in short supply, such as butter and fresh fruit. My mother would come later with the babies to pick up the rest of the items.

I can remember being taught to knit at Brownies so that I could knit socks for the boys in the army. I could still hear Mother say, "The war will be over before you get one pair done." During the war, things got better for us as a family because my father was given jobs painting the temporary buildings that were required in the city of Ottawa. When the war was over, my brother Jack and three other boys from our street came home at the same time, so we had a big party.

🍁 Thelma L. Toner

I was born on a new land farm in northwestern New Brunswick, the second child and first daughter in a family of six. The Depression and World War II greatly affected my growing-up years. As a child, I learned to help any way I could. We lived with the barest of necessities, but had great plans and dreams for our future. I believed that hard, honest work would get me the things I coveted. I never once dreamed that war could affect my plans in such a drastic way.

In September of 1939, I was enrolled in a one-room country school in Grade 9. We were fortunate to have a male teacher who could teach the first year of high school. Immediately after the declaration of war, he left us to join the army. The trustees were unable to replace him with a licensed teacher, so they hired a university student who finished out the year.

In order to take further schooling, I had to board in town and my dad paid the tuition for me. I worked for my room and board and passed Grade 10. The next fall, I started studying Grade 11 by correspondence. Because so many young men and women had joined the Forces or left to go work in the cities for the war effort, many one-room schools had no teachers.

The war had not affected my life a great deal at this point. We had ration books for butter, sugar, gasoline, etc. My mother constantly asked us to not use a lot of soap for washing dishes, as it was so hard to find. Neighbours traded coupons if they had some they didn't need. I vividly remember the adults gathering around the battery radio listening to war news. I began to have an uneasy fear as I heard the adults discussing the war and possible consequences. None of my immediate family was involved, but I did have an uncle overseas and several friends my age had enlisted.

As schools prepared to open again in September 1941, several smaller ones had no teachers. The Department of Education came up with a plan. This plan was to go to the high schools and recruit girls who they felt could manage a small, one-room school. I was thrilled to be chosen and I felt I could continue to study by correspondence. I had always dreamed of being a teacher.

At the age of 17, I was sent to a country school with 12 to 15 students. I found a boarding place and walked back and forth a distance of two and a half miles each way. This one-room school was heated by a woodstove, water had to be carried from the neighbours in a pail and the bathroom was an outhouse. I enjoyed teaching, even though I keenly felt the lack of training. I had most of my own schooling in a one-room school with all grades. I watched and listened as the teacher worked and so I had an idea of how to find time for all grades.

While teaching, I found wartime presented me with some new problems. My ration book had to go with me and I felt I wanted to dress well. Some items of clothing were not easily obtained. It was almost impossible to buy nylons, underwear and other necessities. I was lonely too, as most of the young people were in the service or the war effort.

When my first year of teaching was over, I was overjoyed to learn that we "pinch-hitting" teachers were to have a summer crash course at Teachers College in Fredericton, all expenses paid. I passed my exams and was granted a War Emergency License. This license was extended every six months on condition that I carried out my responsibilities well. Usually that meant a visit from the inspector of schools to evaluate my work. I don't remember much about these visits, except that we were always given the rest of the day off.

I worked for the next two years in a different school. My mother kept in touch by mail. I missed my family, especially my two younger sisters. My parents wanted to come and get me for a weekend or holiday, but often there was no gas for the car and tires were impossible to buy. I began to feel a great deal of frustration. There were always drawbacks to getting where I had dreamed of going.

I discovered a unique way of getting home. I would walk to a small, nearby CN station where the stationmaster would flag down a train for me. He stood on the track and waved a kerosene lantern. The train would stop; I would board and get off at a station close to home.

Getting paid was also a problem. My wages were $35 per month and that often depended on enough taxes being paid. At times, my landlady would have to wait for the $2.50 per week that she charged. We managed by helping each other and knew that once war was over, things would improve.

There was great excitement when boys came home on leave. This usually called for a party. The family I boarded with at this time had only one son who was in the air force. They received word that he was missing and had probably gone down in the Atlantic. As I watched them grieve and saw their tears, I realized for the first time what a huge sacrifice some families made.

I watched the older women knitting gloves, socks and hats to put in parcels for our men and women in service. Now that I had some money of my own, I took note of posters encouraging us to buy War Bonds. I wanted to do more and decided I could contribute by writing newsy letters to soldiers from our community. I had a number of stamps stored in a new envelope and mistakenly sent a letter off in it. Later on, in one of my mother's letters to me, I was mortified to read the following, "Vernon thinks you must be very anxious to hear from him because of all the stamps you sent." Of course, news travels fast in a small community. This was a boy I was not especially fond of and the embarrassment cured me of my desire to write letters for the war effort.

There was great happiness on VE Day, which was also my birthday. I remember my teen years as full of dread and worry and also too much responsibility. Limited resources had kept me from realizing my ambition. One of the benefits of the war years was that I had ten years of teaching courtesy of my War Emergency License. One of the lifelong benefits of living through the war years was having learned how to be resourceful.

🍁 Ann Vandenbosch

During the Second World War, I lived on a farm in the Netherlands. I was 7-years-old at the beginning of the German occupation of our country. In anticipation of the war, around the time that Germany invaded Poland, Holland mobilized its army, including my father. On April 12, 1940, my mother gave birth to her sixth child and my father was given special leave from the army. His leave was short-lived, however. A few days after my brother's birth, Dad learned via a special news bulletin on the radio that all soldiers on leave were to report back to their stations with the first available transportation, because war was imminent. So Mom was left with six small children and a farm with livestock. She did have help in the home and her brother sent his hired man to help with the farming.

The Germans invaded Holland on May 10. In a few short days the fighting was over and the Netherlands, like many other countries, was under German occupation. As a result of the fighting, all communication services were out of order and Mom did not know where Dad was, or if he was still alive. Those were terrible days of uncertainty. Many soldiers had been killed, and many more had been put on ships to be taken to England.

Since there continued to be no news about Dad, one of Mom's brothers

*The farm (1942) where Ann lived during the war. The straw stack
where the downed RAF pilot slept for two nights is in the background.*

and a brother-in-law decided to go looking for him. First, they biked to the
place where Dad had been stationed, and started asking questions. At every
place they were told the same thing - the soldiers have retreated to the next
village. They kept bicycling and kept asking questions until they finally
found him, halfway across the country. What a happy day that was for Dad,
to see his relatives and find out that everyone at home was alive and well.
My uncles returned to our place to bring the news that they had found Dad
and that he was in good health.

Dad was still with his same unit, but they were now forced to serve
Germany and their fate was in German hands. Within a few days, however,
word came that the farmers among them could go home. The German Army
needed to be fed I guess. Dad arrived home on May 27 and life returned to
normal, as far as that was possible under German rule.

This was the beginning of the war for me, but the story I really want to
talk about happened in 1943. With the German occupation, civil servants,
just like the soldiers, were suddenly serving a different government. Most of
them were not happy about that, but had no choice in the matter. Almost
instantly, a network of underground workers was created to work against the
Germans whenever possible. Civil servants who joined the underground
were terrific assets because they had inside information, which was key for
any kind of sabotage. Because the civil servants were ostensibly working
for the Germans, the occupying forces were satisfied if all irregularities and
special incidents that ordinary citizens came across were reported. From a
Dutch perspective, with luck, these ordinary citizens were reporting to civil
servants who were also members of the underground.

On May 30, 1942, the Allied bombing of Germany started. One thousand
bombers went on that first mission to bomb Cologne. Almost every night,

throngs of airplanes flew over our area on bombing raids to Germany. The sky would be full of planes. The Germans shot at the planes with anti-aircraft guns; many airplanes were shot down and went up in flames. The crew would jump with parachutes taking the risk of being captured by the Germans. Many got back to England safely via the strong underground organization.

Helping these pilots was a great risk and anyone caught in the process was most likely killed by the Germans. Dutch citizens who encountered a Royal Air Force (RAF) pilot were required by the Germans to report him immediately to the local police. My mother had always said that if she ever came in contact with a pilot, she would report him to the police. She said, "However badly I will feel about that, the risk is too great."

Most everyone knew that an underground organization existed, but many citizens did not know who these people were. Dad had once travelled with our local police officer, Constable Derks, who told him that if he were ever in a situation to need the underground, to come and tell him. He said, "Then you have done what the Germans want and I will look after the rest." Well, it happened!

On a Saturday evening in November 1943, around seven o'clock p.m., there was a knock at our door. I was 11 at the time and I opened the door. There in the dark stood a stranger who said something I could not understand. When Dad came to see who was there, he heard the man say RAF. Dad knew immediately what that meant. Our visitor was an English pilot. Dad let him in and locked the door. At the time, Mom was busy putting the younger children to bed. By that time there were eight of us - the youngest six months and the oldest 12.

Dad told Mom to put all of us to bed right away, to lock the door and not to open it for anyone. He would go by bike to inform Constable Derks. He left, and there was Mom with eight children and a frightened English pilot who did not know where he was or what was going to happen to him. My parents did not speak a word of English at the time. So we were all rushed off to bed and Mom told us never to talk about this to anyone. The three oldest, including me, understood it all too well. After we were in bed, Mom tried to feed her pilot. She offered him a sandwich and a glass of milk, but he seemed nervous and did not take anything.

Dad did not fare so well. The people who boarded the police officer did not open the door. At the same time, someone came to our door and, of course, Mom did not open it either. So Dad decided to find the neighbour's son Leonard who was engaged to the daughter of the family where Constable Derks boarded; surely they would open the door for him. They did, but informed him that the police officer was on leave. Dad was in a predicament and explained to Leonard why he needed the police officer.

Constable Derks had advised Leonard as well. If something unusual happened when he wasn't there, he advised going to Mr. Robbers, who lived in the next village. Dad bicycled on without light because curfews were in place and we weren't allowed to be out so late. Mr. Robbers came to our house riding on the back of Leonard's bike. He spoke English, so he at least was able to finally put the pilot at ease. Mr. Robbers told him that he was with good people and that they were working on getting him back to England. The pilot relaxed, drank the milk that was still standing in front of him, lay down on the couch and fell fast asleep.

Mr. Robbers went to the police in his village, hoping the police would take the pilot and know of a way to get him to freedom. That way Dad, Leonard and Mr. Robbers would have done their duty as required by the Germans - handed him over to the police. But that police officer didn't dare take the pilot. He said, "I will never let on if you try to get him to freedom, but I won't help you." He added, "I would feel a lot better if I had never known about it." He wasn't the only one! So this second plan failed and far too many people were involved in the situation.

Mr. Robbers then contacted the town clerk and a friend, both of whom belonged to the underground. They arranged a temporary secret hiding place for the pilot who was taken there by bike later that same night. The pilot explained to his liberators that the compass in the plane didn't work after they were shot and they weren't even sure which country they were flying over. He had a small map the size of a handkerchief and on that he pointed everything out. When the plane began to fall, they all bailed out. He fell near a small wooded area close to our house, where he had hidden for two days. At night he slept on the straw stack near our house. The pilot was only 19-years-old and came from Dover. For safety reasons, we were not given his name and he was not given ours.

The two underground workers had noticed how frightened Mom had been through the whole ordeal. They thanked both Mom and Dad for the good deed they had done and said that they would be rewarded. At the time, Mom had a 16-year-old girl helping her with the housework. She happened to be staying over at our house that weekend. Like the rest of us, she was also sent to bed and told to never talk about the experience to anyone.

The next day, Sunday morning, the police officer who refused to be involved came to our house to talk to the three older children and Mom's helper. He warned us to never mention the pilot to anyone. He said that if the information ever came out, we would all be shot. I was convinced; I would never talk about it.

From the underground, we later learned that "our" pilot had returned safely to England. Three other crewmen were hiding in a nearby barn, where the farmer found them standing behind the cows. We heard that the farmer had given them clothing and that they tried to find freedom dressed as civilians. Whether or not they were successful, we never heard.

After the war, Dad received a citation from the Dutch Government, thanking him for services rendered to the Allied Service Personnel during the German occupation.

In 1953, our whole family - ten children by then - immigrated to Canada.

Not much was ever said or thought about our pilot. We had far too many new things to learn and do.

In 1984, however, the memories were unexpectedly revived. A niece of mine was on vacation in the Netherlands. At one stage she met a man who came from the same village as we did, so she told him her mother's maiden name. "My father," the man said, "picked up a pilot at your grandparents place during the war." The man's father was the town clerk!

When my niece returned to Canada, she brought along the name and address of the famous pilot. I wrote to him immediately, thankful that we no longer had a language barrier. Here is how he described his return home: "I remember having to leave your home because the risks were too great with so many children. I was taken via the escape line to Eindhoven, from there to Brussels and Paris. After crossing the Pyrenees into Spain, I was taken to the British Embassy in Madrid, and from there I went to Gibraltar, finally arriving home on January 4, 1944."

My parents were still living at the time, and were delighted to hear first-hand that the pilot had made it home safely and survived the war.

🍁 Wilhelmina Vanstrien

I was 9-years-old when World War II started. I lived in the southeast part of Holland in Gemert, near the German border. When the Germans invaded Holland, we were evacuated to a safer place about 10 to 15 kilometres from our farm. Because the bridge had been blown up over the canal, we crossed a small footbridge by foot or bicycle. The people did not have beds for us where we were billeted, so we slept on the wooden floor, with only a blanket. It was very hard! My dad stayed behind and took care of the home farm; nothing happened there, so after a few days we got to go home.

During the four years under German rule, we had bombers coming over from England. They flew over around two o'clock a.m. and returned home between four and five o'clock a.m. Some planes were hit and some times they were on fire. In one 10-week period in 1943, we had seven planes downed in our area. One of the planes still had its bombs loaded, which exploded in mid-air, killing all on board and spreading the whole plane in pieces over a wide area. It looked bad! There were body parts hanging in the trees. Some of our windows in our house were broken. We were still in bed, but at once we were wide-awake and frightened. These bombing attacks occurred throughout 1943 and 1944.

In September 1944, the Canadian and English had their cannons positioned near our house aiming for a town where the German troops were held up. When they let the cannons off, we were rocked back and forth on

our chairs. This went on until they had conquered the town; the whole town was in ruins. In October 1944, Canadian and English soldiers were stationed in our yard and fields for two to three weeks until they moved on.

Wilhelmina (second from right, front row) and her family posed with some Canadian soldiers.

🍁 Daisy Wannamaker

A soft gentle rain was falling on William David Street in east end Montreal on that evening in September 1939 when war was declared. I was walking home from my girlfriend's house and my tears were falling with the rain. I had a terrible foreboding that our lives would never be the same again. I was 16.

I was still in high school and graduated in 1940. I lived in a flat on Ste. Catherine Street with my mother, father, one older and two younger sisters. My father was a diesel engineer employed by the Molson family on their private yacht. I went to business college after high school. I started working at 17 as a typist at the head office of the largest insurance company in Canada, the Sun Life Assurance Company.

Employees from different departments of the company took on various volunteer jobs to help out the war effort, including selling War Savings Stamps, acting as Air Raid Wardens and taking First Aid Courses. The main volunteer effort, however, was entertaining servicemen twice a week at dances at the Red Triangle Club run by the YMCA. The Thursday dance ran from 8:00 to 10:30 p.m. and the Saturday one was held in the afternoon. The Club was in Philip's Square, downtown Montreal, close to Eatons, Simpsons, theatres and the main CNR Station.

The "Y" attracted all the servicemen – Aussies, New Zealanders, Free French, Poles, Brits, a few Americans and, of course, all of our own military. There were several rules that had to be followed. We had to wear white blouses and dark skirts. We were not allowed to leave the canteen with a serviceman, so instead we'd just say, "I can meet you at the corner later." And we could not refuse to dance if we were asked, even if the guy was shorter than you. The Brits were the best dancers. You could always pick them out – mostly air force. "Swing" was in, so was the "jitterbug." The band consisted of piano, sax, trumpet and drums.

If anyone became a little rowdy, they were escorted out the door. Refreshments were available at minimum cost, but alcohol was not served. On the whole, it was a respectable place, and most times you met someone interesting and enjoyed the company. Many were lonesome I suspect; some were merchant seaman who had just gone through some harrowing experience. But on the whole they didn't elaborate on what had happened to them. They were there to have fun and meet the local girls.

Often my mother would call the "Y" and invite two or three servicemen for Sunday dinner. They appreciated my mother's good basic cooking and the girls looked after the dessert. The conversations focused on their countries and families, how long they'd been in the city and did they like it? Warnings not to divulge information were seen on billboards everywhere. We took that seriously, so you kept to general topics.

I volunteered as an Air Raid Warden. After some training I was issued a hard hat, a flashlight and an arm band with "Air Warden" on it. I was assigned a block in the downtown. All lights had to be off, or dimmed with curtains. I remember one instance where a couple was going through some lovemaking and it was rather embarrassing. You had no recourse, you just had to observe the "lights out" rule and then leave.

Daisy as an Air Raid Warden, September, 1943.

Going to the movies was our "life." In Quebec you had to be 16 before you were allowed into a show. But, if you were tall, wore lipstick and high heels, the teller overlooked the age barrier. I never knew anyone that was refused. We saw maybe four movies a week. There were always two films on a program. You could stay and watch them over again. The cost was 12 cents during the day and 25 cents in the evening.

My father enlisted in February 1941, and was immediately granted the rank of Chief Petty Officer in the Canadian Naval Reserve. After basic training, he spent most of his time on the East coast, including Newfoundland and the Eastern seaboard of the US. The ships were minesweepers and the odd converted yacht, all armed with depth charges. At times they encountered submarines. In freezing temperatures, the heavy seas iced up the ship so badly that it had to be chipped off with axes for fear of sinking. We were always writing Dad letters to keep him happy. He was good at writing back.

On January 1, 1943, Dad's name appeared on the King's Order List published in the *Canada Gazette* as being mentioned in despatch for distinguished service; his name was sent by the Minister of National Defence for Naval Services. He was able to straighten out a bent shaft and stop the ship in dangerous waters within close proximity to submarines. For this he was given an Oak Leaf to be added to his war medals.

While my father was gone, my mother had four girls at home. We were well trained in housework and were taught sewing skills and some cooking. So when my mother died suddenly at 45, we were on our own. We had no relations, all were in occupied Holland, but we had many friends. My dad was granted compassionate leave for a time and spent the rest of his career installing engines in our ships being built for the navy in local dockyards.

October 15, 1942 – I remember it well. I spied six soldiers striding in together. They seemed to have a distinctive bearing. They had flashes I had never seen before – "S" for Surveyor, a small diamond red patch that denoted attachment to the Artillery Regiment. We knew all the badges, insignias and ranks going, so it was an easy way to start a conversation. Montreal was in close proximity to many bases – army, air force and navy - and many men gravitated to the clubs that were free, and also provided some recreation. They could play pool, write letters, play cards or just relax.

The six men were taking a course relating to the Survey Regiment to which they were attached. They were billeted at the Motordrome on Sherbrooke Street. I don't suppose many had been in Canada's largest city before, a rather lively place to be stationed for two and a half months.

We met in a "Paul Jones." There were always too many girls in a circle, but when I turned around here was a chap, 6 feet, 3 inches tall, by the name of John that made that evening memorable in a way that changed my life. One thing you never did at age 17 or 18 was to get serious. We were too young for that and, after all, it was wartime, "Here today and gone tomorrow." I met John several times after that. He came to our flat, stayed for meals, met my folks, was polite and inclined to be shy. He had a farm background in Ontario. He had two brothers, one in the army, and a sister. He was 23. When it came time for his group to go overseas, we agreed to write. I still have two bundles of letters, his and mine. I must say we got to know each other that way.

While in England, John couldn't adjust to the diet, became ill, was hospitalized and then sent home. He was based at Fort Frontenac in Kingston waiting for discharge, which came in April 1944. We had become engaged on Valentine's Day with plans to be married in August. It became imperative that I meet his parents. The first thing his mother asked me was, "What colour are your eyes?" And coming from Quebec she was a bit curious as to my religion. After that we took a drive to the farm we'd be buying from his dad under the Veterans Land Act. They encouraged farmers to go back to the land.

Farming was a new venture to me, but youth was on my side; I was only 20. We worked hard and it was a good life.

🍁 Klazina Wasylycia

In May 1940, when the war in Holland started, I was 17-years-old and living in the small town of Assen in the province of Drenthe. I remember the first day of the German occupation well. All the bridges over the canal were blown up and we had to cross in a small boat to get to work. I was working in the office of a publishing company at that time, where the equivalent of the *Home and Country* was published; it was called *De platte lands vrouw*.

That same year, my mother died, so it was a difficult time for us – my dad, my sister and myself. We had to learn fast how to do housework and deal with the ration cards for food and fuel. Because we lived in a rural area we were never hungry, like so many people in the western part of Holland. There were always potatoes to eat. During the five years of German occupation, however, things gradually got worse. It was a fearful time. Friends were taken away to concentration camps or to Germany as slave labourers.

In 1944, we had hopes of being liberated. The Allied troops had reached the southern part of Holland, but it took another six months before the rest of the country was free. Some people from the southern parts were evacuated to the north, where we lived. I had joined the Red Cross and it was our task to look after these people. Finally, in April 1945, the Canadian Army liberated us. It was a time of celebration. How good it felt to be free. People came out of hiding; even some we thought had been killed.

Canadian soldiers were welcomed everywhere. Some of them were stationed across the road from our office. This caused quite a bit of excitement and curiosity among the office staff. One of the Canadian soldiers, after finishing his guard duty, walked into our office and introduced himself as Harry Wasylycia. Some interesting conversations followed as we were trying out our high school English. From then on, Harry was a regular visitor. Neither of us had seen any movies for a few years, so Harry invited me to see one and we started dating.

Harry stayed in Holland as long as he could, but had to leave with his regiment, the Governor General's Horse Guards, in December. We promised to write each other, which we did for a year and a half. After

Klazina (right) with her sister and father in Rotterdam before leaving for Canada, June, 1947.

Harry returned to the family farm in Alberta, procedures were started for me to immigrate to Canada. In the meantime, I travelled with the Red Cross to accompany a trainload of undernourished children from the western part of Holland to Denmark where food was more plentiful. The children stayed for a couple of months, but we came back in a few days.

In May 1947, I received word that a place would be available for me in June on the first immigrant ship to leave Holland after the war. My trip on the *Waterman*, a troopship, would be at my own risk. Now I had to make the final difficult decision to leave my family. With only a month to get ready, preparations had to be made in a hurry, like medicals, official papers and baggage. On June 17, 1947, with my family seeing me off at the port of Rotterdam, I left for Canada. The trip took 10 days. The ocean was rough, accommodations were poor, I had to sleep in a bunk bed and stand in line for food.

I was seasick and homesick and vowed to go back home as soon as possible. We arrived in Montreal on June 26 and before disembarking I had to arrange travel to my destination.

From the boat we were taken by bus to the train station in Montreal. We had a lot of time to spend there. I remember buying oranges, which were still not available in Holland. This was the first immigrant ship to arrive in Montreal and there was some confusion. The train conductor had trouble communicating with the large Dutch families going West. They asked me to make some announcements over the intercom regarding travel accommodations.

Harry had moved from Alberta to Kitchener. However, not knowing the difference between CP and CN, I ended up in Galt, where Harry was waiting for me. He was working at Uniroyal and boarding in Kitchener. I stayed in a hotel in Waterloo. We were married on July 26 in Kitchener, with only a few of Harry's cousins present.

❧ Mae Wayte

I was 19 and working in Napanee doing housework. I had been going with a nice boy for three years and we were thinking about getting married and enjoying life. When war broke out and he enlisted, we decided to get married and have some time together. I went with him to Peterborough where he was stationed, then to Petawawa. He went overseas from there, and I went to my parents in Newburgh for a few months until I gave birth to twins, a boy and a girl.

I was lucky to have a loving mother and sister to help me. When the children were a bit older, I bought a house because I always thought renting was a waste of money. My sister went with me to help with the children. The Gibbard Furniture Factory in Napanee got an order for shell boxes, so they needed more workers. My sister didn't want to work out, so she kept the children. I worked there for a couple of years and got my machinist papers. I had to quit when my sister got married. Then I rented some rooms to a newly married couple until they could find a house and I took in a friend when she started working in one of the stores in Newburgh. I managed pretty well throughout the war. I had no husband to help me and the children had no father for almost four years.

When the war ended, my husband wrote that he wanted to buy a farm. He said he had enough of being told what to do and when to do it. I got a chance to sell my house, so I had $1,000 to help out. Along with help from the Department of Veterans Affairs (DVA), we got a nice farm just west of Napanee.

One thing I found about wartime was that women were able to get jobs of all kinds and had more freedom in the workplace. Many will think it was a dull life. Maybe so, but it was a busy one. I was lucky to have my husband come home safe and in one piece. His nerves were not too good for a while, but otherwise he was fine.

❧ Joyce Anne Welch

I can remember quite clearly the day that World War II began. It was 11:00 a.m. on Sunday morning September 3, 1939. My face was covered in soap and my mother said that the Prime Minister was about to make an important announcement on the wireless. So I quickly rinsed and dried my face and went to hear what was being said. In a solemn voice Prime Minister Neville Chamberlain told the whole country that Britain was in a state of war with Germany.

I was 15-years-old at the time and like most young people had no idea how this war would affect my life. But my parents, having experienced World War I, were shocked that this could be happening all over again. Our home was in the County of Kent in the small town of Strood, on the north side of the River Midway. The city of Rochester was on the south side, and that part of Kent through to the coast was known as "Hell Fire Corner" during the war. We were directly across the English Channel from the French Coast, and so were the closest to what became the enemy's front line.

The first time the air raid sirens sounded, it was a rather scary experience. I remember the large air raid shelter that was built of concrete at the end of our street, inside the grounds of the Workman's Club. My sister and I used to stand outside watching the fighter planes dogfighting, until our mother insisted that we come inside the shelter.

Later on, corrugated iron shelters were put in the back gardens at each house, and that is where we spent a lot of nights when the air raids were really bad. My sister and I were always the last ones to get out of bed and go into the shelter. One night, we had just left the back door when large pieces of shrapnel started to fall; luckily we were not hit by any of it. Another time an unexploded bomb landed in the middle of the road at the top of our street. The people living close to it had to evacuate their houses until the bomb squad had defused it.

Having just left school, my first job was in a small store. From there I went to work in the Short Brothers Aircraft Factory, where the big Sunderlands, or "Flying Boats" as they were called, were built. This was classed as essential war work. In 1942, after I turned 17, I told my parents that I wanted to join the air force. I don't think they were too happy about it, but they finally gave their permission. Six months later I went for my medical and became a member of the Woman's Auxiliary Air Force (WAAF).

This was my first time away from my family and it was quite an experience for a young girl. But I found that most of the girls that I met were just the same. The first place that we were sent was Innsworth Lane in Gloustershire, where we learned to march in formation on the barrack square. What a sorry sight we were when we first arrived! After about six weeks of training, we were marching along and saluting with the best of them.

When I joined the WAAF I had wanted to be an MT driver. But in 1942, they had all the drivers they needed so I had the choice of being a cook or doing general duties. I chose to be a cook. After leaving Innsworth Lane, I was sent to Melksham in Wiltshire. I had helped my mother with cooking at home, but this was another eye-opening experience for me and for everyone. I had never seen such large amounts of food on such large boilers and in such large ovens. Again, in the space of about eight weeks, we learned enough to be sent to our first posting and we parted company with the friends that we had made.

My first permanent posting was at Detling, near Maidstone in Kent. I was within a one-hour bus ride from home. The airdrome at Detling had been bombed about two weeks before I arrived, so the MT section was moved about two or three miles from the main camp. That is where I was sent to cook for the drivers and mechanics. The cookhouse was small and we were billeted with some local people close to our work. It was ideal for me. I was able to get on a bus and go home whenever I had time off, and best of all I spent my eighteenth birthday with my family.

Unfortunately my run of good luck being posted so close to home did not last long. By mid-December I was on my way to the "Home of the Air Force," Cranwell in Lincolnshire. There were quite a lot of new arrivals from different parts of the country at this time and most of them were not too happy about being posted just before Christmas.

The camp was huge and there were thousands of RAFs (Royal Air Force) and WAAFs. My billet was a Nissen hut at the west camp. There were rows of these corrugated iron huts and about 20 girls to each one. The only heat was a black pot-bellied stove halfway down the hut and over to one side. If you were lucky enough to have your bed close to the stove, you were quite warm. If you were at either end, you spent a lot of chilly nights with your great coat on top of the bed for extra warmth. The bathhouses were a revelation - a large hut divided into cubicles with a tub in each one and no heating at all. You had to line up to have a bath, and if you were lucky the previous bather had cleaned out the tub.

The only times that I encountered the V-1 flying bombs and the V-2 rockets were when I was home on leave in 1944, while I was stationed in Wales. My family told me about them, but until I heard and saw them myself, I could not have imagined how much fear they caused. The sound of the engine was loud. But when the motor cut out, the bomb fell at that spot and the loss of life and damage was devastating.

My next posting was to Langham in Norfolk. It was while I was at this station that the war in Europe ended. We knew that something important was happening. The sky was dark with planes flying overhead for days. Then on May 8, 1945, it was announced over the tannoy that the war in Europe was over. It was VE Day. Of course, there was a lot of celebrating in all parts of the camp. From that time forward the pace of the war slowed down, at least in Europe, and everyone began talking about getting back onto "Civie" Street.

People were being posted all over the country from Langham. I was on my way again. This time to Devonshire; Torquay was my destination. This was a beautiful place. We were billeted in big hotels and worked in bigger ones. My workplace was the Grand Hotel right on the seafront. What a difference from all of the other camps. Most of the hotels in Torquay and the smaller places in the area had been commandeered to accommodate the many Canadians who were arriving daily. This was a repatriation station for Canadians on their way home. I worked at the Grand Hotel for about two months and was then sent to a small town just outside Torquay called Babbacombe. The hotels were much smaller there, but the work was the same. The Canadian boys went through on their way home.

After a week at this new place, I met my future husband in August 1945. We got engaged at Christmas and I went home to tell my parents that I was getting married. We were married on February 22, 1946, and so I became a Canadian war bride. Just before we were to be married, I was posted again to a camp in the Midlands. My future husband went to Germany. From there I was sent to a Demobilization Camp, and so ended my air force career. I went home to await my husband's demobilization order. After the order came, we had a month together before he left to return to Canada. I followed him in September.

❦ Patricia Woodruff

I lived in a small village near the city of Croydon, southeast of London. In 1939 I had just completed a secretarial course and had started my first job in London in September. This entailed a journey by bus, train and another bus. But most young people gladly paid the price in time and expense to work in the most glamorous city in the world!

The radio, newspapers and newsreels at the cinemas showed gigantic rallies of Hitler Youth saluting and chanting "Sieg Heil," as well as Hitler's ravings and threats. On a sunny Sunday morning in early September, the whole country sat anxiously listening to their radios at 11:00 a.m. to hear that we were at war. A few minutes later, we heard the air raid siren for the first time, but fortunately it was a false alarm.

Certain measures went into effect right away. Everyone was issued a gas mask that you were required to have with you at all times. Children in the London area were evacuated to country villages and towns. Anderson air raid shelters were supplied to each household to be erected in your backyard by excavating three feet, installing the corrugated steel and then covering it with sandbags. They were designed to take damage from blast or fallout; but nothing could save you from a direct hit. When the siren went off you got out of bed and went to the shelter until the all-clear sounded. How we hated to get out of a warm bed!

Later on, we had a reinforced concrete shelter installed in our house. When the raids became nightly, we just went to bed in the shelter. We even kept our best clothes and jewellery in it. There were also huge public and office shelters, and once a warning sounded Air Raid Wardens cleared the streets and you had to take cover.

A total blackout came into effect right away. All buildings had to have heavy black curtains or boards to put over all windows at night. If even a tiny chink of light showed, the Air Raid Warden knocked at your door and you could be fined. As there were no street lights you had to carry a torch, or a flashlight that was covered with tape, that allowed only a slit of light to show. Similarly, all vehicles had their headlights covered. Every street had a head firewatcher and each household was allotted one night a week to be alert for incendiary bombs. You also had to stay one night a week at your place of work to do firewatch duty. It became a ritual with everyone to listen to the latest BBC news.

Once food rationing became severe, it was difficult to provide a tasty meal. Women would travel on a bus for an hour or more if they heard a shop was selling unrationed fish or rabbits. This is when queuing-up started. How we hated powdered eggs and milk, but we were glad to have them. With clothing, the slogan was "Make Do and Mend," and this we did with a vengeance! We altered old clothes, darned stockings and reknit old wool sweaters. A friend made me a sweater in a Fair Isle Pattern using tiny skeins of embroidery wool that were not rationed.

From September 1939 until the spring of 1940, it was known as the "Phoney War" because we didn't see any action in Britain, but this quickly changed after the fall of France. The 1st Canadian Division, the proud "red patches," was the only equipped defence force in England, as the British Army had to leave their equipment at Dunkirk. There was also a Home Guard formed by older men and the young men who were waiting their call up. Although ill-equipped, they met and drilled regularly and patrolled the country areas, as there was a big danger of enemy paratroopers being dropped at strategic places to sabotage.

In the summer of 1940, the Battle of Britain began in the air; you could sometimes see dogfights in the sky. As I lived between four airfields - Hendon, Kenley, Biggun Hill and Croydon - we saw a lot of activity. The failure to subdue Britain, due to the heroic efforts of the air force, led to the nightly bombing raids on London. When travelling to work on the train, I could see houses that were just piles of rubble or buildings sliced in half with beds, etc., hanging down.

I decided to work locally because I would barely get home from work before the nightly sirens sounded. The droning of the German bombers going over on their way to London was a frightening sound. Sometimes a shower of incendiary bombs was released, which lit up the area like fairy lights. A house on the next street was burned and a house behind us was flattened in a daylight raid. Fortunately, there was minimal damage to our house - the front door was blown in, windows were cracked and tiles were blown off the roof by blast damage.

The nightly raids gradually eased up. One evening we were standing on our back porch watching what we thought was a German plane fly over, followed by an explosion and crash. We thought it had been hit by anti-aircraft fire. A few days later we learned it was a pilotless plane, later known as a doodlebug. They did a lot of damage, but we got quite blasé about them. If you could see and hear them you knew you were safe; you only had to worry when the engines cut out. Early in 1945, the dreadful V-2s or "blockbusters" were launched across the Channel from the Pas de Calais. You couldn't hear them coming and they did widespread damage.

During the time of the bombing raids on London a balloon barrage was installed. This was a series of huge silver balloons or dirigibles, each with its own crew of men. The balloons were installed in parks and in the countryside south of London. They could be raised or lowered with heavy chains. On a sunny day it was an amazing sight to see all those silver "elephants" shining in the sky.

I was employed in a reserved occupation at a large utility company. I took a first aid course and then helped relieve staff at a local hospital in the evenings. I also acted as secretary two nights a week to Major Warburton, the head of the local Home Guard. In addition, I helped out when necessary with the work of the local Women's Voluntary Services.

This was the background of wartime life in the south of England. People used to grumble about the raids and rationing, but it never occurred to anyone not to keep going and make the best of things. During the war, the propaganda from Germany in the person of Lord Haw-Haw had no affect on the British public. Churchill's rallying speeches put into words the unstated feelings of the people, and they still bring a lump to my throat when I hear them! We felt he was the right man for the job and that he would bring us through. In many ways it was an exciting time with dances for the local

Along with other Canadian war brides, Patricia (3rd from left in black suit) met G.I. war brides in the middle of the International Rainbow Bridge at Niagara Falls to help promote the premiere of the movie "A Yank in London."

servicemen, new experiences and a feeling that one had to grasp what happiness one could.

One sunny day while playing tennis, I met a lonely young Canadian. He said he would be 21 in a couple of days so I invited him to drop around our house. This became a habit; we fell in love and got married. I wore a wedding dress of ivory satin, the material for which a friend obtained without clothing coupons as it was intended for draperies. For the next 16 months, we snatched every opportunity to be together until his unit was sent to Italy for two years.

Early in 1945 the Canadian authorities urged all war brides to go to Canada. My name came up in May and it was a hard decision to leave. All my worldly possessions had to fit into one large suitcase. The swimming pool of the ship had been converted into three-tier bunks for our use. We were part of a large convoy and the crossing took nine days. We were halfway across when the war in Europe ended, and we sat on the deck and cried about missing the celebrations in London! After a two-day train journey the Red Cross and my mother-in-law met me at Niagara Falls. My husband arrived home six weeks later. Like most returning veterans, all we wanted was to settle down, work hard, raise a family and enjoy the peace.

The war resulted in many unforeseen changes, mostly in the lives of women. In pre-war Britain, women did not work after marriage. During the war, they went into the services or worked at local command posts or in war factories. Women became more independent as they realized they could support themselves if necessary. Styles of dress changed and out of necessity women wore slacks or one-piece "siren suits." I think our daughters benefitted from these changes in attitude.

🍁 Netta Wyatt

My earliest memories of the war were from 1940. I was 6-years-old at the time and my sister was 4. My father had enlisted in the Royal Air Force (RAF) and was posted to Norfolk, England. This left my mother to raise two small children on a small allotment from the Forces.

We lived in a small town called Uddingston, close to Glasgow, Scotland. The houses were basically all the same – row houses with four one-room apartments in each house, separated by a wall and stairs called a close. Each house had a two-foot stonewall in front with the remnants of iron works sticking up, most of which had been removed for salvage in World War I. The one-room interiors were small, containing a living room, kitchen, two "hole in the wall beds" and a coal fireplace. The toilet and laundry facilities were shared with the three other families.

When the air raid sirens started, we were picked up out of our beds and were taken to the shelter. There were many nights we spent in the shelter sitting on the wooden benches waiting for the Air Raid Wardens to sound the all-clear to return home. This happened quite regularly as the Germans were trying to bomb the shipyards at Clydeside in Glasgow about 12 miles away. Sometimes we would peek out the blackout curtains at night and see the searchlights.

We were all given gas masks and had to carry them at all times. If the air raid sirens sounded while we were in school, we ran like hell to a safe house. Mine was at Mrs. McKellar's where we hid under the beds, if there was room! One day at school there was great excitement. During the night a Junker 88 German Bomber was shot down. It had crashed about a half a mile away in Jack's Park. The whole school was paraded to see it. This was something to be proud of, a great achievement!

Everything was rationed. We had coupons for sweets, clothing, coffee, tea and meat, if you could afford it. My mother would send me to the co-operative store for our groceries. Vegetables and fruit were scarce and expensive. We lived on powdered milk and powdered eggs. We had no money to put in the meter to run the gas ring, so my father took some dried milk, powdered eggs and flour, mixed these with water and a dab of butter, and cooked them in the coal fireplace.

When our co-op number came up on the board, we were entitled to buy the special of the week, if we could afford it. Tins of fruit were the steal of the day. The special could also be sweets or Cadbury chocolate biscuits. I remember when my father came home on leave he brought us his sweetie ration.

My best Christmas during the war was when we received a food parcel from Canada. It was wonderful. It contained all kinds of tinned fruits. I had my first Canadian apple from British Columbia. My sister Florence couldn't pronounce Canadian, so she called them Comedian apples. I remember they were big, juicy and delicious.

Mothers took the "weans," or children, to the medical clinic where they were given items like concentrated orange juice, malt, halibut and cod liver oil capsules. My sister and I each received a voucher from the County Council for a new pair of lace-up black shoes. Because most of the men were away in the Forces, things were really tight. The women had to stick together in order to survive with their families. Many times my mother would sell or trade her ration coupons in order to get things we didn't have. It was a tough time for us.

At the end of the war my father came home and worked in the coal mine. Things improved drastically. When I look back I realize how hard life was in those times. I learned to appreciate the sacrifices of the men and women, and the mothers left on their own. We learned to do with less and enjoyed things more.

I was six at the beginning of World War II, the youngest of four girls. I lived in a coastal town in the north of England. It was suggested that the youngest children be evacuated as our area was being heavily bombed; the targets were the many shipyards where new ships were built and older ones were repaired. My memories of my departure day are still quite vivid.

The children in my age group waited with our mothers at the railway station for the trains to arrive. After saying a teary goodbye, we settled in a compartment coach, roughly 10 children to one teacher. I had been told to stay close to my friend Benny who lived on our street; his mother and mine were friends. We really did stick together. We had one stop on the way, at a local school where we had a drink and a piece of cake before continuing on to our final destination. We stopped at a village school, where we stood in line to be picked out by the prospective guardians. My lady picked me because she wanted a girl and I resembled the rest of her family. She had three boys and her baby girl had died.

I remember crying a lot when I got to her home. I was afraid. I was disconnected from Benny too, so nothing was familiar. As the days went by I guess things got easier and I settled in, but my surroundings were so different from my hometown with its seaside beaches and cliffs and the River Tyne. I was now at the heart of Cumberland, with its rural countryside and colliery village; all of the men farmed or worked in the mines.

One rainy day, I remember one of the boys in the house said two strange ladies were at the front door. I ran around the house and found my mother and Benny's mother at the door. We three stood in the teeming rain under an umbrella, hugging and crying so hard. They had made the arduous journey, only to find my two sisters and I and Benny and his brother all in different towns with quite a distance between us. My mother came as often as possible, but mostly because my sisters were unhappy. Her journeys were not good as the trains were packed with servicemen and women filling the corridors of the trains and sleeping everywhere, even on the luggage racks.

Finally, it was all too much for my parents, especially when I started to get attached to my new family. We were brought back home to the frightening situation of air raids, sirens almost every night and spending the rest of the night in a shelter on our street. A particularly bad raid on our street involved both land mines and incendiary bombs. A few doors down, some houses were demolished and people were killed. Our house was badly damaged and our belongings were destroyed. I can remember how my mother held a pillow over our heads to deaden the sounds of the bombs. She told us later that she thought we would be killed that time. It was like a warning to her, so we were sent off to the country again for our safety.

This time, my sisters and I were in the same village, but not the same house. At least we saw each other more often. I was in a large house and I was wanted as a companion to the youngest daughter, who was my age. The older sister had left to go to boarding school. I stayed there a little over a year. Outwardly I seemed to settle into my new life, but I had sleep walking experiences and nightmares. I was an unhappy little girl. When my parents learned about how unhappy my sisters and I were, they decided to bring us home. We had been gone for two years.

Because our house had been so badly bombed, we had to get other accommodations. The only one we could get was a small, two-room upstairs flat, which proved to be too small for a family of six. It was not too long before we were able to get a five-room house to rent. We considered ourselves lucky, as housing was impossible to come by.

My father's job was piloting ships up the River Tyne, either arriving or leaving the docks. He was constantly in a dangerous place as the river was always being bombed in the hopes of hitting ships. My mother constantly worried about him and our family's safety. It was a terrible stress. I know that we all felt the strain of those years.

🍁 Rosalie Yaeger

I was born in London, England. My parents were Canadians who moved to England immediately after their marriage, so my father could take up a pastorate in the Lutheran Church in London. When war was declared in 1939, I was 17-years-old and had just started a three-year course of training in Home Economics at the Battersea Polytechnic College, a residential girls' school. When the bombing blitz became almost a nightly occurrence and the air raid sirens sounded, we had to go down to the basement of the residence to spend the night.

My sister Eunice, who was three years younger, was an evacuee to Toronto. My father's brother invited her to come and stay with him and his family. My mother wasn't too keen about the idea, but the government was urging families to allow their children to get out of London, which was a prime bombing target of the enemy.

Meanwhile in Canada, a certain young man by the name of Ted Yaeger had enlisted in the Royal Canadian Air Force (RCAF) before the war broke out. He was posted to England in February 1940 and was stationed not far from London. In August, being a good Lutheran lad, he sought out an English-speaking Lutheran church to attend Sunday worship. After the service ended, as people were conversing outside, my mother noticed his Canadian badges and spoke to him. Being favourably impressed, she made sure that I also met him.

Ted was the first "foreigner" to come to the church. But after that fateful Sunday, there were other young servicemen who came to church and they would be invited to come "home for dinner" by members of the congregation. It was later determined that there had been over 2,000 "after-church dinners" for the visiting servicemen, the majority of whom were Americans.

Because my home was in London, I was allowed to go home from school on weekends. So I was able to go to my own church to see Ted again when he came. When I finished my course at the Polytechnic, I was contracted to teach girls Home Economics in a local school. It was just a stone's throw from where my mother and stepfather lived, above his bakery in Southwark, so I lived with them.

Ted and I had been engaged for some time and he had given me my diamond ring. Because Ted had already been overseas three years, he got notice on a Thursday in February 1943 that he was to be posted back to Canada, and would be leaving on the following Monday. He immediately asked for leave, came to London and told me that we had to get married right away. I said I couldn't get married because I had my teaching contract.

Nevertheless, we went to the civil office on Saturday, accompanied by my mother because I was underage and she had to give her permission. We had the Lutheran ceremony on Sunday, February 21, as part of the church service. That weekend, Ted went to the RCAF headquarters in London and told them that he would be staying in England. Because teachers weren't suppose to marry while they were under contract, I wore my wedding ring on an inconspicuous chain around my neck.

Ted continued in England until D-Day when he was sent to France. Some time in July, he became concerned because he hadn't heard from me since D-Day. Ted spoke with a superior officer who changed his orders giving him an opportunity to come to London to see me.

What a sight met his eyes as he walked down the street toward my stepfather's bakery. The six row houses that abutted the building were flattened. The far wall of the bakery had collapsed from the concussion. A buzz bomb had come down in the area. I myself had heard the sound of the V-1 bomb and when the sound stopped, I dove under the bed. With the blast, a picture on the wall fell on my bed. That was a close call!

Ted was posted back to Canada in the late summer of 1944; he sailed on the *Mauritania*. Three weeks later in September, I sailed for Canada, also on the *Mauritania*. I was about four months pregnant. We landed at Pier 21 in Halifax; the train en route to Toronto was waiting for us to board. We arrived on Thanksgiving Day. Within a few days we came to Number 6 Repair Depot (6RD) at Trenton.

Shortly after Ted met us in London, he wrote his mother in Toronto telling her that my sister Eunice had evacuated to my uncle's home in Canada. So Eunice got to know my mother-in-law quite well, before I even met her.

Eunice was so happy in Canada that she stayed about 10 years before going back home to England.

Inspection Parade, No. 6 M Depot, Toronto, 1942.

Courtesy of Gladys Bracey

Acknowledgements

The Federated Women's Institutes of Ontario (FWIO) is a non-profit organization whose members strive to better the lives of women and their families. The first debt of gratitude is extended to FWIO for backing *Fighting for Home & Country: Women Remember World War II.* The idea for this book was initiated after the success of *From This Place: Recollections of the Lives of Women in the 20th Century.*

Many people have helped to make this book possible. I owe the deepest debt of gratitude to Linda McMullin and Kathy Harris, my sisters. Their care, concern, advice and counsel, not to mention practical help, over a long period of time were instrumental to its completion.

To the individuals who helped with the initial typing of the war stories - Linda McMullin, Mary Poodry and her daughters Ashley and Teri – I am greatly indebted for the time saved.

The nature of these accounts entailed numerous investigative searches to confirm the accuracy of people, places and things, many of which were conducted by Kathy Harris. Kathy also helped with the initial organizing of the stories and memorabilia to ensure that chaos did not reign.

I am appreciative of Janet Schrade's assistance in verifying the proper use of the German language when it appears in the narratives.

And I owe a special debt of gratitude to the exacting work and eagle eyes of the proofreaders – Linda McMullin, Lynn Lodge and Joan Playle. Their work was exceptional!

The support and enthusiasm of Debbie Thompson Wilson, who designed and laid out this book, is gratefully acknowledged.

Thanks to my family – Gord, Matthew and Beth – for their patience and love while I endeavoured to complete this book amidst the routine of life and work.

Last, and most important, sincere thanks to all the Women's Institute members who documented their experiences and shared photographs and memorabilia from their personal collections. This book is for you.

Janine Roelens-Grant

Index

Red Cross parcel wrapper.

Courtesy of Nellie Montgomery

Everett, Margaret – Maple Ridge WI - 74

Ferguson, Delores – Sunny Brooke WI - 75

Ferrier, Jean – Westover WI - 76

Fletcher, Ruby G. – Brooke WI - 76

Folkard, Joan – The Maples WI - 78

Forget, Patricia – Crown Hill WI - 80

Gatien, Ida – Penage Road WI - 84

Gaunt, Alberta – Union Street WI - 85

Gibson, Janet M. – Motherwell WI - 88

Gimbert, Shanna B. – Coningsby WI - 90

Greer, Alina – Mansfield WI - 93

Haferkorn, Laura M. – Community WI - 94

Hall, Jean – Navan WI - 96

Hambly, Mary Belle – Grandview WI - 98

Hawker, Iris – Mountain View WI - 98

Hemstra, Dorothy – Langton WI - 100

Herweyer, Willy – Russell Village WI - 102

Hill, Jessie – Thorndale WI - 103

Hill, Mona – Snake River WI - 105

Hodgson, Joyce – Roseland WI - 107

Holt, Marjorie – Pine Ridge WI - 108

Hoogkamp, Narda – Providence-Shaws WI - 110

Howden, Margaret – Riverside WI - 112

Hurst, Muriel – Helena Feasby WI - 112

Isaacs, Pat – Roslin WI - 115

Jennings, Ruth E. – Bethany WI - 116

Jermey, Kathleen – Crown Hill WI - 117

Kelly, Dorothy – Appleton WI - 120

Kenney, Eileen – New Flos WI - 122

Korbyn, Lynn – Binbrook WI - 123

Kulmala, Jean – Penage Road WI - 125

Leenders, Freda – Coningsby WI - 128

Lefler, Shirley – Oakland WI - 130

Lehman, Marlene – Ponsonby WI - 131

Lindenstruth, Berta – Ferguson Falls WI - 132

Lindop, Annette – Lombardy WI - 133

Lowcock, Joan – Camilla WI - 134

Lynch, Katherine – Violet Hill WI - 136

Lyttle, Sheila H. – Carluke WI - 137

Macaulay, Grace A. – Chesterville WI - 138

Maitland, Liane – Winterbourne WI - 141

*Airgraph Christmas Card
sent by Allied Forces, 1944.*

Mann, Winnifred – Listowel West WI - 142

Marsland, Bernice – Braemar WI - 143

McKenna, Catharine – Brigden WI - 144

McManus, Iris – Nelson WI - 144

Metcalf, Ruth – Eady-Grenard WI - 145

Miller, Mary F.S. – Highland Creek WI - 146

Montgomery, Nellie – Rednersville WI - 148

Moore, Shirley – St. Vincent WI - 150

Morrison, Ruth – Motherwell WI - 150

Muir, Hilda – Maple Grove WI - 151

Nesbitt-Thom, Marjorie – Williamsburg WI - 153

Nichols, Muriel – White School WI - 155

Noble, Adrienne – Gowanstown WI - 156

Orr, Shirley E. – Mansfield WI - 157

Osske, Veronika – Bethesda-Reach WI - 158

Ottokar, Zina – Spanish River WI - 159

Parker, Lois M. – Maggie Johnson WI - 161

Pattenden, Bertha – Vandorf WI - 163

Phoenix, Jean – Calton WI -164

Purvs, Inta - Coningsby WI - 165

Rabstein, Cynthia – Coningsby WI -168

Rath, Delight – Grand Bend WI - 169

Reid, Myrtle – Coningsby WI - 171

Riggin, Doreen – Violet Hill WI - 173

Roeper-Boulogne, Ada – Ivanhoe WI - 174

Rowsell, Blaikie – Solina WI - 179

Sciarra, Sheila – DeCew Falls WI - 180

Scott, Lydia – Englehart WI - 183

Serbey, Leona – Hillview WI - 186

Slangen, Corrie – Oakcrest WI - 187

Smith, Jane C. – Maple Grove WI - 190

Snelgrove, Juanita – Dunrobin WI - 190

Stewart, Doreen – Kent Centre WI - 191

Sweezey, Gerry – Cathcart WI - 193

Ten Hove, Elizabeth – Lily Dempsey WI - 196

Thompson, Bernice – Tyendinaga East WI - 198

Timbers, Fay – Brucedale WI - 199

Toner, Thelma L. – Canfield WI - 200

Vandenbosch, Ann – Crumlin WI - 202

Vanstrien, Wilhelmina – Browns WI - 206

Wannamaker, Daisy – Rednersville WI - 207

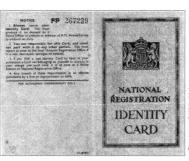

*Postcard notifying family of
a soldier's return date.*

*Outside cover of a
British National Registration Card.*

Wasylycia, Klazina – Winterbourne WI -210

Wayte, Mae – Grandview WI - 212

Welch, Joyce Anne – O'Connor WI - 212

Woodruff, Patricia – Niagara Falls WI - 215

Wyatt, Netta – Burnstown WI - 218

Wyss, Margaret – Stardale WI - 220

Yaeger, Rosalie – Mountain View WI - 221

Farm Service Force Certificate.